DARE
to be
JESUS

DARE
to be
JESUS

Christ is Here to Take Over – You!

Molly McCoy

Carpenter's Son Publishing

DEDICATION

This book is dedicated to my Father in Heaven and His Eternal Kingdom. God's Love, Mercy and Grace have made it possible. All Praise and Honor and Glory to the God of All Creation – the God of our Salvation! With much thanksgiving, I dedicate this book to God's Son, my Lord and Saviour Jesus Christ. In His Great Love, He Saved me and "called" me to send this book out to His "Called-Out Ones." With equal gratitude, I dedicate this book to God the Holy Spirit – our God-Friend, our Good Friend Who sticketh closer than a brother. In Power and Great Glory, the Spirit of Christ indwells every Christian every moment of every day; therefore I dedicate this book to Him (and He will just give all the Glory to Jesus).

This book is dedicated to you, the reader. Read and be Gloriously Saved! Read and be Gloriously Blessed! Read and be Spiritually Touched by the Lord Jesus – Who is quietly reading you. Our Miracle-working Saviour makes all things new. May this book be a Special Blessing from the Lord to His "Called-Out Ones" – whom He is using to build His Church in this generation.

My prayer is for my life and this book to Glorify and Magnify our Great God. The souls who will be in Heaven because I lived on Planet Earth will be to the Praise and Glory of God, and God alone. I thank my Lord for everyone who was a link in the chain of Christians who produced this book – all the way back to the Birth of our Lord's Church. They literally risked their lives to dare to "be Jesus" to their world.

"SOLI DEO GLORIA!"

Published by Carpenter's Son Publishing, Franklin, Tennessee

Published in association with Larry Carpenter of Christian Book Services, LLC

www.christianbookservices.com

The Authorized (King James) Version of the Bible ('the KJV'), the rights in which are vested in the Crown in the United Kingdom, is reproduced here by permission of the Crown's patentee, Cambridge University Press.

Cover Design by Suzanne Lawing

Interior Layout Design by Adept Content Solutions

Printed in the United States of America

9781949572964

CONTENTS

INTRODUCTION I

"And I heard a loud Voice in Heaven saying,
Now is come Salvation and strength, and the
Kingdom of our God and the Power of His Christ!"
(Revelation 12:10).

My Friend, does your life have meaning? *Serious* meaning? Well, take a deep breath ... because in the Providence of God, you have just picked it up. This book is your **Divine Appointment** with the **Lord Jesus** Who is about to give *Serious Meaning* to your life. And don't tell me you're not interested. If the **True and Living God** didn't intend for your life to have meaning, He would never have put such a deep hunger for it in your soul. That's why you *long* to involve yourself in "Something Bigger" than just *you*. That is why your soul *tingled* when you read the above verse. And yet, deep in your heart, you *know* the truth: You've been spending your life (time, *same thing*) searching for meaning in all the wrong places. This book is "Jesus" whispering to your hungry heart, *"You only find True Meaning in the only place you find True Love – in **Me**!!"*

So, are you finally ready to dedicate your time (life, *same thing*) to *Something* that will outlive you on this Earth – as well as follow you into **Eternity**? If so, you are in the right place at the right time. Your Heavenly Father is smiling upon you today as He entrusts you with a **Greater Destiny** than you would ever have chosen for yourself. It is a *Blessed Privilege* to be "Called" by God to surrender your God-given life to His **Kingdom Work**. This book is God's Invitation to **you** to participate in His "Greatest of all causes" on Planet Earth – the Salvation of lost mankind through the proclamation of the Gospel *(Good News!)* of Jesus

1

Christ our Lord. Should you choose to accept the Lord's Invitation, it will be a *Divine Transaction* between no one else except the Lord and you – Spirit to spirit.

There is an ole saying amongst Christian Preachers that goes like this: *"When Christ comes back, He's not coming to take sides … He's coming to **take over!**"* Well Friend, the Lord has *Breaking News* for you today: **Christ is already here!** If you are a Born-Again Christian and you don't see Jesus, just go look in the mirror. At the moment of your Salvation, God made **you** a "New Creation in Christ Jesus," and whether you can see it in the mirror or not, the Spirit of your Saviour, the **Lord Jesus**, is *actually living* in your inner "spirit-man." Yes siree, and it's high time you *let* your resident **Lord** take you over. **"Jesus in you"** has waited long enough for you to start giving **Him** the control of **you**. Your Lord Jesus is quite ready, and as of today, He's starting the process of getting *you* as ready as *He* is. Jesus won't be denied any longer. At precisely the right time, *Jesus the Saviour* knocked *Saul the Destroyer* off his horse, told him what for and turned him into *Paul the Apostle*. From then on, Paul loved calling himself "the bond-slave of Jesus Christ." When you and I become "bond-slaves of Jesus Christ," **we** will start turning *our* world upside-down, inside-out and right-side-up … the way the Apostle Paul did. *Mercy Me!*

"Be still and know that I AM God" (Psalm 46:10). Have you ever met "The 'I AM' God"? If you haven't, you're about to. He is a *Supernatural God* with ways past finding out; He is *so* in control, *so* in charge and *forever* on His Throne. His Name is the **Lord Jesus** … and you are going to fall in love with Him. Whether you are a Born-Again Christian or the most reprobate sinner on Planet Earth, Jesus' *Supernatural Love* is able to work a *Miracle* in your life – no one is beyond Jesus' reach. The Lord is no respecter of persons; He works His Miracles in *anyone* who will humble himself (herself), come to Him and *let Him*. Jesus is just waiting to hear you say, *"I'm done, Lord. I'm ready to give it all over to **You**."*

Tell me, have you ever knocked on *Heaven's Door?* No? Well perk up, my Friend, because according to Revelation 3:20, Heaven is knocking on *your door*. This book is "Jesus" knocking on the door of *your heart*. Jesus is sending His Message "Spirit Express" to Born-

Again Christians. If you are not one (yet), skip over to Chapter One (Ole Slewfoot) and start reading there. You don't need an introduction to this book, *you* desperately need an introduction to **The One** Who gloriously created you; Who intimately knows you; Who deeply loves you, and Who willingly came to this Earth to lay down His Divine Life for **you** on Calvary's Cross to pay the penalty for all your sins (see you later).

Since you're still reading, you are a Born-Again Christian, and this book is for you ... *if* you are longing to have a closer walk with your Lord Jesus. First, as one Christian to another, let me ask you a couple of personal questions. Have you spent your entire Christian life content to just be in "Jesus' Secret Service"? Well, would you be willing to *allow* your Lord to give you a "New Job" in His **CIA** (Christians In Action!)? Your new position will require you to be Jesus' Faithful Servant who lives your life for the *Supreme Purpose* of being spilt-out in the *Divine Service* of your **King.** You will need an on-the-job-training-manual and the best one is God's Word, the Bible. The underlying theme of *this* book came from *that* Book, and, simply stated, it's just three words: **Christ in you.** The title is *Dare To Be Jesus* because our exalted Christ Jesus has *Supernaturally* sent the Person of *His Spirit* from His Throne in Heaven to "live" in *your spirit* here on Planet Earth. You, Christian, are *Spiritually* united with the *Living Christ* once and for all, now and forever. **You** are "living proof" that Jesus arose from the grave and is **Alive** today because **Jesus is Alive in you!** My prayer is for the *reality* of that Truth to literally *explode* in your soul so that you will *let* Jesus be **"Jesus in you!"** Your Lord *longs* for you to know Him in this very personal way. Adam intimately *knew* Eve, and she gave birth to a son. Jesus intimately *knows you,* and when you intimately *know Jesus,* the **Eternal Son of God** will give birth to a *Miracle* in your life!

So, let Jesus take you on a little tour of His Heart ... and yours. Jesus will show you *His Great Love* for you and *His Will* for you. You can fill in the blanks, but His over-arching Will for you is: *"And they overcame (satan) by the Blood of The Lamb, and by the word of their testimony, and they loved not their lives unto the death"* (Revelation 12:11). There is a *Spiritual Battle* to be engaged in and a *Glorious Victory* to be won. The *Power* to win is in Jesus' Blood, shed on Calvary's Cross

for the sins of the world. The *Strategy* to win is the proclamation of the Good News of "Salvation in Christ Jesus" *and* your own personal Christian Testimony. The *Spiritual Activation* behind the *Power* and the *Strategy* is *Prayer*. You *never* pray a prayer your Heavenly Father doesn't hear; so pray as you read because your Father is listening ... to your heart. Spirit-inspired prayer opens the very windows of Heaven and unleashes the Power of God into your life. *"When you pray, you draw Heaven into History – Eternity into Time! Prayer is the place of Supernatural intervention"* (Tony Evans). You need the Power of your **King** in order to live under His Rule and do His Will ... and He knows it. *Now*, Jesus is just waiting to hear you call out to Him telling Him that **you** know it. *Christ-Centered* prayers springing from a heart of **Faith** transform *Jesus' Presence* within you into *Power Incarnate!* *"I fear the prayers of John Knox more than all the assembled armies of Europe!"* (Mary, Queen of Scots). *"I fear the prayers of (your name) more than all the armies of the world!"* (satan, lord of the flies). *"O God, give us America, ere we die!!"* (Born-Again Christians, Servants of **King Jesus**).

So, are you ready to wake up from your sleepwalk through life and dare to "be Jesus" to this world? If you are, then draw up close and listen with your heart ... because **you** are the one to whom the Lord sent this book. The mystery of your life is no longer a mystery – this is *Jesus' Revelation of the Meaning of Your Life*: You have been sent here by your Heavenly Father on a "Divinely Supernatural Mission" of **Eternal** importance! **God** chose you. *"I know whom I have chosen!"* You chose **God**. *Hallelujah! Now*, God is choosing to conscript you into "The Service of The King!" *For the Glory of His Kingdom and the Honor of His Name!*

On August 21, 2017, the moon totally eclipsed the sun in America. *Newsflash!* God's enemy *satan* has been eclipsing the Son of God in our unhinged (from God) drifting Nation for decades! We **Christians** are God's only "Plan" for averting the disaster of a total eclipse of "The Son" in America. We *must* turn back this tide of demonic corruption being flooded into our Beloved Country by our worst enemy – **satan**. And we *can* ... because *The Battle is* **The Lord's!** So, take your dark glasses off and look directly at the Son of God – Who is looking directly at **you**! In Jesus' hand are a pair of "new glasses" –

and He is offering them to *you*. Your Lord wants you to start looking at your life the same way *He* looks at your life – and when you do, you'll see that Jesus is not only looking at *you*, but He is also looking at this world – *through your eyes!* The mission of this book is to get you looking at **"Jesus in you"** as **"Jesus in you"** looks out of *your eyes* at this world *He came to redeem. "That the world through Jesus might be Saved!!"*

"But (they) had certain questions against (Paul) ... of One Jesus, Who was dead, Whom Paul affirmed to be alive!" (Acts 25:19). Right on, Paul! I *also* affirm that this same Jesus (The Living Word of God) is *indeed* "Alive!" **Jesus' Living Presence** "in me" is reaching out to *you* to prove that *He is here.* At this very moment, Jesus is *praying for you!* I have already prayed for you. I don't know your name, but **Jesus** sure does. As you read, listen *(with your heart)* for Jesus' Voice "calling" *your* name. We all have defining moments over our lifetime, and *this* could be the moment your **Living Saviour** adds something new to *your* Christian Life. Our Lord Jesus is the One Who makes our lives "new every morning," and today is a new day full of promise for those with *Spiritual Eyes* to see and *Spiritual Ears* to hear. Listen for the sound of *Destiny's Door* ... turning on its very small hinges. This book could be the "small hinge" God uses to turn **you** into a *Faithful Witness* fit for your Master's use. Your Lord could even use *you* to wake up our satan-drugged Nation and change the *Destiny* of America. Start thinking what God's thinking: *He could!* Yes siree, since everybody else is leading a revolution in our Country these days, you may as well let **God** use lil ole **you** to start a *New Revolution* in America – **"A Jesus Revolution!"** Never forget, years ago a small band of courageous American settlers took on the mighty English Empire – **and won!** *Now*, we Born-Again Christians *must* be courageous enough to take on *satan's* evil empire of darkness and death ... before "The Light" goes totally out in America. Just look at the UK today. It was once the greatest bastion of **Christianity** in the world! What a difference a devil makes.

What a difference a Christian makes!! *You*, my Friend, are on this world-scene *right now* – and it's no accident you are here. You aren't just some happenstance of nature. *Oh no*, **you** are the **Plan of God!** He knew you before you were ever born, and He has placed you here *for such a time as*

this. **You** are a Member-in-good-standing of that "Chosen Generation" Peter told us about. That makes *you* the **Chosen Servant of God** – and He has work for you to do. Are you ready to do it? God is ready when you're ready. The life your Lord gives you is a *Precious Gift* – use it wisely. The clock is ticking. *Every second counts!* Don't waste your life (time, *same thing*) in cyberspace. You weren't born with a smarty-pants phone in your hand, for pity's sake! Put it down long enough to put your feet on Earth's terra firma and go talk to some flesh-and-blood folks who are heading for **Eternity!** You know where *you* are going when *you* die, but they don't have a clue. *Newsflash!* Jesus wants to "clue them in," and **you**, Christian, are His Plan. Jesus' Plan for you isn't a milk-toast plan. *Oh no*, His Plan for you is: **Dare to "be Jesus" to this world!!** If you will dare to do that *now*, **He** will gloriously "be Jesus" to *you* in Heaven – *forever!* **"Do you think I would rather have arms and legs or Eternal Purpose?" (Nick Vujicic).**

I was listening to my little squawk-radio the other day when I heard a Preacher say, *"Would you be excited to see Jesus if He came back today?"* Immediately, my heart lit-up as I sang out, *"I'm excited to see Jesus every day ... because He's already here – in me!!"* My heart's desire is for you to come to *see* your Lord Jesus like you've never seen Him before … **in you!** And when you do, my prayer is that you will come to *love* Jesus like you've never loved Him before … with all your heart. May you become keenly aware of *Jesus' Living Presence* dwelling within you, loving *you* like *you've* never been loved before! Michelangelo's painting on the ceiling of the Sistine Chapel shows God *almost* touching Adam. If you are a Born-Again Christian, my Friend, God is not only touching you, He is "dwelling" in your inner spirit-man *hugging* you (in the Person of His Son's Spirit). "Jesus in you" would *love* for you to hug Him back. Hug Him so close that you can feel His heart beating … for *you, His Favorite Child.* Jesus is inviting you to step into *His World* – a World of His **Great Love** with no boundaries and no end. As Rod Serling would say, *"A World of Another Dimension."* Pastor Brad Waters often prays, *"Lord, we need a touch from Another World!"* My prayer is that the **King** of that Kingdom will *Supernaturally* reach out from *His World* and touch your heart. Christ Jesus longs to lovingly shake you up, wake you up and draw you up closer to Himself than you have ever been before. Jesus is reaching

out His nail-pierced hand to soothe your battle-weary soul and cool your brow from "this fever called living." Jesus quietly leans over your slumbering spirit and softly whispers,

"Awake, My Love, My Bride! Awake out of your deep sleep.
My Spirit's Holy kiss upon your heart softly awakens your soul.
Arise, My Love, My Bride! Arise to Renewed Life!
I AM forever with you, making all things Eternally New!"
Signed: Jesus, your Heavenly Bridegroom.

Christian Friend, let your Lord Jesus *quicken your soul* as you pray your way through a book that points you to *Him* and *His Eternal Kingdom* over and over and over again. Take a deep "Spiritual Breath" and let Jesus (Who abides within your spirit) breathe more of *Himself* into your soul. Then, let Jesus breathe **His Life** out again – through *your mouth!* **That** is what Jesus is in you to do. So, do you dare to go out into this world *actually believing* that **Jesus** is the One Who will be speaking *through you* to those lost people you encounter every day? **Do you dare to "be Jesus" to this world?** That is the question. Only you have the answer. May this book be the catalyst that catapults you into a "Brave New World" of radical trust and faithful obedience. This New World is actually "Jesus' World" (and it's not very far away). Jesus' World is different from your world. You are the leader in your world – **Jesus** is the Leader in *His World*. Do you dare to place yourself under the Kingdom-Rule of King Jesus and follow *Him*? Jesus promises that should you choose to accept the assignment of following *Him*, He will make you "a fisher of men." **That** is His agenda for you. That is what this book is about – welcoming you into "Jesus' World" where you will discover *Jesus' Divine Agenda* for your life (time, *same thing*). Do you dare? It may be the worst of times, but it is also the *best* of times, and "Good Things" are happening in Jesus' World. This book is *Jesus' Divine Invitation* to **you** to come join Him in His *Spiritual World (of Witnessing)*.

"*Prayers outlive the lives of those who uttered them; outlive a generation; outlive an age; outlive a world!*" (E. M. Bounds).

Much prayer has gone into the writing of this book. God moves when *somebody prays.* The *one thing* I desire this book to be above all else is: *Anointed by God!* It will just be a dust-catcher on your shelf *unless* it has "God's Anointing" on it in a *Supernatural Way.* Only *God* can *Save* a soul and *totally transform* a soul (I'm just His unprofitable servant doing my duty to the Lord I love). My prayer is for you to receive a fresh Anointing from God and then *let* Him use *your life* in a *powerful way.* We serve a "Miracle-Working God" Who works *Miracles* every day – and today is *your* day. As I pray for you, Christian Friend, you are presented to *God* upon the Golden Altar before His Throne in Heaven (Revelation 8:3-5). There you are … being filled by your Lord with His *Holy Spirit Fire* so that He can use you to create quite a storm down here on Earth for His Eternal Kingdom. Our Lord Jesus calms storms … *and causes storms!!* *"And if I be lifted up from the Earth, I Will draw all men unto Me!" Signed: Jesus, Lord and Saviour* (John 12:32).

"WELCOME TO MY WORLD!"

This concludes Part I of the Introduction. I realize that many of you are wondering how this book came to be called *Dare To Be Jesus.* I cover that in Introduction II. But for now, I know that all you movers-and-shakers of this modern world are always in such a mad rush. After all, the world is out there turning … *without you. Mercy Me!* So, if you have a plane to catch and you're on a tight schedule, I understand. Just skip on over to "Welcome To My World" and start reading there. *And hurry up!!*

Now, for all you "laid-back-rest-takers" who enjoy the challenge of seeing how much detail-information you can get to stick in your brain, it's *"Intermission Time."* So, take a break, get a healthy snack, get something healthy to drink; then return to your comfy chair – as the curtain rises on Part II. Just relax (and don't tell the "movers-and-shakers" that, unbeknownst to them, I call Part I my *Introduction for Sissies*).

ONWARD CHRISTIAN SOLDIERS!

WARNING: Before you read this book, I must warn you that it is a **CHRISTIAN BOOK.** In it, you will be presented with THE CHRISTIAN GOD, THE CHRISTIAN SAVIOUR, THE CHRISTIAN BIBLE, THE CHRISTIAN FAITH, THE CHRISTIAN LIFE, THE CHRISTIAN DOCTRINE and THE CHRISTIAN OPINIONS of the author. If you have a problem with what **GOD'S BIBLE** says about *all* of life, don't read this book. It makes no attempt to be "politically correct" – aka "Biblically Incorrect!"

INTRODUCTION II

"I AM come 'The Light' into the world!"
Signed: Jesus, God the Son (John 3:19).

Ahh! Now that all the "Marthas" have hurried out to the kitchen, *we* can relax while I tell all of you "Marys" a little more about this unusual book (and its unusual author). Erma Bombeck once wrote a book with the amusing title: *When You Look Like Your Passport Photo, It's Time to Go Home.* Well, I'm an ole widow lady who looks *worse* than the picture on her driver's license, so I know it will soon be time for *me* to go Home. However, as long as my Lord leaves me here, I want to try and make myself useful (hopefully, you will find this book useful). It is my Legacy to the next generation. I'm taking Dennis Swanberg's advice and planting a shade tree for others to sit under. David Barton wisely observes that "Revival" occurs when we Christians train the next generation. Therefore, this book is the "Baton" of the **Gospel of Jesus Christ** passed on to those following behind me. *"When I am old and grey-headed, O God, forsake me not; until I have showed Thy Strength unto this generation and Thy Power to everyone who is to come"* (Psalm 71:18).

If there has ever been a generation in the history of the world that needed God's help, it's the next generation in America. They are hurting, confused and desperately searching for meaning in their life. They are totally clueless to the fact that they are being blinded, lied to, indoctrinated, shackled and enslaved ... by *satan*. **But Jesus** hasn't forgotten them; He knows that they will never be fulfilled and content until they find their place in *His Kingdom*, joyously serving *Him*. True satisfaction can only be found in the **Presence of Jesus**.

11

"Happiness is something you stumble over on your way to serve Jesus!" (Adrian Rogers).

The Lord is reaching out to touch His World, His Church, His People and, most importantly, Jesus is reaching out to touch **you!** However, He has chosen a most unlikely person to do it through – **me!** I'm just a lil ole widow lady who is definitely **not** a professional writer. I've never been to College, but I *have* been to the same School many of you have attended: The University of Adversity (if that counts for anything, or not). My only Master's Degree is bowing my knee to *The Master of the Highest Degree,* **Jesus Christ** – which is how I received my BAC (Born-Again Christian).

So, when my Lord called me to write this book, I responded much the same way Sarah did when the Lord told *her* she was going to have a baby, *"Lord, I'm too old to write a book. I don't know how to write a book. I'm no writer. I can't write a book, for pity's sake!"* (Notice all the "I's"). Well, there are times when your Lord has to open a door … then push you through it. So, He did. *Miraculously,* Jehovah Jesus placed a baby into Sarah's hands, and amazingly, He placed this book into *mine.* And *now,* the Lord has just as miraculously placed it into *your* hands (the book, not the baby).

When I finally answered my Lord's "Call" and started obediently writing (while praying for "God's Unseen Hand" to be upon me), the book just seemed to flow out of my pen. So much so, that the Introduction turned out to be one of the longer chapters in the book. I do apologize, but then whoever knows what a beginner is going to do. Even the title is strange. I know you're having a problem with that, and I don't blame you … so did I. I kept asking my Lord to let me name it something else, **but Jesus** kept *insisting* that *Dare To Be Jesus* was to be the title (and you know how He is sometimes). Every time I asked Him, *"Lord, who is ever going to read a book with a title like that?"* His answer was always the same: *"Those I 'call.'"*

So, here it is … strange title and all. However, I do feel that I owe you an explanation of how this book came to be called *Dare To Be Jesus.* Do you remember the Christian song, "Who Will Be Jesus To Them?" by Bruce Carroll? Have you ever wondered how many people listened to it, agreed it was a good idea but went their merry way without it ever impacting their lives? Well, I know of at least

one. Yep, the one with the pen in her hand. Back then, I witnessed *occasionally* but only out of a sense of duty. I was more interested in living *my* life than I was in living *Jesus' Life*. But as you probably know, our Lord doesn't give up on us easily. In fact, He never gives up on us *at all*. And when there is a heavy-duty, industrial-strength job to be done, Jesus comes Himself.

However, I have also noticed something else about my Lord. When He walked this Earth 2,000 years ago, He was never in a hurry. So, in keeping with His personality, it took Jesus many years to get around to revealing to me what I'm about to share with you – but He finally decided that the time was right. It happened one day when I was reading the story of Jesus and Nicodemus in John Chapter Three. Jesus said, *"Nicodemus, you must be born again!"* Poor Nick didn't have a clue, so he asked, *"Lord, how can I enter my mother's womb and be born again?"* I could empathize with Nick because I got to thinking about the day the Lord *Saved me*, and I realized that I wasn't literally born again either. So, what really *did* change about me at the moment of my Salvation? As I was asking my Lord to explain this to me and poor Nick, I could "hear" Jesus' still small Voice speaking to me deep within my spirit, *"My Dear Child, on the day that I 'Saved' you, you weren't The One Who was born again ... I WAS!!"*

Wow! Like a lightning bolt, the "Light" went on in my soul, and I could *see* and *understand* what Jesus was revealing to me. The first time Jesus came to Planet Earth, He was born into a baby's body in Bethlehem ... but *that* body is long-gone. Since God never leaves Himself without a Witness, *Jesus* came and was "Born Again" into *my body* on the day He *Saved* me! With that revelation, my whole Christian life was radically transformed. I had always "served the Lord" up in Heaven seated at the right hand of His Father. I knew that He had sent His Holy Spirit to always be with me, *but* I was not yet living the "Abundant Life" of always being with *Him* ... until that moment. Never had so many things suddenly become so crystal clear as when my Lord said to me, *"I was The One Who was Born Again ... in you!"*

Over the years, I had heard preachers talk about having a close, intimate relationship with Jesus, and I would always wonder if *I* did (a pretty good sign that I didn't). Looking back now, I realize that *this* was the moment my Lord chose to transition from walking *with me* to

abiding *in me*. I wrote this book in hopes that *you* won't have to wait as long as I did to have a "Jesus in me" relationship with your Lord Jesus.

The Bible I read from says that Jesus' words, *"You must be born again"* could have been translated, *"You must be born from Above."* You must be born *from Above* because the day you are born down here below, you arrive with your "spirit" DOA. You walk around on Planet Earth physically alive, *but* with your spirit inside of you stone-cold dead … until … the moment of your Salvation! The *Divine Spirit* of your Heavenly Bridegroom enters into His Betrothed Bride with His **Divine Presence** and makes you **Spiritually Alive!** *"For this cause shall a Man leave His Father … and cleave to His Wife, and they twain shall be one flesh" Signed: Jesus, your Heavenly Bridegroom* (Mark 10:7-8). You and Jesus don't need **eharmony.com**; you are *already* a perfect match (a Marriage made in Heaven). You need Jesus' Spirit, and He needs *your* body. **Jesus** is now able to walk around on His Earth *again*, doing His "Greater Works" using *your* flesh-and-blood body. *Wow!* What an honor! What an awesome privilege!

You get to be like the "never-before-ridden-colt" that carried Jesus into Jerusalem on Palm Sunday. *(Wouldn't you just love to know what that little donkey was thinking? When Jesus spoke to him, he heard the Voice of the Eternal Son of God – the same way we did at Salvation. So, I'm pretty sure that little "Called-Out Donkey" was thinking the same thing I think every day: The Son of God chose* **me***! Jesus needs* **me** *to help Him do something very important … today!).* **You** get to carry Jesus wherever *He* wants to go – and never forget, if our Lord could speak through Balaam's donkey, He can certainly speak through *you*. ☺

Not long after my *new* revelation of the New Birth, I was driving down a highway when I spotted a large billboard featuring a smiling young lady advertising her seminar entitled "Dare To Be A Diamond." I thought about that for a minute, then shared my thoughts with my constant Companion, *"Lord, maybe I should go around the Country teaching a seminar and call it 'Dare To Be Jesus.'"* They say that if you want to hear God laugh, tell Him your plans. Well, even though I couldn't hear Him, I'm sure He was laughing. That's because my Lord knew I wasn't able, and besides, He had other plans. *Better Plans.* He always does, you know. And when Jesus led me to write this book, He told me to name it *Dare To Be Jesus.* So, I took a deep breath, trusted

my Good Shepherd and followed His leading ... because God knows what He's about. Our Lord moves in mysterious ways, and He always has a reason and a purpose for *everything*. And now you know how this book got its strange title. But don't let it get in your way. *Dare To Be Jesus* is Jesus' *Better Plan* for *your* life. So, just get over the title and keep reading about it. God's "Big Plan" for you is to come join the "Greatest Movement" *ever* on Planet Earth. Your Lord is waiting for **you**. Don't keep your Heavenly Bridegroom waiting any longer. **"Let us be glad and rejoice and give honor to Him: for the Marriage of The Lamb is come, and His Wife hath made herself ready!"** (Revelation 19:7).

When Jesus walked our Earth 2,000 years ago, He was always dealing with *Spiritual, Eternal* matters. Jesus was definitely a "Man on a Mission." This book is also on a mission because **Jesus** is on a mission to turn "ho-hum Christians" into **"Gung-Ho Christians!"** *The Lion of Judah is on the move!* I believe that the *Windows of Heaven* are open wide and **God's Spirit** is being poured out just like the Prophets predicted. To everything there is a season and a time to every purpose under Heaven. Could *this* be the time the Lord has chosen to bring you into "God's Divine Purpose" for *your* life? God "called" Moses at the Burning Bush, and the Lord Jesus "calls out" to *you* day after day after day. Christ's Spirit seeks to ignite a **Holy Fire in your bones** that will compel you to respond to God's "Call" upon your life. My prayer is that you will have ears to *hear* and a heart to *believe* that your Lord has sent **you** to Planet Earth on a mission – a *Divinely Supernatural Mission* – an **Eternal Mission!** God's "Called-Out Ones" will hear God's "Call" ... and take off their sandals. *"**World Changers** are focused on what really matters in life!"* (Greg Laurie).

May this book "be Jesus" to you as He presses you into your *Divine Destiny* that He had planned for you long before you were ever born. Jeremiah isn't the only one our Lord knew in his mother's womb. Jesus even knew **you** from the *Foundation of the World!* Jesus knew you then; He knows you now, and He knows that the time has come for you to *let Him "live" through you.* The first time "Jesus in you" gives His Gospel to someone *who is receptive* to Him, you will know beyond a doubt how *significant* and *valuable* you are to your Lord and His Eternal Kingdom. Jesus doesn't just want good things for your life, He wants the "Best Things" ... and He knows that the *Best Things* are **Eternal Things!**

This novice-author book isn't a "how to" book but a plea to your heart. "Jesus" is pleading with you from its pages to listen with your heart to *His* heart and hear His still small Voice speaking to *you*, *His Favorite Child*. This book is "Jesus" challenging you to give your attention to *Him* for a change, set your affections on *Him* above this world, talk with *Him* as your "Best Friend Forever" (because He *is*) and *yield* your very life to *His Supreme Being* dwelling within you. When you answer Jesus' "Call" and *do these things*, you are showing your Lord just *how much* He is worth to you – and I promise you, **Jesus** will spend all of **Eternity** making *very sure* that you know just how much **you** are worth to **Him!**

This book is "Jesus" looking for *peculiar people* to be His "Called-Out Ones" in a world of disinterested people. Is Jesus looking for you? *Of course, He is.* The fact that you're holding this unusual book in your hand is proof of that. Now the question on the Floor is: Are **you** looking for **Jesus?** *Seriously* looking for Jesus? Are you willing to go after **Jesus** the same way He was willing to go after **you** when He left Heaven and came to this Earth *to die for you?* Are you ready to quit wasting the precious life (time, *same thing*) your Lord has given you … and give it all to **Him?** Are you ready to be one of Jesus' peculiar people?

I'm one of Jesus' peculiar people. I fill my purse with Gospel Tracts and go out into this busy world. I walk up to people wherever they are, whatever they're doing and interrupt their life with **Jesus Christ**. Actually, I let **Jesus** interrupt their life *Himself*. He's good at that. Jesus *loves* interrupting our life. When you least expect it, Jesus will interrupt your life and jerk you around so that you're facing **Him** for a change. Jesus has many ways of interrupting your life. This book is one of His gentler ones. So, be wise; *don't make Jesus come get you.*

Young folks reading this book may be a bit confused at times. That's because I'm an ole-timer, and I draw ole sayings, language and values from an era before they were born (a land before time). I just figure that *someone* needs to pass along ole-timey talk and wisdom to the next generation, for pity's sake (now if *they* would just start helping *us* understand *them*, we could start closing the generation gap). There was another ole-timer who did this one time without even realizing it. You've probably heard of the Christian Band "MercyMe." Ever wondered how they got their name? Well, according to legend, Bart Millard (the lead singer) and his newly formed band were trying to come up with a good

name for the group. One day they were all sitting around suggesting ideas and shooting down ideas until they were all out of ideas. Just then, Bart's phone rang. It was his Grandmother.

"Hey Son, whatcha doing?"

"Hey Grandma, the guys and I are just hanging out trying to come up with a good name for our new band."

"Well, Mercy Me! Why don't you get out and get yourself a *real* job!" And the rest, as they say, is history (His Story). So you see, us ole-timers are sho nuff good for *something.* Yes siree and a bob-tail bull, when you belong to the Lord Jesus, He fixes you up by filling you up; then uses you up right down to your last breath on Earth. *But wait!!* There's more! It ain't over when it's over. Nope, your Lord raises you up in Glory, takes you up to Heaven, loads you up with His Joy and celebrates with you up and down Heaven *forever! Mercy Me!*

Many will object, no doubt, to the humorous stories I have included in this otherwise serious discussion of our Lord Jesus and His Eternal Kingdom. Well, I would like to submit to you Proverbs 17:22: *"A merry heart doeth good like a medicine."* And I won't even be sending you a bill ... *but* to my *critics,* I'm sending my defense: *"If you only knew how much I held back, you would be proud of me."* Laughter really is quite good for you, and the joy Jesus brings to your soul is immeasurable! Someone has said that laughing is like jogging on the inside. People who know such things tell us that laughter even boosts your immune system! If you haven't discovered by now that God has a sense of humor, then *Lighten Up and Live*! Right, Ken? I rest my case.

There is so much repetition in this book it will drive you bananas, trust me. One reason for the repetition could be that I just forgot I had written it somewhere else. At my age, I have trouble remembering what I had for breakfast (don't laugh; your day's comin'). So, just think "mind over matter" – when you've lost your mind, it doesn't matter. Just don't monkey around and throw it down. *No*, that's not God's plan. This book is *part of* God's Plan. He is in the process of conforming you to the Image of His Son Jesus, and He has many ways of doing so – like a book that teaches you temperance. So, just take a "patience pill" and read on. Relax and enjoy the journey ... with Jesus. *Don't fight the process.*

With you in mind, I tried to fill my book with "Spiritual News you can use." If I failed to achieve my goal, you can always use it to read

at night in bed … to put you to sleep. However, my prayer is that our Lord will use it to *wake you up* instead. Jesus has given me a life that has been many things, but it has never been boring. The way I see it, boredom comes from the *inside* of us – not from the outside (tell *that* to your kids the next time they're moaning about being bored). The time has come for your Lord to give *you* a life that is anything *but* boring. It's time for Jesus to grab ahold of you and turn you ever which way but loose! To journey through this world on *Assignment* with the God of this Universe is an adventure you *don't* want to miss! God chose to give you life on Planet Earth; then He chose to give you *Eternal Life* through His Son Jesus … for a reason … *an Eternal Reason. Get all excited, go tell everybody that **Jesus Christ is Lord!!***

You may have decided to read this book because you think it's going to be *mystical*. Well, you're right; the Christian Life *is* mystical. Actually, it's *Supernatural* … just like "The One" we belong to, **King Jesus** – Who *Supernaturally Saves* us and *Supernaturally Lives* in us. Christian, you were *Saved* believing that the Lord would *Save* you. *Now,* Jesus wants you to *live* your Christian life *believing* that He is "living in you" and "working through you." That's what **Jesus** wants. What do *you* want? Your Christian life will only be as *Supernatural* as you want it to be and decide it will be. *You* are the one who chooses to take Jesus at His Word and live in a close "Relationship" with Him … or not. All things are possible to him who *believes*. So, tell your indwelling Saviour, *"Lord, I believe!!"* Then, live out your Christian life proving to Him that *you do. "Faith always has legs on it"* (Jeff Schreve).

As you read, you will see one "!" after another. That's because in **Jesus' World** *everything* is "!" I want my whole life to be "!" for my Lord Jesus. Don't waste your God-given time (life, *same thing*) on unimportant, trivial, *earthly* pursuits. Come join Jesus in *His World*, and He will make *your* life count for *Him!* Then, He will put lots of "!" in *your* life too. Those football games you worship won't matter one whit when you are taking your last breath. *Jesus' Eternal Kingdom will!!*

There are also quite a few "( )" in my book as well. Except for Scripture and credits, they are just peripheral thoughts that aren't a part of the main text (feel free to skip over them if they break your concentration). Without a doubt, we Americans *must* be entertained at all times. However, our Lord doesn't want this book to just entertain

you; He wants it to change your life – *your Destiny!* What you choose to do with the **Lord Jesus Christ** *now* will determine, no doubt, what *He* will choose to do with *you* for all *Eternity!* Take your position as *Ambassador for Christ* very seriously … *now.* I once bought a bumper sticker that said:

> ## "ON JUDGMENT DAY YOU WILL WISH YOU HAD BEEN A *FANATIC* FOR JESUS CHRIST!!"

As an elderly Christian who loves her Country, I got up on my "soap box" a few times to give you my views on some of the controversies we're all dealing with in America these days. Don't write me letters; I'm too old to change. I've been standing on *The Rock* too long to move now. Just consider the things I've shared and ask the Lord to give *you* some *Godly Wisdom* – America needs all the help she can get. As long as I'm here, I have purposed in my heart not to sit by silent while satan's slaves drag my Lord's Honor and Glory through the muck of this wicked world. My Lord can count on me. I'm standing with Him on the *Firm Foundation* He laid in His Holy Word. Here I stand! I can do no other. May God help me! Amen. *When you come visit me in jail, bring my cloak and the parchments.*

"Welcome To My World!" You will see those words throughout the book. I'm not referring to *my* world but to **Jesus' World.** My prayer is for everyone who reads this book to receive a *Supernatural Touch* from Another World – **Jesus' World!** May you come "Face to face" with your Saviour – and think. Then, enter into the "Spiritual Work" of giving Jesus' Gospel to the lost – *without thinking twice.* Jesus is waiting for you to come join Him in *His World* … before you leave this one. Those who walk with the Lord Jesus, walk in a different *World.* "*Come unto Me!!*" You will also see the words **"But God"** and **"But Jesus"** in bold print throughout the book. That's because I believe they are two of the weightiest words in the Bible. How 'bout you? Do you remember when *your* life was a major mess and you were dead in your trespasses and sins – **But God!!**

English teachers will frown upon some of my "improper" grammar and words; so let me explain. I was raised by a perfectionist-father

who expected me to do everything perfect – every 'i' dotted, every 't' crossed. My grades had to be perfect; my grammar had to be perfect; my conduct had to be perfect; everything had to be *perfect*. After all, I was *his* daughter. That's a lot of pressure to put on a kid. Now that I'm old, however, I have learned the wisdom of Ken Davis who says, *"Lighten Up and Live!"* I'm with ya, Ken. So, don't worry about the grammar; it's all legit. I know … I checked it out with the *McCoy Manual of Stylish Writin'*, circa 1894.

(Side-note: Many years ago, I went for a walk on a dark, cloudy day, so I took along an umbrella *just in case*. As I was walking down the sidewalk, I looked up to see an elderly gentleman slowly approaching. He was holding an umbrella in one hand and the hand of a very tiny girl in the other. As we neared one another, the little girl's big blue eyes were riveted on *me*. When we were just a few yards apart, she excitedly exclaimed, *"Look, Grandpa! She has a brunella too!"* With a twinkle in his eye, he looked at me and smiled as he answered, *"Yes, Sweetheart, she has a brunella too."* I smiled back at him in agreement with his soft answer to her. If that had been my Daddy and me, my error would *not* have been permitted. I would have been corrected and drilled until I could (hopefully) say it right. But this wise grandfather knew that the day *would come* when his granddaughter would be able to correctly say "umbrella." In the meantime, he knew that she was doing the best she could. There are times when we need to strictly discipline our children in the admonition of the Lord – and there are times we need to be loving and gracious … like Jesus. I have never forgotten that humorous moment. I was witnessing a loving grandfather graciously "being Jesus" to his precious little granddaughter. Today, that family may still laugh about her child-like creativity with words. And who knows, they may still call umbrellas "brunellas" in remembrance of the child she was. You may think I'm a strange bird, but from that day to this, I have called an umbrella a "brunella" … in tribute to that wise grandfather who was showing tender love and grace to his little granddaughter. *"This is My Commandment, That ye love one another, as I have loved you"* Signed: *Jesus, our Gentle Shepherd* {John 15:12}).

Young folks and ole folks live and move in two different dimensions. When you're young, you only have one speed: **House afire!** *But* when you get old, you feel like the house has already burned down, and you're just

sitting amongst the embers waiting for the fire-rescue-guys to come get you. My Grandmother used to say, *"It takes me all day to do nothing."* Back then, I thought that was funny. Today, I say the same thing myself. Therefore, this book has been years in the making. So at times, you may feel like it's a trip in a "time-machine" because some of the current events I wrote about back then are now "ancient history."

I had to include one of my all-time favorite Pastors, Adrian Rogers. If you aren't familiar with Adrian, you can go to his website: **lwf.org** and get some of his sermons. You will be blessed. He is with our Lord now, and I'm looking forward to seeing him in Heaven and saying, *"Thank you, Brother Adrian."* And he will just point to Jesus and say, *"Thank Him. All the Glory goes to my Lord Jesus!"*

Pastor Tony Evans is another of Jesus' Special Shepherds who loves lifting up the Mighty Name of **Jesus.** And that is what I want to do in this book. **Jesus! Jesus! Jesus! Sweetest Name I know!** Tony and I are determined not to give any of you a moment's rest until **Jesus** is "Alive!" **in you** *and* powerfully flowing **through you** to this lost world He came to *Redeem.* You can get acquainted with Tony and get some of his sermons at: **tonyevans.org.**

"Jesus is just sitting on ready!" Pastor Charles Stanley (**intouch.org**) often uses that phrase to describe our Lord Jesus. I love hearing him say those words because they are so true. I am convinced that there are so many "Greater Works" our Lord is eager to do on this Earth ... but guess who is dragging their feet. Right. So, your Lord is using *Divine Intervention* to get **you** as ready as **He** is. Jesus loves to use us ordinary people to do extraordinary things. Are you willing and ready to be one of those people? With the **Supernatural Saviour** dwelling in *you*, you are anything *but* ordinary. Come live in Jesus' World, and you will find out just how truly extraordinary **Jesus** is *and* how extraordinary *you* can be – *in Him.* **"If Jesus Christ is Real, and He is here, then we need to put Him to work!!"** (Kamal Saleem).

I'm quite sure there will be rebuttals, arguments and challenges to this book. People will say, *"If you think you're Jesus* (I can hear them already), *then why don't you just Save everybody and heal everybody?"* Well, consider this: When Jesus walked this Earth in Israel, not everyone got *Saved*; not everyone got healed. The rich young ruler was witnessed to by **Jesus Himself** ... and walked away! Not everyone who sat under the preaching of Spurgeon, Whitefield, Wesley, Moody, Graham and many

others got *Saved* or healed. As Born-Again Christians, we faithfully speak forth "The Word" of our Lord and *leave the results with Him*. It's not our job to *Save* or heal anyone. Our job is to be obedient Servants and faithful Witnesses of our Lord Jesus. When we do our job, He faithfully does His. *"Duty is ours … results are God's"* (John Quincy Adams).

Years ago, I drove a friend to see her doctor whose office was on the 17th floor of a high-rise building. While waiting, I decided to get some exercise by walking down and back up the stairs. So I took off, and gravity helped me get all the way down to the 2nd level. At that point, something told me it would be a good idea to turn around and head back up. When I did, I suddenly discovered gravity all over again – only this time, it was no longer my friend. I struggled upward, but the higher I got, the slower I went. My legs felt like jell-o, and my lungs couldn't seem to get enough air. I felt dizzy … but I didn't stop. I couldn't. I knew that if I passed out in the stairwell, my friend wouldn't be able to get home. So, I panted and plodded on. I figured that if it didn't kill me, it would be good for me. When I finally approached the 17th floor, I saw a hand-written sign that someone had taped on the wall facing the people going up (and about to pass out). It read: **If It Does Not Challenge You, It Will Not Change You!**

So, Fellow-Climber, expect your Lord Jesus to challenge you from the pages of this book. Expect *Jesus* and *His Will* to confront you at every turn – at every intersection of His World and your world – two ways, one choice. Expect "unseen forces" to try to pull you down and hold you back. Expect to struggle … but don't stop – if you pass out reading this book, some of your friends won't be able to get *Home*. So, keep going. Persevere on to hear *Jesus' Voice* and feel *His Presence*. Our Lord is alive and well on Planet Earth; He is *Mighty* to *Save*; *Mighty* to challenge; *Mighty* to change. Jesus' World and your world are about to collide.

Decades ago, Jesus' World collided with *my* world, and, *Praise God*, I ended up in *His!* With *great joy*, I met my Saviour, received His forgiveness and entered into His heart – a Heart overflowing with His deep love and deep thoughts. Today, I'm interrupting your regularly scheduled program to let you know that I saw *you* there (in Jesus' heart), and I know what He's thinking about you. Are you ready? Take a deep breath … because **Jesus** has chosen **you** to enter into His **Spiritual World** and do His **Supernatural Work** of giving His **Glorious Gospel** to the lost! *Hallelujah!!* It's too late to turn back now – you've already started reading. But trust me, entering **Jesus'**

World is a whole lot easier than walking up 15 flights of stairs! *"Come unto Me, and I will give you rest in your labor."*

I don't know what you paid for this book (maybe 25 cents at a yard sale), but it came to you at a very high price. It cost God His Son. It cost Jesus His life. It cost me my life (time, *same thing*), a lot of hard work and a bunch of Ben Franklins – but Volume I is finally here. May God anoint it and use it to *bless you* and *draw you* into a closer walk with His Son. As you read, pray … and let your Heavenly Bridegroom have *His Way* with you, His Bride. Don't say you're too old or too tired. I'm old *and* tired, **but God** decided to use me anyway. **Jesus** was more tired than all of us Sissies as He tried to carry His Cross (our Cross) to Calvary's Hill. But His Heavenly Father gave Him the strength He needed to finish His God-given task – and He will do the same for you … and for me. May this book **"be Jesus"** to you as He reaches out and softly touches your heart:

"My Love, My Bride, awake!!
You are sleep–walking your way through life.
I AM come to give you a very different life.
I AM opening your Spiritual Eyes to see that
I AM making you more 'Spiritually Alive!' in Me.
I AM so 'Powerfully Alive!' in you that our hearts beat together.
Supernaturally joined at the heart, we
are The Divine Dream Team!
Wake up, My Love, My Bride!!
Wake up from this satan-induced-spell the deceiver has you under.
He can't steal your Salvation, but he can sure blind you to
My Supernatural Presence within you.
Arise, My Love, My Bride!!
Take My hand, and I will raise you up to Renewed Life.
I AM right here with you, and I love you deeply!"
Signed: Jesus, your Heavenly Bridegroom.

DARE to be JESUS

A book that challenges you to *"be Jesus"* to this world may strike you as being a bit "radical." Well, in case you haven't noticed, **Jesus** was a *Radical Messiah*. The Pharisees probably called Him *"A Right-Wing Conservative Religious Nut!!"* **But Jesus** just smiled ... because He knew that He didn't come to this Earth to please *anyone* – except His Heavenly Father. Jesus said that He came to do only His Father's Will – and He did (John 6:38). Jesus said that He came to say only what His Father told Him to say – and He did (John 8:28). Jesus said that He came to go only where His Father told Him to go – and He did ... even when His Father said, *"Son, go to Calvary."* So, He did ... and He died. Through it all, Jesus pleased His Father (John 8:29). If **you** want to please your Heavenly Father more than anything else, love the **Lord Jesus** more than anyone else. Do what Jesus tells you to do. Say what Jesus tells you to say. Go where Jesus tells you to go ... *even* ... then feel God's smile upon your life.

Jesus is a Radical Messiah, and when you follow *Him*, He may "call" you to do some radical things. Jesus may "call" you to stand with Him when no one else does; believe His Word when no one else does; speak His Truth when no one else does; sacrifice your time (life, *same thing*), personal ambitions and possessions when no one else does; love someone when no one else does ... or even dare to read a radical book when no one else does.

"One of the greatest injustices we do to our young people
is to ask them to be conservative.
Christianity is not conservative ... but revolutionary!"
(Francis Shaeffer).

"WELCOME TO MY WORLD!"

As we come to the close of Introduction II, I want to thank you for persevering *all the way through*. The Sissies dropped out at the end of Part I. They didn't know that this Introduction was just a test – from the Lord. They didn't know because God doesn't send us a telegram informing us He's testing us (the young folks are saying, *"Like, what's a*

24

telegram? Doesn't she mean Instagram? "). The Teacher is always silent during the test. Therefore, they didn't realize that this Introduction was just their Lord *testing them* (the young folks think I meant to say "texting them"). Our Lord is always looking for those who have what it takes to be His Mightiest of Warriors in His war against satan and his evil kingdom of darkness and death. You see, Jesus has already counted the cost, and He knows *what it will take.* Now, He's just looking around to see *who has what it takes.* Case in point: the writing of this book. My Lord called me to write it because He had already tested me at some point in my life and I somehow managed to pass His test (only by the Grace of God!). Therefore, Jesus knew I could do it. I didn't know I could, but that didn't matter … I didn't get a vote. *Mercy Me!*

So congratulations, my Friend, you have passed your Lord's test! You are now *officially* one of **Jesus' Spiritual Giants** – ready for your **Master's** use. You have proven to Him beyond a doubt that *you* are definitely *not* the faint of heart. Anyone who could conquer such a lengthy introduction to a book will find battling satan and his evil demons "a walk in the park!" *Now* you are ready for your Lord to take you out of His C.i.a. (Christians inactive) and put you into His **C.I.A.** (Christians In Action!). No more being in Jesus' Secret Service for *you!*

"ONWARD CHRISTIAN SOLDIERS!"

The Fellowship of the Unashamed

I am part of "The Fellowship of The Unashamed."
The die has been cast. I have stepped over
the line. The decision has been made.
I am a Disciple of Jesus Christ. I won't back up,
let up, slow down, back away or be still.
My past is redeemed, my present makes
sense and my future is secure.
I am finished and done with low living, sight
walking, small planning, smooth knees,
colorless dreams, tame visions, worldly talking,
cheap giving and dwarfed goals.
I no longer need pre-eminence, prosperity,
position, promotions or popularity.
I now live in His Presence, walk by Faith, lift by
Prayer, love with patience and labor with Power.
My pace is set, my gait fast, my goal Heaven,
my road narrow, my way rough,
my companions few, my Guide reliable, my mission clear.
I cannot be bought, compromised, deterred,
lured away, turned back, diluted or delayed.

I will not flinch in the face of sacrifice,
hesitate in the presence of adversity,
negotiate at the table of the enemy,
ponder at the pool of popularity
or meander in the maze of mediocrity.
I won't give up, back up, let up or shut up
until I have stayed up, stored up,
prayed up, paid up and preached up for the cause of Christ.
I am a Disciple of Jesus Christ.
I must go 'til He comes, give 'til I drop, preach
'til all know and work 'til He returns.
And when He comes for His own, He will
have no problem recognizing me.
My banner will be clear.
"For I am not ashamed of the Gospel of Jesus Christ,
for it is the Power of God unto Salvation to everyone who
believeth."
(Romans 1:16).
(Author Unknown).

OLE SLEWFOOT

*"Blessed are they which are called
unto the Marriage Supper of The Lamb"*
(Revelation 19:9)

Congratulations, my Friend! **YOU ARE CHOSEN** ... to read this book. Someone put it into your hands – but not the one you think. The **Lord** of Heaven and Earth has a "Supreme Purpose" for *everything*. *He* is **The One** behind every "coincidence" of life. I know, I know ... you're thinking, *"I don't believe that."* But why not wait until you finish reading this book to decide. *Someone* will make it very clear. He is the **Master** of making things clear. For instance, He said, *"All that The Father giveth Me shall come to Me" (John 6:37)*. That bold proclamation rings out as clearly today as it did the day it was first spoken by the **Master** of everything – the One and only Son of God, the **Lord Jesus Christ.**

Perhaps, He was thinking of that moment in a wedding when the time comes for the Father to walk the Bride down the aisle and give her over to her waiting Bridegroom. *Perhaps* ... Jesus was thinking of *this moment*. Does Jesus know that **your** time has come? Did you pick this book up to read because this is *your* **Divine Appointment** with your future Bridegroom, **Jesus Christ**, or ... because you're just a curiosity-seeker wondering how *you* can "be Jesus" in ten easy steps? At this point, only the Lord knows. Very soon, *you* will know. You are about to answer the question, *"What will you do with **Jesus** ... Who is called The Christ?"*

For now though, if you're wanting to "be Jesus" on this Earth, my Friend, and you have never had an encounter with Him of the *Supernatural, Divine* kind, then *you* are the number-one person the

Lord wants to read this Chapter. Jesus knows you need Him; I know you need Him, and I wrote this Chapter just for *you*. Even though I don't know who you are, I know **The One** Who *does* know who you are. I also know that He loves you enough to come to this Earth and die on a Cross to *Save* your *Eternal Soul!* You need for the *Supernatural Power* of the **Lord Jesus** to reach out to you through this Chapter more than anyone else. **"Verily, verily, I say unto thee, Except a man be Born-Again, he cannot see the Kingdom of God!" Signed: Jesus, Lord and Saviour!** (John 3:3).

However, the rest of this book is written to Born-Again Christians. *So*, if you are just reading this book on a dare, and your mind is already made up and your heart is locked up to **The Son of God** ever entering in, then you may as well just put it down now ... because nothing else I have written will apply to you. Don't waste your time reading about "a Life" lived in "a World" you will *never* be a part of ... **by your own choosing.** Just throw it aside and forget you ever picked it up ... and spend the rest of your life wondering what *might* have happened if you had not allowed **satan** to win the day **(and your soul)**. *"Come unto Me and find rest for your soul!"* *Signed: Jesus.*

(Wait....wait....wait....)

You're still reading. Does that mean you would *like* for this book to apply to you?

OK, good. Here's how it can. We'll start with "the science." Scientists are now telling us that all people everywhere have descended from just *one couple*. How 'bout that; slowly but surely, science is catching up with **God** – Who has already told us in His Holy Word (the Bible) that *He Created* the Heavens, the Earth and the first man and woman, Adam and Eve, to live upon this Earth in perfect harmony and fellowship with Him. God reigned upon His Heavenly Throne and in the hearts of His Spirit-filled couple. All was well in God's Glorious World ... *until* ... along came Lucifer (the original hell's angel) to cause trouble in Paradise. That ole serpent slithered up to sweet Eve and somehow persuaded her to obey *him* rather than God. (And no, I don't think Eve was blonde; however, I *do* wonder why she would waste her time listening to a talking snake, for pity's sake – but I can't throw stones at *her*; I do the same thing myself sometimes.)

30

Anyway, that smooth-talking, shifty serpent "spoke with forked-tongue" and promised Eve that if she would just listen to *him* and eat that forbidden fruit, *she* would be "as God." The devil made it sound so delicious that she swallowed his lies ... as well as the forbidden fruit. Then, she gave some to Adam and became the first woman on Earth to bring a good man down. *"Adam's rib ... satan's fib ... women's lib!"* (Adrian Rogers).

(Note: I realize that since you aren't yet a Christian, you most likely believe in evolution. I devote an entire Chapter to satan's evil **lie** of evolution in a future book, but if you can't wait, go on-line and search for "scientific proof of how evolution works" {hint: It doesn't}. Then, go to *Answers in Genesis* and get *God's Science.* The *Truth* of God's Word (the Bible) condemns satan and his lies. However, if you have ever read the Bible, you know that God doesn't *force you* to believe it. Nope, God isn't a terrorist; He merely presents you with **His Truth**; then leaves the struggle to believe it between His Holy Spirit and you. Ditto for this chapter; this is your chance to struggle with **God** over His very existence and the **Truth** of His Word. However, be forewarned: I am praying for you.)

Adam and Eve foolishly chose to believe the *lies* of satan rather than trust the *Truth* of the God Who created them (and *you*, my Friend, are still doing the same thing today). When they obeyed satan, they switched "gods" and allowed *the spirit of evil* to enter into their soul. The God (god) you obey is the God (god) you belong to. Adam and Eve broke Covenant with God, and God broke Fellowship with them. With the entrance of the devil's demonic power into their soul, God departed their spirit. And when God went out, His Spirit went out with Him. The Light of God's Spirit was withdrawn from *their* spirit; the darkness of sin moved in, and they were left "spiritually dead" in their inner spirit-man. However, since they were still *physically* alive, they had children (just like their own miserable selves) who had children (just like their own miserable selves) who had children (just like their own miserable selves) ... right down to *you.* **"Wherefore, as by one man sin entered into the world, and death by sin; and so death passed upon all men, for that all have sinned"** (Romans 5:12).

At the moment Adam and Eve sinned, they died ... just like God had told them they would. Their *spiritual life* with God immediately

died because He immediately took His *Holy Spirit* from them – which caused them to die *progressively* in their soul and *ultimately* in their body. God created you a triune person (spirit/soul/body), but your *spirit* is presently severed from Him and very dark. At *this very moment,* **you** are in the same desperate condition as Adam and Eve were at *that moment.* The devil's diabolical lie is still bearing fruit today – the lost condition of all mankind at the moment of birth. **"Your birth certificate is also your death certificate!"** (Tony Evans). *Mercy Me!!*

My Friend, you have a very grave problem – you're headed for the grave. You are infected with a disease much more deadly than the coronavirus. It's the disease of **sin**, and *you* are terminal! If you doubt me, just take a look at a picture of yourself taken ten, twenty, thirty, forty or fifty years ago. You are slowly dying under God's judgment of **sin** with every breath you take – and no matter how many antioxidants you take trying to counter the deadly effects of oxygen … you are going to lose the battle. *Sorry 'bout that,* but you were in the loins of Adam when he rebelled and sinned against God, and Adam has passed his spiritually dead, morally bankrupt condition down to **you.** You have gone astray from your birth and have turned to your own miserable way. Your **sins** have put you under the same sentence of death *(from God)* as Adam's **sin** did. When God asked Adam, *"Where art thou, Adam?"* God knew where Adam was. God just wanted to make sure *Adam* knew where he was. In a heartbeat, he was *a long way* from God. And you (Adam's great, great, great …) took *your* first breath a long way from God as well. *"The seed of every **sin** known unto man is within my heart"* (Robert Murray McCheyne).

Amazingly, your biggest problem in life is one you don't even know you have. Yep, ole slewfoot deceives you, blinds you and keeps you away from *anyone* who just might tell you the *Truth.* **But God** has foiled the devil's plans by getting this book into your hands, and *now,* you will learn *God's Truth.* The unseen "Spiritual World" is *very real* and *very near.* In it are two separate kingdoms: God's Righteous Eternal Kingdom and satan's evil kingdom of sin and death (which God presently *allows* to exist). Your inner spirit-man exists within **one** of those two spiritual kingdoms – which are your *only* two options. There is no middle ground. **None!** Because of our inherited **sin**, every soul born into this world arrives

in satan's kingdom of *spiritual death*. No exceptions. **None!** Satan has power over you, and that power is **sin**. You were born in **sin** and in satan's power.

"The spirit of the age" is actually *the spirit of satan* because that diabolical devil controls the soul of every person who comes into this world ... without their knowing it (including *you*), and apart from the *Divine intervention of God*, you are just the pitiful slave of "the demon-god of this world." You are at the mercy of your unmerciful master, and until you *let* the Lord Jesus "Redeem" you ... you are on *death row*. Listen to me, my Friend, you don't go to hell because of *what you do*. Oh no, you go to hell because of *who you are* – **a slave of satan**. *"The question posed on the cover of this book asks, 'Is ole slewfoot trackin' YOU down?' Truth is, if you aren't a Born-Again Christian, the answer is, 'No – **he already has you!**'"* (*Ole Slewfoot*, the book). *You are badly in need of "The Way" of escape.*

However, you may be just having a big laugh over all of this because *you* are one of the many atheists these days whose mantra is: *"Not afraid of burning in hell."* You think that *you* are the master of your fate, the captain of your soul – a real tough "In-Your-Face-God" atheist. When people like me try to warn you of the eternal fate awaiting those who follow *prideful, arrogant satan*, you just laugh and call us crazy, fanatical, religious nuts. That sly ole devil has you deceived into believing his **big lie**: *"Satan is just a myth. Yeah, you don't have to be afraid of him ... or hell ... because there isn't really a hell awaiting anyone after they die."* The deceiver has you boldly declaring, *"I don't believe in hell,"* but I've noticed that it's one of your favorite words: *"Hell, yes!" "Hell, no!" "We had a hell-of-a-good-time!" "He's mean as hell!" "Go to hell!"* So, why would you tell someone to go to a place you claim you don't believe in? I'll tell you why. The evil-one *you don't know you belong to* knows that if he can get you treating hell as a joke, he can convince you that it really *is* just a joke – and he's doing a heck-of-a-good-job.

But Jesus tells you the **Truth**: *"I will forewarn you Whom ye shall fear: Fear God Who after He hath killed hath Power to cast into hell, into the fire that never shall be quenched, and where their worm dieth not."* (Luke 12:5, Mark 9:44). The **Lord Jesus** spoke more of hell than anyone else in the Bible because *He created it* for satan and

his demon-angels. Hell is the place of total separation from **God** ... *forever*. And *now*, you have decided to condemn *yourself* to spending **Eternity** there as well. *But* if God ever gave you just a tiny taste of hell, you would find out that you're not such a tough guy after all – and you would beat a path to the foot of **Jesus' Cross** faster than you could say, **"Lord, have Mercy!"**

Without the light of the sun, there is no life on Planet Earth. Without the "Light" of the Son of God, there is no "Life" within the spirit of man. Enter: the atheist – **you**. You walk around physically alive but "spiritually dead;" therefore you keep falling for the whole bag of tricks and pack of lies satan is deceiving you with. *Someone* needs to tell you that if ole slick is successful in keeping you "spiritually blind" until the day you die, you will **die** *"spiritually dead."* Then, the **Lord Jesus** *will* condemn your spiritually dead soul to the *place* of **"spiritually dead souls"** – the place satan is telling you doesn't even exist. Yep, you will find out (when it's too late) that you weren't big enough to fight with **God** ... and win. You will meet **The Truth**, and you will know the **Truth:** *"The fool hath said in his heart, 'There is no God'"* (Psalm 53:1). The moment you die will be the moment you *cease* to be an atheist. Death will bring you to your knees as you *bow* in **Judgment** before **The One** you are presently mocking – and you will shockingly discover Who the **Real Master** of your fate really is. *Surprise! Surprise!* You just *thought* you were free from God when you proudly proclaimed, *"It's my life, and I'll live it any way I want to"* ... because God will say to you, *"You were wrong. It's **My** life – and now, I will do with you anything **I** want to."* The Lord's Angel *will cast* you into Hades, but not before you (the former atheist) *bow* your knee to **The One** satan told you didn't exist and confess: **Jesus Christ is Lord of all to the Glory of God the Father.** *Praise His Holy Name!!* **"You can laugh your way into hell, but you can't laugh your way out once you get there"** (Adrian Rogers).

You and your fellow-atheists ridicule and mock us Christians for praying to **God**. Well, you had better hope we do ... because there is no fear of God before *your* eyes; so if *we* don't pray for you, who will? The mark of those who belong to satan is this: You sin and are *proud* of it. The mark of those who belong to **Jesus** is this: We humbly pray and intercede for the lost because *we* know what you don't: Even **you** aren't

beyond the **Mercy** and **Grace** of the **God** Who *created* you – and you are desperately in need of **God's Mercy**. You will never find true *Peace* and *Joy* until the **Lord Jesus** "lives" in your heart and spirit. But don't despair, my Friend, because whether you realize it or not, your decision to continue reading this book unleashed **The Hound of Heaven** onto your trail. *The Lord Jesus has finally tracked you down!!*

At this point in your life, satan has power over you. But you always have the *power of choice*. Therefore, you can choose to have *power over satan* – by choosing the **Lord Jesus** and *His Power* over that devil. *However*, should you choose **not** to choose Jesus, you have just chosen your path … as well as *your Destiny* – a Destiny ole slewfoot would rather you **not** think about … **ever!** Yep, that devious demon hopes you *never* think about the fact that there is a **death** to die, a **God** to meet and a **Judgment** to face – a **Judgment** as sure as death. With every beat of your heart, you get closer to your *last one*. **"Life isn't over when it's over. On the other side of your last heartbeat is Eternity!"** (Charles Stanley).

> *"Until this moment, I thought there was neither a God nor a hell.*
> *Now, I know that there are both, and I am doomed to perdition*
> *by the just Judgment of The Almighty!"*
> (The final words of Sir Thomas Scott).

"Then shall the dust (your body) return to the earth as it was, and the spirit shall return unto God Who gave it" (Ecclesiastes 12:7). *So*, have *you* ever thought about it? What do you think is going to happen to *you* when you take *your* last breath and leave Planet Earth for good? Aren't you glad you kept reading? I know what you're thinking, *"This is the most depressing book I've ever read. Why would anyone write a book about such morbid stuff?"* Answer: Because I want *you* to be able to "be Jesus" to lots of lost folks who need Him, and I know what it's going to take. Jesus was crucified on a Cross. And that's exactly what's going to have to happen to *you* … if you want to "be Jesus" on this Earth. Fallen man is so corrupt and so evil he can't possibly be reformed. Death is the only cure. *Mercy Me!*

So, what *is* going to happen to you when you die? I'm pretty sure I know your answer: *"I don't know."* The reason you don't know what's going to happen to you when you die is because satan doesn't *want* you to know. Therefore, your evil slave-master comes up with an idea that will keep you from ever thinking about **your death**. Yes siree, he makes you "the *life* of the party!" *Whoopee!! These are the days, my Friend! They will never end! Eat, drink, dance, sing and make merry – forever and a day!!* Shifty satan will do everything in his power to keep you from ever thinking about the fact that the *day is* coming when the party is going to be over, the lights are going out, and **you** are going to **die!** *But* **Someone** with *Greater Power* than satan has sent me to you in **God's Power** with the truth. The world you're living in is doomed and self-destructing – but ole slewfoot doesn't want you to know.

Nope, satan's not about to tell you that you're doing 90 miles-an-hour down a dead-end street ... heading for death, the grave, judgment and *eternal damnation!* You get around faster driving your flashy sports car, but you *still* don't know where you're going. And the devil wants to keep you that way – strapped into a dead-end life with *him* hitting the accelerator! **Sin** is an addictive drug that holds you in its grip. Each and every **sin** you commit feeds a **beast** within your soul that grows and grows until it is so strong and so powerful you can no longer control it. *So ... it* controls **you.** As your beastly **sin** grows stronger and you grow weaker, you are helplessly tormented by demons in your *soul* ... and two-legged devils in your *life*.

Those evil demons you've invited to your "party" aren't living rent-free in your soul, you know. Not hardly; they are extracting an extremely high price from you – your relationships, your health, your possessions, your joy, your sanity, your very soul and most importantly ... your *Eternal Life!* The devil doesn't care anything about your *Eternal Soul – he hates you!* Little by little, satan is gleefully stealing, killing and destroying everything in your life. Sadly, the **Joy of Jesus** and the comfort of **Jesus' Love** are completely foreign to you. You've chosen instead to get *your* "high" from the wine of the wickedness of this world. *But* a sobering day *is* coming. It's called: *The moment of your death.* That's when you discover what a fool you've been. Yep, you will find out (when it's too late) that you've been playing footsy with ole slewfootsy,

"the playboy-demon of the world." Satan is an earthy, devious, sensuous "player" who has just been playing you … because *now* he has no power to deliver you from eternal suffering in the horrors of *outer darkness.* So, you may be "livin' it up" right now, but the day *is* coming when you are going to have to "live it all down" … down there … *forever.* **"Welcome to satan's world!"**

Friend, if you ever come down from your "high" long enough to get depressed and think about killing yourself, forget it … you're already dead … *spiritually dead.* The Lord is trying to warn you that if you really dig the things of the devil, the devil is gleefully digging your grave – your **eternal** grave! Like Judas, satan gives you the "kiss of death" – *but* the last thing he wants you thinking about is "the moment of your death" and what's going to happen to you *then.* Satan keeps you thinking only and always about all you have *(in this world)*, all you've done *(in this world)*, all the $$$ you've got squirreled-away *(in this world)* and all the people who think you hung the moon *(over this world).* Ole slick doesn't want you to know that when you *do* die *(and you surely will)* and stand before **God** *(and you surely will)*, all **God** will care about is what you did with His Son **Jesus** – Who hung on the Cross and died for you *(and He surely did).* Nope, satan doesn't want you to ever hear about the **Saviour** Who died for you. **But God** doesn't care *what* the devil wants because *He's* throwing a monkey-wrench into satan's plan – *monkey me.*

I know you. You think that all you need is your smarty-pants phone and speedy fingers and the world is yours. *Surprise! Surprise!* Just a few more ticks of the ole Timex and this world is going to be … **gone.** Then what? *Then*, what world will be yours? While you're thinking about your answer, let me confess to you that I was once where you are now; so I know first-hand what your life is like in *this world* … as the ole Timex ticks: You're just a lost soul, wandering around over Planet Earth, seeking you know not what, you know not who, you know not where and you know not why *(only a Miracle of God could have ever gotten this book into your hands).* You're always looking for *something* – just around the corner – *or* halfway around the world. The god of this world keeps you racing madly down roads … to nowhere. The enemy of your soul keeps you crossing bridges full-speed-ahead … to nowhere. You have spent your time (life, *same thing*) searching for meaning in

a meaningless world – a quest doomed to dismal failure because the evil-one you belong to has nothing better to offer you. Satan's world is meaningless because it's hurtling toward total annihilation. *Lord, have Mercy!!*

Yep, *that* is your only hope: **God's Mercy.** The **Lord Jesus** sent me here today to tell you that God has *indeed* had *Mercy* on you, and **He** is "The One" Who is trackin' you down through this heart-piercing, life-giving book He has placed in your hands. The Saviour is seeking you because He *knows* that you are just a little lost Lamb who needs the **Good Shepherd** to pick you up in His strong arms, hug you close and carry you *Home ... before dark.*

I know you. You have a huge hole in your *soul* ... and you know it ... because you've been stuffing everything imaginable into that hole trying to fill it up and give you some satisfaction – but to no avail. Right? Of, course. But you may as well just give up. Nothing on God's green Earth will ever satisfy you. There's not a possession, a position or a power that will ever do it. There's not a person on the face of this Earth who can give you the *"love"* you are longing for ... and need. You are desperately trying to fill a spiritual void with physical things. You will never succeed. You're rolling down the road of life in the pitch blackness of night as misery-on-wheels, and that light at the end of your tunnel is just an on-coming train. *Mercy Me!*

"You know there is something missing in your life ... you just can't remember what" (Jeff Wickwire). The truth is starting to dawn on you that this painful life you're living is your own creation. As everything unravels and your world caves in on top of you, you have all but given up hope. Life seems so pointless, and ever so often, when satan isn't looking, you *do* think about your death. You look into the face of a loved-one in a coffin, and you have no answers, only questions. *"They were here, and then ... they were gone. What happened to them? Where did they go? Is there really a Heaven ... a hell ... a God?"* As you long for a ray of hope, there *are* those fleeting moments when you're sure you can almost hear, from a World away, the faint Voice of **Someone** vaguely familiar, speaking these words: *"He who is not with Me is against Me"* ... and His words just keep echoing off the walls of your soul – a dark, lonely cavern of no light, no love, no hope ... and *no happy future.* **"Vanity of vanities; all is vanity. What profit hath a man**

of all his labor which he taketh under the sun?" Signed: Every Son of Adam (Ecclesiastes 1:2-3).

Oh, Friend … you with the homeless heart … turn your eyes upon **Someone** Who has been watching *you* all of your life. **The Watcher** is now wanting entrance into your lonely heart – but you're not sure you can trust Him. Well, open your heart up to the **Lord Jesus** , and He will reveal Himself to you in such a way that you will *know* beyond a doubt that He *did* come out of that tomb; He *is* "Alive!" today, and He is knocking on your heart's door *right now* with the *Power* to **Save** you from *eternal death*. I know beyond a doubt that the Lord Jesus is *very much* "Alive!" … because He is **"Alive in me!"** And He is just a heartbeat away from being **"Alive in you!"** You may have lost your way, but **The Way** has finally found **you!** Jesus is *very present* at this *very moment* in the "Spiritual Realm" reaching out to you through *my spirit* and revealing Himself to *your spirit:* "*O, Precious Little Lamb, I love you!! Come to Me and I will give you rest!"*

So, take the advice of one who was once where you are now: **Answer Jesus' "Call" and open your heart's door to Him!** I can promise you, Jesus will *Supernaturally* come into your open heart with His *Eternal Love!* You are already in *Jesus'* heart; *now*, He wants to enter into *yours*. You have a Jesus-shaped vacuum in your soul only *Jesus* can fill … and He knows it. Listen closely, my Friend; **"Jesus"** is pouring His Heart out to **you**, "*O, Little Lamb,* **I AM** *so near to you.* **I AM** *God's Son … come close to Me and let Me touch you, and your fear and trembling will cease. I want to give you* **Eternal Life** *and pour rivers of* **The Living Water of Life** *into your dry soul! Then, I will use you mightily as My Ambassador on Earth and one day take you Home to Heaven to be with Me and all My Saints – forever! Listen to My Voice as I unfold to you 'The Way' for* **you** *to become one of My Little Lambs."*

Without Jesus, your life is just one long, mysterious journey in the dark. And you will never solve the mysteries of life … *until* … you are able to break the code. To break the code, you need the correct password. Well, the moment has arrived for you to break that code because the One Who has all the *Answers* to the mysteries of life is revealing to you His Password: **#1JESUSCHRISTLordandSaviour!!!** Satan is hoping you lose the piece of paper you wrote that Password

on. But if you do, you'll be stuck with *his* password to misery: <0satanbornloser!!!

The "demon-god of this world" *does not* want you to know that the *True and Living God* is a merciful God Who loves you so much that He has provided *The Lamb* (His Son) Who is *The Way* for you to be rescued from his clutches and delivered out of his evil kingdom of death. *But Jesus* wants you to know *all* of that; so He's typing that Password in for you, and … *Wa La* … up pops:

TheBestBreakingNewsYouHaveEverHeard@ *SalvationInChristJesus*.org!

But first, do you remember the worst *broken news*? Yep, *sin* has broken your fellowship with God; *sin* separates you from your Creator. So, how can your *sin* ever be blotted out? *Good News!* Your *Eternal Salvation* is possible today because 2,000 years ago *God's Son* came *Himself* to this doomed Planet as *The Lamb of God* and gave *His Precious Life* on a cruel Roman Cross to pay the penalty for all of *your sins* (even though you may not believe that {yet}, it's *still true*). *"For as by one man's disobedience many were made sinners, so by the obedience of One shall many be made Righteous … even so might Grace reign through Righteousness unto Eternal Life by Jesus Christ our Lord"* (Romans 5:19, 21).

Jesus is willingly laying His Life down on that Cross – for *you!* The Blood flowing from His body is the Precious Holy Blood of *God* – spilling out for *you!* The Love holding Jesus to His (your) Cross is *God's Love* – spilling out for *you (but the devil doesn't want you to know). Jesus* wants you to know that *you* are the reason He prayed to His Father to *forgive* those who were crucifying Him … because that includes *you.* God's Great Love, Mercy, Grace and Forgiveness are *still* being poured out for you – through His Son Jesus. *"Behold, the Lamb of God Who taketh away (your) sin"* (John 1:29).

Worthy is "The Lamb" Who was slain! The Lamb upon that Cross is "The King" within my heart *(My Heart: Christ's Throne)*. But satan is determined that Jesus will never be *your* King. So, he *blinds you* to the Radiant Glory of God's Son on that Cross *(Divine Love Incarnate!).* The devil doesn't want you to ever see how *Holy* and *Righteous Jesus* is … and how sinful and rebellious *you* are. The enemy of your soul hides the *truth* from you: *Your sins* nailed Jesus to that Cross. *Your*

hard heart was the hammer that drove those nails. *Your* rebellion was the whip that beat Jesus' back. *You* should be on that Cross! **But Jesus**, God's Son, is taking your place. Until you "see" how much it cost God to *Save* your Eternal soul by sacrificing His Son, you will never *feel your heart break*. **God's** heart broke that day He had to watch His Precious Son die, hanging on a cruel wooden Cross. **But God** kept thinking of you ... and how much *He loves precious you*. **"The price paid for something determines its value, and nobody but nobody paid a higher Price for you than God did when He reached into His wallet and pulled out His Son, JESUS CHRIST!!"** (Tony Evans).

You, my Friend, are sorely in need of the Lord's *Mercy* and *Forgiveness*, but until you are able to humble yourself before Jesus' Cross, you won't seek either. So, turn your eyes upon **Jesus** – the One big enough to rule this Universe and yet small enough to become a humble Servant ... all the way to Calvary's Cross. The *Humility* of Jesus and the *Love* of God enabled the *Power* of God to be *Victorious* over evil satan (leader of the "human pride parade"). Christians call this *Divine Power* "Calvary Love." Have you ever heard of it? Well, I'll tell you about it. *Calvary Love* goes to a cruel wooden Roman Cross to agonize, suffer and die there for people who hate You. *Calvary Love* forgives the ones who beat Your back, hit Your face, pull out Your beard, drive the nails and crush the crown of thorns down upon Your bloodied head. *Calvary Love* sacrifices and gives *to the death* for those who curse You, mock You, beat You and spit upon You. *Calvary Love* makes the *ultimate sacrifice* to deliver from hell those who have put *You* through it. At *this very moment*, God has drawn you to the foot of His Son's Cross to reveal to you His **Great Love** for you ... even if **Jesus Christ** is your favorite curse word. And why does the Lord love you so? I'll tell you why He loves you so: *Just because He loves you so*. If you can't figure that out, don't worry; you're not alone. None of us can. But we don't turn it down – and neither should you. The Lord Jesus wants to teach you all about "Calvary Love." And then ... He wants to fill you with it. *Let Him.* **"But God commendeth His Love toward us, in that, while we were yet sinners, Christ died for us!"** (Romans 5:8). *Thank You, Lord Jesus!!*

When Jesus, God's Son, was dying on the Cross to pay the penalty for the sins of lost mankind ... He was thinking ... about **you!** And

Jesus is *still* thinking about you. *"I AM the Good Shepherd, and know My Sheep, and am known of Mine."* Signed: Jesus (John 10:14). **Jesus Loves You!** And Jesus' Love for you is *stronger* than all the hate the devil can bring up out of hell. The Son of God wants *your* heart for His very own. Now, I know what you're thinking, *"So, why doesn't Jesus just go ahead and come into my heart?"* Answer: Jesus is patiently waiting for you to throw out your *pride*, humble yourself before His Cross, confess your **sins** to Him and admit that you are a lost sinner who *needs Him* to be your Saviour. Jesus waits for you to become like the prodigal son who came to his senses and suddenly saw himself for what he was – a sold-out-to-sin lost soul, drowning in shame and regret. *The Light* went on, and he *knew* what he had to do. So, he did it. The prodigal *arose,* came home to his father and said, *"Father, I have sinned against Heaven and in thy sight." "If I am to go in, I must go in on my knees"* (Alistair Begg, truthforlife.org).

O, Precious Soul, quit running and listen! Jesus is *calling out* to spiritually dead **you** to come Home to **Him** for **"New Life in Christ!!"** You may be in a bad place, a sad place, a tight place or the wrong place; but when you come to the foot of **Jesus' Cross**, you've come to the **Right Place!!** In the Presence of Jesus, you hear Him "calling" you … in your heart. Respond to Him … with your *whole heart.* The Saviour Who loves you is calling you *by your name.* **"My Sheep hear My Voice, and I know them, and they follow Me."** Signed: Jesus, The Good Shepherd (John 10:27).

"You can't say, 'The Lord is my Shepherd' if you're one of satan's goats" (Adrian Rogers). My Friend, it's time for **you** to *rise up* outta that pig sty you're wallowing in and come *Home* to your Father – your **Heavenly Father.** Once you humble your heart in *repentance* and *faith* and accept "Jesus' Atoning Death" for you, He enters your inner spirit-man, fills you with *Himself* and makes you "Spiritually Alive!" for the first time in your life. *Yes!!* Take heart, Dear Heart, your sad lonely heart is just one heartbeat away from being a heart filled with Joy … because a heart full of **Jesus** is a heart full of **Joy!** Jesus isn't a kill-joy – He's a fill-Joy! *"You can seek happiness all your life and you won't find it … until you find Jesus … then happiness will find you!"* (Darrel Campbell).

However ... if you've decided you *like* 'livin' it up" on the *born-loser's* bandwagon (eatin' up his **lies**), then just go ahead and curse, smoke, drink, do drugs, live loose and party ... Party ... PARTEEE!! Hurt others at will, destroy whatever or whomever you choose, steal whatever you want *(sound like our riots?)* because there is nothing after death to even be concerned about. Nothing matters. Just waste your life ... because it's all just a big waste anyway. Right? Satan says, *"Right!"*

However ... if **God** is "Right" and there really **is** "Life" after death, then you had better wake up **now** and consider some things. Your flesh-man is having a blast ... as long as your Earthsuit lasts. **But** there is coming a day when the storm clouds shall rise – and your Earthman **will** fall. Then, your *spirit-man* **will** rise out of your dead-man and go to **God's Judgment**. You **will** be judged for every moment you lived on Planet Earth. So, you may be controlling things pretty well right now, my Friend, *but* after the date on your Earthsuit expires ... you won't have that luxury. This is literally a matter of life or death – **Eternal Life** ... *or* **eternal death!** *"And as it is appointed unto men once to die, but after this the Judgment!"* (Hebrews 9:27).

At this point in your life, satan has you spiritually bound. Your soul is locked up in your flesh; your flesh is controlled by your soul, and your soul is controlled by satan – who has it locked up in his chains! **YOU NEED JESUS!!** You need to *let* Jesus die for you! When you do, Jesus applies His Precious Blood to your inner spirit-man; it breaks satan's chains and sets you free! *He whom The Son sets free is free indeed!* New Hampshire's State Motto is: Live Free or Die! That is also the Christian's Motto. You either live your life "free in Christ" or you die – a double-death – physical *and* spiritual. When you live your life without God's Spirit living in *your spirit*, you are "spiritually dead" (separated from God). When you **die** that way, you *stay* separated from God – *forever!* (Revelation 21:8). If you don't believe me ... try it. *"Christ's Spirit is to your inner spirit-man what blood is to your body"* (Adrian Rogers).

People are always marching through our streets demanding "justice." Well, don't ever march up to **God** and demand justice. If God gives you justice, you will end up in hell ... because that's what you (and all the rest of us) deserve. The wages of **sin** is *eternal death*, and we have **all** sinned

... against God! *"You aren't standing before The Judge because you stole a car. Oh no, you're standing before The Judge because you stole HIS Car!"* (Tony Evans). What you desperately need is God's *Mercy*; you need for God to withhold from you that which you so justly deserve. And when you humbly ask God for His *Mercy*, He smiles and bestows His *Grace* on you as well. God's Grace gives you what you need but in no way deserve.

> *"And this is the record, that God hath given to you*
> *Eternal Life, and this Life is in His Son.*
> *He that hath The Son hath Life, and he that*
> *hath not The Son hath not Life.*
> *And we know that The Son of God is come, and*
> *hath given unto us an understanding*
> *that we may know Him Who is True, and we are*
> *in Him Who is True, in His Son Jesus Christ.*
> *This is the True God and Eternal Life"* (I John 5:11-12,20).

The Lord knows you need Him. Do *you* know you need Him? You do *now!* At this very moment, you are in the Holy Presence of God *(but satan doesn't want you to know)*. **Jesus** wants you to know that He has been waiting all your life for *this moment* – the moment His Father would draw you to the foot of His Cross where He is dying to *Save* you. And now, He's dying to meet you ... **you!** The Lord has *Saved* too many billions of people over the centuries to turn *you* down now. So count on it; you're just one heartbeat away from **"New Life in Christ!"** Don't let the devil keep you "spiritually dead" any longer. *No!* This chapter is a "Light" that, if followed, will lead you to "The Light of the World" – **Jesus Christ.** Your spiritually dead, dark spirit desperately *needs* the Light of the Lord, but satan is frantically trying to block God's Supernatural Light from opening your *spiritual eyes* because he knows that if you ever "see" the *Messiah* with your heart, you will cry out, **"Oh, Lord Jesus! You are dying for me on that Cross! You're paying for my sins there. Oh, thank You, Lord! THANK YOU!!"**

As the Spirit of Christ draws near, the devil tightens his grip on you, hoping you won't realize what is happening. In all of Time and Eternity, *this* is your "Divine Appointment" – *the Time of your Visitation* from the God of this Universe! God's *Irresistible Love* and *Awesome Power* are reaching out to you *right now*. This is *your* "date with Deity." *But ole slewfoot* is trying to blind you with his darkness. Engulfed in satan's darkness, you can't *see* Jesus' Light – and you can't keep your "date" with Him. Your dark soul can't look down the corridors of Time into Eternity and *see* that you *will* be there – either in the Glory of God's Heaven *or* in the terror of eternal hell.

So, here you stay ... deceived by satan in his darkness ... not realizing that the decisions you make on this Earth determine your *Destiny*. **But God!** Yep, the **Saviour** has shown up to reveal to you *His Truth:* "Eternal Life" isn't just a long time or a faraway place. **Eternal Life** is a very real, very personal, very intimate "Relationship" with **God** through His Son, the **Lord Jesus** (John 17:3). Yours can begin *right now.* **Yes!!**

Satan screams, **"NOOOOO!!! I AM YOUR MASTER!!"** The enemy of your soul wants to keep you wearing his demonic dark glasses so that *The Light of the World* can't illuminate your dark spirit. The prince of darkness grim knows that as long as you belong to *him*, you will hate "Jesus' Light" and flee away from it ... because it exposes your dark, evil deeds. *So* ... wearing the devil's demonic dark glasses, you stay stone-cold dead in your trespasses and sins – just the way he likes you – just the way you are. And may I add, just the way I was before my Lord graciously *Saved me*. During those many years, ole slewfoot kept *me* walking around in darkness as he blinded me to the "reality" of the *Spiritual World*. With satan's blinders on, I just couldn't "see" the *Spiritual Realm* – where the **Lord Jesus** dwells – Who gives us **Eternal Life**. *"I AM the Light of the World; he that followeth Me shall not walk in darkness, but shall have the Light of Life!" Signed: Jesus* (John 8:12).

The devil loves it when his darkness is your ole friend; it keeps you close to him – so close that you can't *see* the truth: *You are firmly in the death-throes of satan's grip!* The devil's plan is to keep Christians (like me) from ever shining the Light of Jesus into your dark soul. Your

slave-master is afraid that if you suddenly saw the *Truth*, you might try to escape. *Never!* Satan wants you to stay just the way you are right now – *spiritually dead* in your **sin**. So, the question on the Floor is: *What do you want?* I know what the Christians praying for you want. I know what I want. In fact, I am praying for everyone who reads this book. I'm asking **God's Holy Spirit** to quicken the words to the heart of the reader and *Supernaturally Save* every lost soul who reads it! Big Prayer. **Bigger GOD!!**

"*Young man, I say unto thee, Arise!*" *Signed: Jesus* (Luke 7:14). What a *Mighty God* I serve! My Friend, I know that my Lord is big enough and powerful enough to *deliver you* from satan's death-grip. Satan knows it too ... and he is *so* afraid he's about to lose you as his slave. *Oh*, how he's hoping you don't know how close God is to you right now – **Jesus** is knocking on your heart's door! Satan is panic-stricken and loudly screaming, "*Don't listen!!*" **But Jesus** just keeps on knocking and whispering in your spiritual ear, "*O, Weary Soul, if you will open your heart up to Me, I will come in. I really will! My Precious Blood will wash you clean of all your sins; My Spirit will come and Supernaturally dwell in your spirit (your inner-man) forever, and you won't be spiritually dead anymore!!*" "*Verily, verily, I say unto you, He that heareth My Word and believeth on Him Who sent Me, hath Everlasting Life, and shall not come into condemnation but is passed from death unto Life!*" *Signed: Jesus* (John 5:24).

Jesus is God! He has the *Supernatural Power* to *Save* your Eternal soul and give you **Eternal Life** – and that *Power* is in His Blood. Satan is scared to death of the Sacred Blood of Christ Jesus! Much to satan's great dismay, when you say, **"YES!"** to Jesus, His Spiritual Blood flows over your soul and washes you clean of every sin you have ever committed. *Yes!!* Satan screams, "*No!! You're happy just the way you are!!*" The devil is terrified that you are about to experience the *Power* of **Jesus' Sacrificial Death** on your behalf – which atones for all your sin for *all Eternity!* God's Blood flowing out of Jesus' body on that Cross is paying the tremendous debt you owe God for all those sins. "*There is a Fountain filled with Blood drawn from Immanuel's veins, and sinners plunged beneath that flood lose all their guilty stains*" (William Cowper). *But* "you know who" doesn't want you to

46

experience the sweet Peace of God that comes to you when all your sins have been wiped away by the Precious Blood of Jesus. Satan doesn't want you to have the calm assurance of knowing that you are a *Blessed, Forgiven, Redeemed* Child of God with a Home in Heaven when you die. **But Jesus** and I do. We want you to know that even though you were born in satan's grasp, God is offering you **The Way** not to die that way: *Jesus is Alive and you're forgiven; Heaven's Gates are open wide!! "Therefore, being justified by Faith, we have Peace with God through our Lord Jesus Christ" Signed: Every Born-Again Christian* (Romans 5:1).

You may be reading the words of this book through tears ... because you haven't had any *Peace* in *your* soul for years. Your heart is so heavy that you actually feel like you're in "hell" today. If that is you, my Friend, take heart ... Jesus is with you in your hell. He is reaching out to you *right now.* If you will take Jesus' Divine Hand of Mercy, Love and Grace with your hand of Faith, He will walk you out of your "hell." *But* you must humble yourself and *let Him.* If you're wondering how the Lord is able to deliver you from hell, listen with your heart, my Child, and I will tell you.

When the Lord Jesus came to this Earth, He came as "God Incarnate" (God in human flesh). When Jesus went to the Cross, He went as *God Incarnate.* God the Son could have slain all His enemies with a Word! Jesus didn't *have to* die on that Cross or shed one drop of His Precious Blood. He didn't have to ... but He did. So, why did He? I'll tell you why He did it. Jesus knew that only the sinless Son of God could ever pay the *Price* required to redeem lost, sinful, fallen mankind – so Jesus willingly went to the Cross for us. And while He was there, Jesus looked down the corridors of *Time* and saw this day – the day a certain lost, sinful, fallen person would need for Him to be on that Cross (in the Spiritual Realm) as the *Sacrificial Payment* for all of their sins. And now, Jesus is patiently waiting for that certain lost person to come to Him (on His Eternal Cross in the Spiritual Realm) and accept *His death* on their behalf. Jesus knows who that lost "someone" is ... and so do you.

This is a *Divinely personal* moment between Jesus and you – Spirit to spirit in the *Unseen World.* Jesus' Spiritual World is *so real* and *so near* to you that you can enter it through your heart of *Faith ... beating*

for Jesus. In the *Spiritual Realm*, in a *Supernatural Way*, Jesus is waiting on that Cross for **you.** So, just come – come to Jesus' Cross, bow down very low ... and come all alone. *Jesus' Heart of Love* is reaching out to *your* lonely heart even now, *"O, little lost Lamb, come to Me through My Blood that I shed for you on the Cross. I know what you need. I AM what you need. Just come!"* **"Greater Love hath no man than this, that a Man lay down His Life for His friends." Signed: Jesus, Friend of sinners (John 15:13).**

The Cross of Jesus Christ is *Eternal!* His Precious Blood is *Eternal* – and is being spilled out for **you!** God's Perfect Lamb has been sacrificed on His Eternal Cross for **your** sins. Some two thousand years ago, Jesus died *physically* on the Cross. Today, He is in the "Spiritual Business" of trackin' down us lost Sheep and applying His *Spiritual Blood* that He shed there to our *Eternal Soul.* Only *"The Great I AM"* could ever pull off such a Supernatural Miracle. The moment you accept Jesus' death for you, Christ's Spirit enters into *your spirit* and makes you *"Spiritually Alive!"* Then, Jesus and you can walk right out of your "hell" ... *together. "We are Ambassadors for Christ, as though God did beseech you by us: We pray you in Christ's stead, be ye reconciled to God!"* (II Corinthians 5:20).

Many years ago, I was *Saved* when I said *"Yes!"* to the Lord Jesus! But I didn't just say a word; oh no, it was *the cry of my heart!* My Salvation was like a marriage ceremony, but instead of standing before a minister, I stood before **God**, made a commitment of love and faithfulness by saying *"Yes,"* pledged myself to His Son ... and received the **Lord Jesus** as my Heavenly Bridegroom. I didn't just a say word ... I received *"A Person!"* Our Marriage will one day be consummated in Heaven, and until then, Jesus has placed His Holy Spirit in my heart as a constant reminder of His Great Love for me. *Ahh! "I found Him Whom my soul loveth: I held Him and would not let Him go!" Signed: Molly* (Song of Solomon 3:4).

Mere words could never describe the *Wonderful Love, Heavenly Joy* and *Deep Peace* I experienced at the moment my Lord *Saved* me. *Heaven came down and Glory filled my soul!!* The most profound evidence of my Salvation was the *amazing transformation* that took place deep inside of me at that moment and has worked its way from the inside out since that glorious day. If you are a skeptic who is

doubtful that a Christian's Salvation could possibly be "for real," there is only *"One Way"* you will ever be able to find out for sure. *"This is the Work of God, that ye believe on Him Whom He hath sent" Signed: Jesus, The Saviour sent for you (John 6:29).*

I wrote this chapter just for you … to bring you into the Lord's Holy Presence *now*, while He is still reaching out His nail-pierced Hand to you as your *Saviour.* If you refuse Him *now*, you will one day have to stand before Him as your *Judge* – and all the hosts of Heaven and hell are watching you to see what you are going to do. *Mercy Me!! "What will you do with Jesus? Neutral you cannot be. Someday your heart will be asking, 'What will He do with me?'"* (Albert B. Simpson). While you're thinking about what you are going to do, let me ask you this: When you are lying on your deathbed, crying out with your last breath of life for *someone* to please help you … who, pray tell, is going to show up? *"I AM the Resurrection and the Life!" Signed: Jesus, Lord and Saviour (John 11:25).*

"Your doom is sealed!!" That is what the ole-timers used to say to someone who had made a bad decision in their life. *But Jesus* is saying to *you, "In spite of all your bad decisions in your life, I AM still offering you the "Key" to the door of satan's evil kingdom that has you doomed. That "Key" is my Precious Blood I shed for you on Calvary's Cross. Here!! Take it!!" "And when I see the Blood, I Will pass over you, and the plague shall not be upon you to destroy you" Signed: Jehovah Jesus* (Exodus 12:13). *"Your response to Jesus Christ will determine your condition in the sight of God – redeemed or condemned"* (Ian Thomas).

My Friend, please listen to me; don't let your family and friends be standing around your casket one day crying their heart out because they *know* you didn't make it into God's Heaven. *No! Today* is the day of Salvation – *your* Salvation. You have this moment *today* to let the Lord *Save* you and give you a *know-so Salvation. This* will be the first day of the rest of your life – your *Eternal Life!* You will have the *Joy of Jesus* … and so will your family and friends. They will still be standing around your casket one day, but their tears will be tears of *Joy* … because they will *know* that *you made it in! Praise to the Perfect Lamb of God! "Seek ye The Lord while He may be found. Call upon Him while He is near!"* (Isaiah 55:6).

Salvation is a *Supernatural Miracle* of God the Father, God the Son and God the Holy Spirit. It occurs when: (a) God reveals His Son *to*

you; (b) You receive Jesus' death *for* you; (c) Christ's Spirit comes to "live" *in* you. The "in you" part is what the rest of this book is about – which doesn't apply to you … *unless* … Christ's Spirit is "in you." So, is He? Is Jesus "Alive" *in you*? If not, He wants to be. One day, God will give you His *"Final Call"* … and *this* could be it. You may be a drowning man, **but God** is reaching out His Divine Hand of Love, Mercy and Grace to you, *and* He is offering you a Gift: *"The Hand of Faith." It's free!* So, take it and use it to grab the Hand of the Saviour (Jesus) Who loves you with an **Everlasting Love.** Just *accept* God's Gift of **Faith**; then, as a trusting little child, use it to **receive** His Gift of His **Eternal Son.** The Lord has the Power to *Save* you from an eternity in hell, but *you* must make the choice to humble yourself and *receive in Faith* the Power of Jesus' Sacrificial Death *on your behalf.* God has sent you a **Saviour** … *if you will just let Him Save you!!* Jesus is waiting; His hand is extended … take that first step of **Faith** toward Him *right now! "Accepting Jesus as your Saviour isn't a twelve-step program … it's a one-step program"* (Greg Laurie).

This very moment, the Lord is looking into your broken, repentant heart and listening to the cry of your soul. If you want to know for sure that God is *Real* and has the *Power* to *Save* you, just call on Him from your heart; from the very depths of your soul. Say to Him those words He's longing to hear:

*"O Father, I confess that I have sinned against You,
and I'm lost for all Eternity! Please forgive me, Lord.
I know now that Jesus is Your Son, and He died for me.
Please wash all my sins away with Jesus' Precious Blood.
Thank You, Lord Jesus, for dying for me. I now trust You as
my Lord and Saviour. Yes, once and for all, now and forever,
I'm letting You die for ME … and I receive You into my heart.
Come and SAVE me, Lord! This very moment – Save ME!
Sweet Holy Spirit, come and fill me! Thank You, Lord!
I promise: I will never ever be ashamed of You.
In the Mighty Name of Jesus, Amen."*

The God of all Compassion *will hear* the heartfelt cry of your needy soul and send the **Spirit of His Son** into your spiritually dead spirit. *Jesus' Radiant Presence* will illuminate your inner-man so that you can "see" His *Marvelous Light*, deeply "feel" His *Glorious Love* and joyously "live" His *Divine Life!* **"For whosoever shall call upon the Name of The Lord shall be Saved!"** (Romans 10:13).

The Lord is very near to you right now – and so is someone else. You may not realize it, but at this very moment, you are involved in intense "spiritual warfare." Satan, your demonic enemy, is fighting hard for your **soul!** You **dare not** let him win and take you to that horrible place he is trying so hard to take you to *forever*. *Now* is the time for *you* to fight hard against *satan* ... by running into the open arms of **Jesus.** Only **He** has the Power to deliver you from that demon and the terrible fate awaiting those who die in his grip. Open your heart to Jesus, and He will open your *spiritual eyes*; then reach out your *spiritual hand of Faith* and touch the nail-prints in Jesus' hands. When you do, the love Jesus has for you in *His* heart will enter into *yours*.

"That if thou shalt confess with thy mouth the Lord Jesus, and shalt believe in thine heart that God hath raised Him from the dead, thou shalt be Saved!" (Romans 10:9). My Friend, if you said **"YES!!"** to Jesus like I did, *Welcome to His World! "There is Joy in the presence of the Angels of God over one sinner that repenteth!"* (Luke 15:10). Now, you can lift up your voice with the rest of us Born-Again Christians and declare to this watching world: *"I am crucified with Christ, nevertheless I live: yet not I, but Christ liveth in me; and the life which I now live in the flesh, I live by the Faith of the Son of God, Who loved me, and gave Himself for me!"* (Galatians 2:20). See, I told you that you were going to be crucified – but that's good! The "ole you" had to die so that the "New You" can live. And what *is* the "New You"? **"CHRIST IN YOU!!"** Aha! *Now* you can dare to **"be Jesus"** to this world – He's "living" right on the inside of you. *Praise the Lord!*

"Therefore with Joy shall ye draw Water out of the Wells of Salvation!" (Isaiah 12:3) Jesus' Banners of Love, Mercy and Grace are flying over your soul ... with beams of Eternal Light ever before you. You have a "New Song" to sing: The Song of The Redeemed! **Jesus** is now your Love Song within your heart – a heart exploding with the **Joy of Jesus!** Joy is **Jesus** singing within your soul. *Let Jesus sing out of*

your soul! Take a deep *Spiritual Breath* and rejoice! **YOU ARE FORGIVEN** of *all* your sins. You may not be perfect, but you *are perfectly forgiven.* **"Thank You, Lord Jesus!!"** You are now a Masterpiece of God's Mercy and a Miracle of God's Grace! You can never lose Jesus' Love for you or His Presence within you. Your Lord has given you a new *heart,* a new *mind,* a new *life,* new *eyes* and new *ears.* You will never look at life the same, and you will start hearing the still small Voice of Jesus as He speaks to you deep within your heart. In fact, you may be hearing Him right now saying,

"WELCOME TO MY WORLD!"

NOW YOU KNOW THE ANSWER.

God did indeed give you to His Son Jesus.
And now, God has miraculously given
His Son Jesus to you.
Mercy Me!

Yep, that's it, isn't it?
God's Mercy bestowed on me, and
God's Mercy miraculously bestowed on you.
Hallelujah! What a Saviour!
Thank You, LORD.

"The Lord liveth!
And Blessed be my Rock!
And let The God of my Salvation
be exalted!"
(Psalm 18:46).

WELCOME TO MY WORLD

"My Kingdom is not of this world!"
Signed: Jehovah Jesus (John 18:36).

"Welcome to My World!
I've been expecting you. So, won't you come on in?
Enter into the Joy of My Love! I love you
more than you have ever known.
We are beginning a Journey together, you
and I ... that will never end.
I have much to share with you and much
to show you as I walk along
with you on this Journey ... one glorious
step at a time ... into Eternity.
I greatly enjoy our time together. I love
the pleasure of your company.
My Father loves you too and has arranged
for us to be married ... soon.
My desire is for you to always enjoy My Presence with you as well.
So, I have prepared some Angel Food Cake, Heavenly Manna,
for us to share all along The Way.
Come, My Love, My Bride ... let us begin."

DARE to be JESUS

Your Heavenly Bridegroom, the **Lord Jesus**, has come to *Personally* welcome you into "His World" – *and* into a *Divine Journey* with Him as you walk through yours. If Rod Serling were here, he would say, *"You have just entered a World of Another Dimension."* You came from that World on the day you were born, and your showing up on Planet Earth was the manifestation of the *Presence* of a *Supreme Being* with *Supernatural Power* in "Another World" – the *Spiritual Realm*. In other words, *you* are the evidence of things not seen *("Someone" not seen)*. That *Someone* is the **Ruler** of the *Spiritual Realm*, and He actually *was* seen on Planet Earth at one time. It was when our **Lord Jesus** came and proclaimed: **"My Kingdom is not of this world!"** And guess what, as a Born-Again Christian, *you* were escorted into "Jesus' World" by His Holy Spirit at the moment God *Saved* you. *Praise the Lord!!*

The only problem is, if you're like me, you didn't realize it at the time. I had never been a Churchgoer or read the Bible, so I was totally unaware of the amazing *Miracle* which took place in the twinkling of an eye! God *Supernaturally* transported me into the Heavenly Realm "in Christ Jesus," and I had much to learn about my "New Life." My Lord taught me that I am not just a body; I merely *have* a body. I am actually a "spirit being" living in a physical body – which makes it possible for Jesus to have a "Relationship" with me once *His Spirit* makes *my spirit* "Alive!" in the *Spiritual Realm*. And that is exactly what happened to *you* at the moment of your Salvation; God *Miraculously* birthed His Eternal Son in you and *Supernaturally* birthed *you* into His Eternal Kingdom. *New Birth!! New Birth!!*

Therefore, you (in the person of your inner spirit-man) are already in Jesus' Spiritual World by virtue of the fact that God birthed you into it at Salvation. Now, you just need to wake up from your "cataclysmically-stormy-world" and *see* that you have landed in "a Land" even more magnificent than Oz. It may have taken a terrible storm to get you here, but that is often what it takes for God to "birth" an *on-the-run-from-God* lost soul into His Spiritual World. That mighty wind wasn't a tornado but *The Spirit of The Living God* breathing His Breath of *Eternal Life* into *your* spirit. And now, you can relax. In Jesus' World, you can talk with your King anytime you wish. And you don't have to come in fear either; King Jesus held out His Golden Sceptre to you on the Cross of Calvary. When you drew near and touched the top of it in love, you

touched His heart as well. Jesus' undying love for you binds the two of you together. Jesus' love will *never* let you down and *never* let you go. At this very moment, Jesus is waiting for **you**. He *loves* to see you coming to Him because *He* really does have the *Power* to take care of you as you journey through this life. There's no place like being "at Home" in Jesus' heart. *O, the deep, deep Love of Jesus.*

"If we find ourselves with a desire that nothing in this world can satisfy, the most probable explanation is that we were made for Another World!" (C. S. Lewis). You weren't created to live in this world (or Kansas) forever. You were created for *Another World* (way better than Oz). Earth is not your Home; you're jest apassin' through. I realize that lots of folks say we will one day come back to a renewed Earth and live here in our new bodies. No one knows for sure, but I agree with C. S. Lewis; I believe that the New Earth will be in *Another Dimension* suited to our new *glorified bodies.* Creating Universes is child's play for our **Great Creator God.** *How Great is our God and Greatly to be Praised!!* One thing I do know for sure; one day soon I will wake up and say, *"Toto, I don't think we're in Kansas anymore!"* *Eye hath not seen, ear hath not heard, neither have entered into the heart of man, the things which* **God** *hath prepared for them that love* **Him**!! (I Corinthians 2:9). *Thank You, Lord!!*

"And the world passeth away, and the lust thereof; but he that doeth the Will of God abideth forever!" (I John 2:17). The moment you received Jesus as your Lord and Saviour was the moment your Journey of doing God's Will and abiding forever began. *Now,* Jesus is adding something new to your Journey – a special pair of designer "Spiritual Glasses" (*Divinely* designed with *you* in mind). Jesus wants you to take them, put them on … and never take them off. You need them to see *Spiritual Realities.* With your "Jesus Glasses" on, you can "see" that *your Saviour* is the **Great Creator God** Who has created everything you see (and don't see). Looking through your "Jesus Glasses" you can look right through this physical world into the Spiritual World … and see **Jesus.** Every time you see a beautiful flower, your soul will cry out, **"Jesus!"** Every time you see a uniquely designed animal or a glorious sunset or a majestic snow-capped mountain or a breath-taking, star-studded night sky, your soul will cry out, **"Jesus!"** Every time you see a *Miraculously Created* Crown of God's Creation (a person), your soul

will cry out, *"Jesus!"* Every time you look in the mirror and see another Crown of God's Creation, your soul will cry out, *"Jesus!"* Each morning, "The Light of the World" will flood your eyes with His brilliant Son-Shine as He awakens His Crowning Creation … and your heart will cry out, *"Jesus!"* Jesus will become *more real* to you than this world He has created … for **you**. *"Your testimony is that you know **Somebody** this world doesn't know!"* (Jeff Wickwire).

Before my Salvation, I had gone to the beach many times and looked around at everything with spiritually dead eyes. Not long after I was *Saved*, I was walking along the beach, looking at all the uniquely beautiful sea shells as if seeing them for the very first time, when I suddenly heard that still small Voice I had heard at Salvation speaking to me once again. Jesus whispered, *"My Precious Child, I love you so much that I created those beautiful sea shells and placed them there … just for **you**!"* My heart leapt with joy as *love* for my Lord flooded my soul!

"When you woke up this morning, God was on His Throne" (Jeff Schreve). When I woke up this morning, God was on the throne … of my heart. And my first thoughts of the day went to *Him*: "Good Morning, Lord. Thank You for sleep and rest. Thank You for loving me, *Saving* me and always being there – on the throne of my heart. The Beauty of Your Holiness and the smile upon Your face are more *Glorious* than the rising sun. I love You, Lord. Thank You for this lovely day full of promise You are giving to me. Use me to tell those joyless people I see in this world about Your *Precious Love* and *Salvation* for *them*. They need You, Lord – and they don't know it. I must bring them to the foot of Your Cross, where You can *Save* them. Thank You for giving me a **Purpose** in life and a **Job** to do – **I must do it.**"

Christian Friend, your Lord Jesus lives so close to you that He can complete your sentences … as well as your life. He Who began a good work in you *will* complete it; then take you Home to Heaven to be with Him. Wake up each morning with **Jesus** on your mind, and He will give you a Spirit-filled, God-Glorifying day. If your days seem to be full of nothing but troubles, try *loving* and *trusting* your Lord Jesus in and through them all – and He will give you a day full of His **Joy!** *Yes!* Then, share **Jesus' Love** and **Joy** with everyone you meet. Tell that last person you ever talk to before leaving Planet Earth how much **you**

love Jesus, your Faithful Saviour. Then, close your eyes and run into His out-stretched arms of **Love**. *Home Free!*

Over my lifetime, I have been at the bedside of several people as they were dying. A couple of them no longer spoke, but their eyes were open, and I noticed a very strange phenomenon. They were looking very intently *past me* into Another Realm ... seeing things I could not see. Their eyes moved extremely quickly ... as if following "something" that was also moving extremely quickly. One Christian friend had not moved for quite some time when he suddenly reached up and tried to grab whatever it was he was seeing. It isn't unusual for dying people to say, *"Wow!!"* (or something similar) as they are passing into **Eternity**. We don't know what they are seeing, but it sure makes one wonder, doesn't it? When I hear stories of dying people seeing their departed loved-ones or Angels, I don't doubt it for a second. Lazarus the Beggar isn't the only one who gets an Angel escort into Heaven. *We are all beggars before our Lord.*

With your "Jesus Glasses" on, you can "see" the *Eternal World* you are already a part of *as* you fulfill your *Eternal Destiny* by doing God's Will here on Planet Earth. You not only see your future in Eternity but you also see God's *Big Plans* for you here on this Earth – and you see that the two are mysteriously linked together ... by God's Holy Spirit. There is so much more to this life than what you can see with your physical eyes. Don't tell the evolutionists but we are **all** "spirit beings" living in physical bodies while here on Planet Earth. That enables Christ's Spirit to indwell *your spirit* at Salvation. Then, God the Son is able to live *again* on this Earth from Heaven through *you* – but only to the extent that you live out *your* dual-citizenship in Heaven from Earth through *Christ's Spirit*.

Christian, you live in two worlds at the same time while two People are living in *you* at the same time. **You** are a "living channel" between two worlds – one seen, the other unseen. Unredeemed people live in only one – the one *you* are presently living in as well. It's a world in the grip of the god of hate, darkness, sin and death. **But God** has **you** right-smack-dab in the middle of it to shine forth like a diamond in a coal mine and show those spiritually dead followers of satan the God of Love, Light, Redemption and Life – *Eternal Life*. You are here to show them **Jesus Christ – The One** Who gave *you* Eternal Life; **The One** Who longs to give

them a "Life" that never ends in a "World" that never ends! And in case you haven't noticed, that's a "job" that never ends.

Jesus has given *me* the never-ending job of giving to others that which He gives to me. My job right now is to reveal to you, my Christian Friend, that *every moment* of your life is **Eternal!** *Every moment* of your life is lived in the *Supernatural Presence* of **God** Himself! *Every moment* of your life is being recorded in the *Divine Books* of the **God** of this Universe! *Every encounter* you have with people is a **Divine Appointment** that has been *Supernaturally* "set-up" by your Lord – Who knows all, sees all, controls all. When these *Truths* explode within your soul, wild horses won't be able to keep you from heading out into this clueless world to have "Divine Appointments" with *Eternal Souls* (in the Supernatural Presence of God Himself) that will impact *all of Eternity!* Starting today, you are going to start looking through your "Jesus Glasses" and *seeing* the invisible, *knowing* the Invincible, *believing* the incredible and *doing* the impossible (with **Jesus** doing the impossible part, of course). With your Lord indwelling your spirit/soul and your "Jesus Glasses" giving you Spirit-Vision, you not only see Jesus but *you also see everything else through Jesus' eyes!*

Nothing is ever wasted in the Kingdom of God. I know that when *I* encounter people, I'm not just handing them a Gospel tract and saying a few words to them about Jesus. *Oh no, something* much more is going on. *Something Divine. Something Supernatural! Something* of **God** that will still be "going on" when *this* world is no more ... because *every person* is an **Eternal Soul!** Worldlings don't believe such things – but I do. I *know* they are true. Do you? If you do, would you dare to step into Jesus' World of the *Supernatural Presence* of **God** and "Divine Appointments" with people? Jesus is waiting for you ... just for **you.** *"I have only just a minute ... just a tiny little minute, but Eternity is in it!"* (Benjamin E. Mays).

God created you, my Friend, to reflect the *Splendor* and *Glory* of your Creator. Since you're a Christian, you *want* to bring God *Glory,* but find yourself wondering how. I believe that the best way to "Glorify" your Heavenly Father is to *show* this world His Glory by making His Glorious Son *visible* to it – through **you.** (Jesus is hiding in America in plain sight. He is here "living" in millions of Christians – who just aren't interested in "showing Jesus" to anyone *through them.*) In order to reflect Jesus' Glory, you must spend some of your life (time, *same thing*)

fellowshipping with Him in His *Spiritual World* and listening to Him in His *Supernatural Word*. As Jesus and you have some "Supernatural Face-Time" together in *His World*, His Glory enters your soul; then shines out of you into *this dark world* all around you. *Glory* is the manifestation of **God** (in the Person of **"Jesus in you"**) on this Earth. **"O magnify The Lord with me, and let us exalt His Name together!" Signed: Every Born-Again Christian (Psalm 34:3).**

Since Jesus is living in "Another World" (the Spiritual Dimension) you will never be able to get into a space ship and go see Him. That's why the Russian Cosmonaut went up into space, came back down and declared, *"I didn't see God."* Some guy heard what he said and retorted, *"Well, if he hadda stepped outta that space ship, he woulda met Him!"* If you've been chasing after God, you can relax; you don't have far to go. To *see* Jesus, all you have to do is just take an "out of this world" trip – into your inner spirit-man – because *that* is where Jesus is (in the Person of *His Spirit*).

Now, I know what you're thinking, *"Well, just how long will this trip into Jesus' World take?"* Answer: Only as long as it takes for you to put your "Jesus Glasses" on and "see" **Jesus** dwelling within your spirit-man, lovingly looking back at *you*. Your soul cries out, **"I love You, Jesus!"** And *immediately*, **Jesus' Love** floods into your heart. Jesus is so near, so real and so in love with you that you don't have to get in a dark room full of spooky stuff with a candle burning on the table and eerie music playing in the background in order to get yourself into an altered-state-of-consciousness so that you can pass through light-years of space and eventually end up entering the threshold of Jesus' World. *Thank Goodness!!* Nope, your "Jesus Glasses" are able to pierce the darkness and *Supernaturally* reveal to you the Spirit of Christ Jesus (The Light of the World) *living in you!* In a heartbeat, you are through the *Spiritual Veil* and into "Jesus' World" – where He lights up your drab soul with *His Glory* and warms up your lonely heart with *His Love*. The fundamental proof that "Jesus lives" on this Earth "in you" is the *Love* and *Fellowship* the two of you share in the intimacy of your soul. In the glow of *Jesus' Presence*, this world just melts away. Your Lord and you are now dwelling in the "Secret Place" (your *Spiritual Soul*) of the Most High as you nestle under the shadow of His Wings. *"Welcome to My World!"*

Christian, you don't have to engage in some kind of mystical "soul travel" in order to go to "Jesus' World" and stand before Him in Heaven. No siree, the moment Jesus *Saved* you, He came and took up residence in your inner spirit-man … *and brought Heaven with Him!* How else could you come before the Throne of His Grace to receive His help in time of need? You can be physically standing at your kitchen sink while *spiritually standing* before Jesus' Throne in *His* World at the very same time! Any Born-Again Christian who says, *"Where is Jesus? He's not showing up in my life these days,"* just needs to put their "Jesus Glasses" on. Then, they would *see* how blessed they are to always live in the *Presence* of **Jesus** Who is constantly before their inner-man, *Spirit to spirit.* In all thy ways acknowledge **Jesus**, and He will make thy path straight … to **Him!** Christians are able to go through this life joyful, confident, content and peaceful because we can already "see" **The One** we are going to when we leave Planet Earth. *Praise The Lord!*

I was standing in the check-out line of a store the other day when I noticed the picture of a woman sitting in the lotus position on the cover of a magazine. As she sat there with her eyes closed, back rigid, legs crossed, hands and fingers just so, I think she was trying to get in touch with her inner-self. Well Folks, God tells me that *my* inner-self is so sinful and desperately wicked that only *He* can know just how bad I really am … apart from Him. I thank God that His Precious Son has chosen to dwell in *my* inner-man and stay in touch with *me* every moment of my life. The *Greatest Blessing* in all of life for *me* is to be in touch with my *Inner-Saviour.* I go through my day with the conscious awareness of my Lord – Who is right there *with* me and *in* me at all times. Now, I'm not against exercising (even sitting in the lotus position), but if I ever get a round tuit, I do it "in touch with **Jesus**" – not trying to "get in touch with *myself.*" "*Henceforth, I call you not servants, but I call you Friends!*"

Albert Einstein was described by his contemporaries as "a visitor from another world." *Newsflash!* We are *all* visitors from "Another World," and we're headed back there when the date on our Earthsuit expires. As far as we know, Einstein never professed Faith in our Lord and Saviour Christ Jesus. He spoke of God but apparently never *knew* Him through His Son Jesus – just more evidence that we can never "think" our way to God. Not me. Not you. Not even Albert Einstein.

No matter how much you know about this physical, material world, you still have to cross over into the "Spiritual Dimension" to meet God – Who arranges the meeting.

Our Lord Jesus was "The Supreme Visitor" from another world – *His World*. And now, Jesus is paying a visit to another world – your world. Jesus is here to reveal to you a World that you can only see through eyes of *Faith*. Centuries ago, Jesus visited Nicodemus' world with the news that only a *Born-Again Christian* can *see* His World and *enter* His World. That's because it takes the *Faith* of "Christ in you" to experience the *Presence* of "Christ in you" (the witness of The Spirit). A person without Christ doesn't have the *Faith of Christ*, which enables them to believe in "Spiritual Realities." Therefore, living a *Supernatural Christian Life* is just nonsense to them – but not to *you*, my Christian Friend. *"I want to live a life that you cannot explain apart from the Lord Jesus!"* (Adrian Rogers).

The Spiritual Presence of the **Living Christ** is visiting your world for the purpose of serving you notice that He is going to be using *your* "Supernatural Christian Life" to bring lost souls to Salvation in Christ Jesus. I have heard many a testimony of people who said they came to "Faith in Christ" watching a Christian live out a life of "Faith in God" before their very eyes. Yes indeed, people will "see God" and *believe*, when they see your *steadfast Faith* in your *Unseen God*. America will have another "Christian Awakening" when **Christians** have a "Spiritual Awakening" – and the Lord has decided to start with **you**.

So, are you finally ready to start living your life *in* and *for* Another World – the Spiritual Realm – where Jesus reigns as **King**? Honor Him as your Lord and don't wait any longer to start living your dual-citizenship in the *Other World* for which Jesus created you. Spend more of your life (time, *same thing*) allowing Christ's Spirit (Who dwells in *your spirit*) to escort your "spirit-man" into Jesus' World where you and your Saviour have sweet fellowship together "in the Spirit." *"When the Spirit of Truth is come, He will guide you into all Truth!"*

Jesus' World and our world aren't really so far apart. We live in our physical world *within* the Spiritual Realm; therefore, we are also living in the Spiritual Realm as we live in our physical world. Years ago, I heard Joni Tada describe it like this: *"Our life on Earth is the 'womb-life' of Eternity. Just as a little baby is in the dark womb of its mother*

awaiting its trip through the birth canal into this big beautiful world, **we** *are in this spiritually dark world awaiting our trip through God's 'birth canal' into Heaven."* In the meantime, the *Spiritual Veil* between our world and Jesus' World is actually pretty thin. We think it's difficult to get into Jesus' World, but He pulls back the *Veil* and says, *"Won't you come on in? Miracles happen here every day. Step into My Heart. Step into My World.* **I AM** *waiting here ... just for you. Welcome to My World!"*

Jesus' World is a physically invisible World, but you don't have to see His World with your physical eyes to enter it. The ever-so-mysterious stairwell that leads into Jesus' World is ascended through *Prayer, Praise* and *Fellowship – in the Spirit –* anytime, anywhere. Christians *Pray* and *Praise* because we have been given the *Love* and *Faith* to do so by **The One** Who hears – and answers. His Name is **Jesus**, and His Door is always open to our every *heart-felt thought* of Him. Softly and tenderly, Jesus is calling. Softly and tenderly, we respond. *"And (Ruth) came softly, and uncovered his feet, and laid her down"* (Ruth 3:7).

So, the secret to living in Jesus' World is going often through *His Door* and connecting with "Jesus in you" in the "Spirit World" of your *soul –* the link between your world and Jesus' World. Since Jesus' Door is always open, you can make your entrance at the speed of *The Spirit!* The very moment you set your soul *(mind/heart/attention/desire)* upon your Lord Jesus, He is able to use that *avenue* to come into your soul and fill it with His Love, Joy, Peace, Faith, Wisdom and so much more. Your spirit-man uses that same avenue to draw up ever-so-close to **Jesus** and give some of His Love back to *Him. What a Joy!* It's one of those "mysteries" of the Spirit-Life. Great is the mystery of *Godliness.* But trust me, when people see you, they will *just know* that you've been spending time with Jesus. You will be so aglow with His deep *Love* and abiding *Joy! "For God ... hath shined in our hearts to give the light of the knowledge of the Glory of God in the face of Jesus Christ!"* (II Corinthians 4:6).

Something incredible happened when God *Saved* you and His Son's Spirit entered your inner spirit-man – He brought with Him *God's Glory!* From that moment to this, Christ's Spirit has been indwelling *your spirit,* radiating Christ's "Glory." You, Christian, are a *divinely radiant, gloriously beautiful* spirit-being living in a physical body! You don't out-

shine the sun – *The Son* shines out of *you!* Yes indeed, the *Supernatural Divine Life* of the Son of God indwells *you*. Just turn your *spiritual eyes* upon Jesus, and He will open your heart and soul up to this wondrous "New World" of *Splendor* that is within you. When Jesus left Heaven and came to Earth, He came as "The Glory of God" veiled in human flesh. Today, Jesus is *still* the Glory of God veiled in human flesh – *yours!* The Lord Jesus hath clothed Himself with *you!* Two thousand years ago, God revealed His Glory on Planet Earth through the Incarnation of His Son *Jesus*. And *now*, God is revealing His Glory on this Earth through the Incarnation of His Son *"Jesus in you."* With the Living Christ "living in you," Christian, you have so much to give to this world. Most of all, you have *Jesus Himself* to give to everyone around you! *You* are "living proof" that Jesus arose from the grave and is *Alive* today because *Jesus is Alive in you!! You* are a "walking Bible" for all to read. *"As I walk through this world, I am just Jesus' overcoat!"* (Bill Bright).

So, tell me something: How could a Born-Again Christian *ever* have "a dark night of the soul"? I'll tell you how. The Spirit of Christ Jesus inhabits your *spirit* – He fills your *soul* by invitation. Therefore, if you want to brighten the corner where you are, you must take off your ole dark glasses and put on your new "Jesus Glasses." *Now*, you have "Spirit Vision" in the *Spiritual World*, and you can go quickly through the "Jesus Door" of your soul (the thin *Spiritual Veil* between Jesus' World and yours) and present yourself before your *King*. In *Jesus' Divine Presence*, you show Him your heart – full of *love for Him*. You remind Jesus of your past – full of *trust in Him*. You reveal to Jesus your present – full of your great *need of Him*. Then, you humbly ask Jesus to come back with you into *your* world and shoulder that heavy burden you've been trying to carry all by yourself. That's all He needs to hear. *In a flash*, Jesus comes into your dark soul and brightens it up with His *Divine Light*. Jesus hugs your lonely heart and warms it up with His *Glorious Love*. *Jesus' Presence* in your soul fills your entire being full to overflowing with His *Great Joy! Praise to The Lamb upon His Throne – my heart! "The Glory which Thou gavest Me I have given them"* Signed: Jesus (John 17:22).

This is the distinct difference between Christianity and all "religions." The world's religions are studied and debated with ideas and opinions of the mind. But when you come to Christianity, the *Living Lord*

Jesus is very much "Alive!" in *you*, flooding your very *spirit* and *soul* with His **Divine Love** – which explodes into "Worship" of your Heavenly Father! As you fellowship with Jesus in your inner spirit-man, He produces in you His Great Joy, Deep Peace and Godly Wisdom. **You,** my Christian Friend, are *the manifestation* of the "Glory of God" on this Earth! *"Without the soul of man, the flesh is of no value. So, without the quickening Spirit of God, all forms of religion are dead and worthless"* (Matthew Henry).

When Jesus opens the *Spiritual Eyes* of your heart to see His Glorious Beauty and Majesty within you, nothing will be able to keep you away. The greatest fireworks in the world aren't on the Fourth of July, nor are they the lightning storms of summer – they happen every day in your spirit between your Lord Jesus and you! Granny had it right when she called courting, "sparkin'." *"Set me as a seal upon thine heart ... for love is strong as death, the coals thereof are coals of fire, which hath a most vehement flame!"* (Song of Solomon 8:6). The greatest romance in the world doesn't come out of romance novels or Hollywood – it comes out of *Heaven* and takes place in your spirit between Jesus and you! The dynamics of the True Christian Life are *real*; they are *constant*; they are *powerful*, and they will *never end*. Don't wait until after you die to find out what you were missing on this Earth. The *Living Presence* of the Spirit of Christ Jesus is "calling" to you *now*. **"Behold, the Kingdom of God is within you!" Signed: Jesus** (Luke 17:21).

At the heart of every man's existence is this **"Divine Romance."** We are all die-hard romantics because **Jesus** our Creator is a die-hard Romantic. Even if you are the most hardened criminal who ever lived, you *still* crave the *Love* of your Creator God ... and He is *still* pursuing you. We Born-Again Christians have found the *Love* of our God in **Jesus** – Who is *forever* pursuing a closer, more intimate "Relationship" with us. So, keep your heart in tune with *Jesus' Heart of Love*. Try tuning *out* the world for a change and tuning *in* Jesus' Powerfully Supernatural World. *Oh*, the difference the **Spirit of Christ Jesus** makes in your heart, your mind, your soul – *your life!* Live moment by moment in the *Spiritual Presence* of the Glory of Jesus. Life will be a "Joy!" – filled with the sweetness and quiet rest of your Lord Jesus – Who is the *Glorious Rewarder* of those who seek Him with *all their heart*. "Jesus' World" in *this* world is just a heartbeat away. The *Veil* is thin. *Divine Love* will lead you in. Jesus is

waiting for you – *just for you*. *"The cure for a lonely heart is to get alone with Jesus"* (John Piper).

There is another way Jesus loves you; He loves you through people. Our Lord calls us to "be Jesus" to this lost world, *and* He also calls us to "be Jesus" to one another by loving others as He loves *us*. I only have a few friends, but they are my very special "Sisters-in-Jesus." No one is poor who has a good friend. When you have a Christian friend who prays for you and loves you with **Jesus' Love**, you are rich indeed – and *that* will cure a lonely heart too. When people in *this world* share a mutual love for Jesus in *His World*, He bonds them together *on Earth* with a love that will last for *all Eternity*.

You know you're old when there is no one left on this Earth for you to bury … but *you*. It's true: I've lived to be the last leaf upon the tree in the Spring. But the good news is that the older I get, the closer I get to going to *Heaven!* And *that* gets me more and more interested in doing something *every day* that will add to Jesus' Kingdom. I want *lots* of folks with me in Heaven enjoying to the utmost those *Eternal Joys* that are only found in Jesus and His Spiritual World. And I want *you*, Christian, to start living for Jesus' World *now* so that you can get a good taste of Jesus' Joy *before* you die.

I had always heard the ole saying about "having one foot in the grave and the other on a banana peel" and thought it was just a joke … until *I* became gravely ill. *Then*, it suddenly became a reality. I remember looking around at this material world and it all seemed so **"unreal."** I remember how it felt for the "life force" (that every person is born with) to totally drain out of my body. I remember looking around at things I needed to do and having no strength to do them. I remember looking around at things I had once loved and having no desire to even keep them. I remember the feeling of how easy it would be to just slip through the *Veil* between this world and the next … and leave this ole world behind. And I was *soooo* ready. I found out that it's true: Our gracious Lord really *does* give us "dying Grace." There are moments in life (and death) when God reveals to us just how thin the *Veil* between His World and ours really is. Nothing matters … **but God.** As the moments tick away, you learn the profound truth that when the Grim Reaper rattles his chains of death at you, he will expose what you *truly believe* about God. Well, I must have really baffled him because I can

also remember how excited I got as I anticipated my soon trip to *Heaven* – where I would be with my **Jesus!!** I kept thinking, *"I can't believe it! It's finally **my** turn to get to go to **Heaven**! Wow! This is soooo exciting!!"*

As I look back now, I realize what was actually going on. It all happened during the writing of my first book *Ole Slewfoot*, and ole slewfoot was *determined* that I would never live to publish it. Satan's plan was to turn me into a *real* "ghost writer." **But God!!** Yep, my Lord voted for me to live and keep working on this book He had "called" me to write – and **His** is the only vote that counts. I don't know about you, my Christian Friend, but I have a Miracle-Working Saviour Who *loves* to work in impossible situations so that this watching world can "see" *His Power* and *His Glory*. With **God** all things are possible! So, the Great Physician showed the Grim Reaper the door, gave me "healing Grace" and here I am today … still harassing that ole devil every way I can *(hee-hee)*. In fact, I'm on that critter's case night and day. I know how to defeat him: **Give lots of lost folks the Gospel of Jesus Christ!**

I wrote *Ole Slewfoot* for the purpose of convincing those lost folks that the "Spiritual Realm" is *very real*; the Lord Jesus is *very real*; satan is *very real*; the devil's death-grip on them is *very real*; their death is *very real* – *but* Salvation in **Jesus Christ** is also **very real.** In this book, I want to "be Jesus" to you Born-Again Christians by getting *you* to focus on the "Spiritual Realm" as well – but instead of convincing you that you need the Saviour, the *Saviour* wants to convince you that He needs *you* … to *free* those poor souls in satan's death-grip. "Jesus in me" wants to encourage you in the strongest way possible to take your position as "Ambassador of Jesus Christ" quite seriously before *your* death and you must face your Lord Jesus with no "Spiritual Fruit" to show for the life you lived here on Planet Earth. *Mercy Me!*

Now here's the situation; satan just *hates it* that he lost you as his slave. But no worries, Mate; ole slick has come up with a plan that will render you ineffective as a Christian. Yes siree, he just keeps you *totally* focused on his "Big Show" he's got going on *all the time* here on Planet Earth (no matter where you live). *Come, one! Come, all! Step right up and lay your money down!!* The price of the devil's tickets to his "Big Show" is extremely high – your time, your life, your soul … *your Destiny.* Satan doesn't give you a minute's rest from *his* world so that you get the chance to go into **Jesus' World** – where all things **Eternal**

are. The overabundance of the things of this world and its wealth can have an intoxicating effect on human beings – including *you*. Now is the time for you to wise-up and realize that you don't *have to* let ole slewfoot coerce you into attending Ole King Nebbie's Rock Concert. Nope, when satan plays his devilish music to **you** and demands that you bow down to his idols, *you* will say, *"I am not careful to answer thee in this matter. If it be so, my God Whom I serve is able to deliver me from your burning temptations, and He will deliver me out of thine hand, O god of this world. But if not, be it known unto thee, O devil, that I will* **not** *serve thy gods nor worship the idols of gold (money) which thou hast set up"* (Daniel 3:16-18). I promise you, there **is** a way for you to lick ole slick – it's **The Way**. Just go to **Jesus** in *His World* and sincerely pray,

"Lord Jesus, I belong to YOU!
You purchased me with your Precious Blood, and
You are now 'First' in my life. This very moment, I surrender
myself to You to use as You will to build Your Eternal Kingdom.
Lord Jesus, use me (yes, me) so powerfully that it would make
satan's ears tingle if he heard of it. So, go ahead and show
this world Your Resurrection Power – working through me!
Thank You, Lord, in advance for all YOU are going to do.
I pray this in the Mighty Name of Jesus, Amen,"
(And HE WILL!).

Now, I know what you're thinking, *"That wouldn't work for me. I don't have any Gifts."* Wrong. You have the same "Gifts" all Christians have: Life, God's Love, Christ's Spirit, Eternal Life, God's Word, the Gospel, Faith, Prayer, the Church, at least one Spiritual Gift and time. But the question on the Floor is: *What are you doing with your Gifts?* Are you *choosing* to spend your life (time, *same thing*) living for this world, *or* ... are you *choosing* to invest your Gifts in those things that will follow you into **Eternity?** Unsaved people don't know *why* they have been given the *Gift of Life* or *Who* gave it to them. Therefore, they are unable to do anything of *Eternal value*. Born-Again Christians know

that *God* gives us the *Gifts of Life and Eternal Life* so that we will invest *our* God-given lives in the only things that *can* follow us into Eternity – *the souls of people.* The Gospel of Jesus Christ is old ... it's new ... it's timeless. There's no time like the present to use the old Gospel to birth a New Child into **God's Eternal Kingdom.** *You miss ALL the shots you don't take.*

Electricity is unseen, yet very powerful. Most people don't understand how it works or how to produce it, but they know beyond a doubt it is real – they use it 24/7. If unbelievers know that an unseen power is making their TV work, then why do they laugh when we tell them that an unseen Power (Spiritual Person) is at work energizing our *spirit*? Answer: Because the *evil-one* they don't know they belong to is secretly at work keeping their soul's energizer batteries *spiritually dead.* Therefore, they don't know what they don't know: *Jesus' World is a Supernatural World that runs on His Supernatural Power.* Our Unseen God has Wisdom, Knowledge and Power that mere mortals can't even begin to fathom. God's ways are so far above ours that we can only perceive them through *Faith. "What is impossible with man is possible with God"* (Luke 18:27).

A Born-Again Christian is a *Supernatural Being.* Our physical body is a "Miracle-Creation" of a Supernatural God Who is now indwelling our inner spirit-man in the Person of His Son's Spirit. If you have ever studied quantum physics, you know that this is not really all that unbelievable. The "Unseen World" is made up of unseen molecules consisting of atoms. Scientists have discovered subatomic particles so small and so fast they can practically be in two places *at the very same time*! A "quantum leap" occurs when an electron disappears from one energy level within an atom and reappears in another *simultaneously. Wow!*

If scientists could go deep enough into the world of smaller, faster subatomic particles, would they eventually enter *Another Dimension*? I don't know; I just know that Jesus, in His Glorified Body, is the *Missing Link* into that Dimension. When Jesus passed through "solid" walls, He was merely demonstrating the "Laws of Divine Quantum Mechanics." Each *subatomic particle* in Jesus' body was able to *very quickly* "go around" each subatomic particle in the wall and come out the other side just like it went in. Jesus was in league with the stones of the field ... as

well as the stones of the walls! *"Welcome to My World!"* *"If you think you understand quantum mechanics, you don't understand quantum mechanics"* (Richard Feynman).

When we all get to Heaven, we will be even smarter than Einstein … for we shall know as we are known. Even now, we know that the "Unseen World" is more powerful than the visible world. You have probably seen films of nuclear explosions. All that **power** comes from within molecules not visible to our naked eye. *Double Wow!* God tells us in His Word that from His unseen Supernatural World *(Spiritual Dimension)* He created the world we see out of things we cannot see. *Bingo!* People of Faith have no problem believing that, but satan makes sure *his* followers have a problem with anything and everything that even hints of a Creator God. Therefore, atheists say that we Christians are ignorant, unsophisticated and insane to believe so radically in something no one can see. Au contraire, God tells us in His Word that we *do* "see" Him … by looking at the things He has created (Romans 1:20). *Yes, indeed!* We aren't "Einsteins" yet, but we're smart enough to know that everything created *must* be created by *someone*. **Someone** powerful enough to *create* the Heavens, the Earth, everything on the Earth and the entire Universe is even *more real* than His Creation – including the puny men debating and arguing His existence with the very brains *He created* and placed within them. *One would think that men as "brilliant" as they are could figure that out.*

Truth be told, all people everywhere *know* in their heart of hearts that God *does* exist because they can *see* all that He has created. An atheist can argue with you about many things, my Friend, but he cannot deny his own existence. Nevertheless, his demonic pride forces him to *insist* there is no God – even though he doesn't know how he got here. If you doubt me on that, just ask him to explain to you how the theory (phony lie) of evolution works – and since they love "following the science," tell him you want to hear how it works *scientifically.*

Another reality staring the atheist in the face (that he cannot deny) is the fact of his own death – but he hasn't a clue where he's going when it occurs. If asked, the clueless atheist will say, *"Nowhere."* The poor fellow needs for you to clue-him-in to the fact that it is his *"spirit"* within his physical body that gives him *"human life."* So … where did his *"spirit"* come from – and where is it going when he dies? An atheist

is an expert on everything … except the things that really matter … for **Eternity.** *"Professing themselves to be wise, they became fools"* (Romans 1:22). The non-existence of God only exists in the minds of atheists … not in the real world. A truly honest man *must* admit that only a *Supernatural God* is able to "Create" a *Supernatural Human Being* – as well as an equally amazing *Supernatural Universe.* No doubt about it, a *Supernatural Designer* created our Universe. If it had *not* been incredibly designed and engineered right down to *the minutest detail,* it would not be able to exist at all – and some well-known scientists are admitting to that truth.

> *"I find it quite improbable that such order came out of chaos. God to me is a mystery but is the explanation for the Miracle of existence; why there is something instead of nothing"* (Allan Sandage).

> *"A common sense interpretation of the facts suggests that a Super Intellect has monkeyed with physics, as well as with chemistry and biology, and that there are no blind forces worth speaking about in nature"* (Fred Hoyle).

Now, go look in the mirror. Every cell of your body contains an *astronomical* amount of "Intelligent Information" and "Divine Energy" which caused it to become that which our **Creator God** designed it to become – **you.** At the moment of conception, all the genetic information necessary to make you **"you"** was instantly encoded into the DNA of every cell of your body (and men have a *different* chromosome make-up in *every* cell than women). Every organ was present and accounted for as you grew in your mother's womb. Nine months later, God presented to the world His "Unique Creation" – the likes of which had never existed before and will never exist again. God has *Infinite Creativity.* You are indeed "one of a kind."

God created Adam and Eve with their genetic information *fixed* and *complete* in the DNA of every cell of *their* bodies … and from

generation to generation, God does the same for each one of us. We *do not* have the ability to change that *Miracle* of God, and it doesn't change itself. Only **God** has the *Power* to change (or add to) the *Supernaturally encoded* **Intelligent Information** contained in the DNA of our cells (mutations may alter the information already there, but they do not add *new* information – they *can't*). A fish **does not** have the *Power* within itself to give birth to a baby fish that looks even the least bit like a reptile (regardless of *what* "they" try to tell us). If fish *could*, we would be seeing half-fish/half-reptile critters in the sea and on the land *everywhere (Duh)*. And where are all the half-monkey/half-man creatures, walking around as *living proof* of evolution?!! Right, the "missing link" is truly missing – and "they" don't have a clue. Sorry satan, your evil *lie* of evolution is a dead theory and a lost cause. You're just kicking a dead horse that will never be able to get up and run – or even limp.

"Thou art worthy, O Lord,
to receive Glory and Honor and Power;
for Thou hast Created all things,
and for Thy pleasure they are and were Created!"
Signed: Every Born-Again Christian (Revelation 4:11).

People who believe in evolution may tell you that certain "scientists" are now saying that they *know* how life on Earth began – it was brought here from outer-space by aliens in spaceships (and since "they" say it, then it *has* to be true). But don't let people who claim to believe those "mad scientists" frazzle you in the least. Just reply, *"Well, tell me this: Who created those aliens in the first place? Who gave life, intelligence and bodies to the aliens? Who created the Universe they live in?"* Hey, my Christian Friend, we don't have to prove that God exists; He proves it Himself. It's the *atheists* who can't even *begin* to prove that God *doesn't* exist. I am constantly amused by all the irrational back-flips atheists do in order to *somehow* disprove our **Great God**. Truth is: **God is Eternal** while *"they"* have only been around for a few years – *and yet*, they want us to

believe that *they* are smart enough to tell all the rest of us, *"God doesn't exist!"* When are they ever going to just give it up and admit that if **God** didn't exist … *Ta Da* … *they* wouldn't exist either!

But, alas, this world is full of people satan has fooled into believing that God doesn't exist. Ole slewfoot is crafty; he manages to keep his spiritual-zombies from ever coming to their senses and realizing that they are thinking the thought, *"God doesn't exist"* with the *very brain* **God** *created* and placed within their body – *which He also created!* The devil keeps his slaves so distracted with the things of this material world that they never wake up and realize they are actually a **spiritual soul** with a *Supernatural spirit and mind* that will continue to live on even *after* their physical body dies. Ole slick has them believing that even if God *did* somehow exist, they could never know this Powerful, Supernatural God *personally* – *or* have a close, intimate "Relationship" with Him.

Well, I have news for them: "The Finger of God" has indeed touched Planet Earth – and His Name is **Jesus!** *"God took a 'Selfie' of Himself and sent it to us – **Jesus Christ!**"* (Tony Evans). God sent His Son to defeat the devil (who holds people captive with sin), and Jesus did that on Calvary's Cross – *but* it cost Him His physical life. Since God never leaves Himself without a Witness, He has chosen **your body** to carry on "The Family Business" through; and now that God has touched *you* with His *Saving Power*, **you** have become "The Finger of God" in this world. **"Jesus in you"** now reaches out to touch those lost folks with God's Love and Gospel Truth: *"Jesus' Blood washes away all of your sins so that His Spirit can enter into your spirit and dwell there in a close, intimate 'Relationship' with you."*

As you speak Christ's Gospel to the lost, God watches over His Word to perform it. **You** make it possible for your Lord to convince satan's "fooled-ones" that He *does* exist; He *does* love them (enough to die for them), and He *has* come *Himself* to tell them so. **"So shall My Word be that goeth forth out of My mouth; it shall not return unto Me void, but it shall accomplish that which I please, and it shall prosper in the thing whereto I sent it" Signed: Jehovah Jesus (Isaiah 55:11).**

Christian, it is your unseen *spiritual mind* (within your spirit) that makes it possible for Jesus to "live" *through you*. Since Christ's Spirit also dwells within your spirit, He is able to put "Jesus' Thoughts" into

your spirit's amazing "mind" and then download them into your physical brain. Once that occurs, you are able to think *Jesus' Thoughts* after Him and do *His Will* for Him. At least, that's the way it *should* be. More often than we care to admit, our "mind" chooses to ignore those thoughts coming to us from our Lord and chooses instead to listen to the *suggestions* coming from our "flesh" *(and we all know what that gets us).* The Christian life is a constant, decided choice, and we make each choice depending on what is in our "heart" – love for our Lord or ... well, you know.

In order for your Lord to always be the One controlling your thoughts, He's going to need a little co-operation from *you*. Turn off the TV, shut down your computer, kill those *"Bings"* coming from your bossy smarty-pants phone and take your **Bible** to a cozy chair. As you read the *Powerful Words* of **Jesus**, your spirit-man will hear Him speaking directly to **you!** Suddenly, you are in "Another World" – **Jesus' World** – sitting at His feet and hanging on His every Word. You were *Saved* bowing at the foot of Jesus' Cross. You *grow* sitting at His feet. (Instead of growing and maturing, some Christians remain "Spiritual Babies" because they never learn to feed themselves ... from the Word of God.) Like an ole-timey miner, you must *dig* to find the "Gold" within the mine. And when you do, it will sparkle in your hand with the *Divine Gold Dust* of the *Presence of* the **Lord Jesus!** *"I will not leave you alone; I will come unto (into) you."*

So, take your Bible, a pick and a shovel and go through the "Jesus Door" of your soul. **Invest** some of your life (time, *same thing*) digging into Jesus' Gold Mine, and your Lord Jesus Himself will reward your investment with *Diamonds in the Dust! "You are only as strong as your last time with God"* (Jeff Wickwire). Your Lord's purpose for spending time with you is to connect you to His Infinite, Eternal Kingdom. As Jesus broadens your horizon, you *see* that you are "on mission" in *this world* while taking your marching orders from your Sovereign King Who rules from "Another World." Jesus is giving you the amazing privilege of investing in that "Other World" – **Eternity!** When you can see *God's Eternal Purpose* for having you exactly where you are right now, you will *see* "your mission" ... and you will be able to endure it. *"You have no meaning in your life because you have no 'Mission!' in your life"* (Jack Graham).

The *Power* you need to fulfill "your mission" of telling lost folks about your Saviour comes from the Spirit of Christ Who lives within you. You can call on Jesus anytime, anywhere to help you, and He will show up in a flash with just what He wants to tell them. *However*, you won't bother calling on your Lord to help you witness for Him ... *until* ... you love Him *with all your heart.* So, take a little trip into Jesus' World and pay another visit to the foot of His Cross, where you met Him for the very first time. Go back in your spirit to that moment you first looked into *Jesus' Eyes of Love* (lovingly gazing into *your* eyes as He gives His Precious Life for you) and fall in love all over again. *"I am my Beloved's, and my Beloved is mine!" Signed: Molly* (Song of Solomon 6:3).

In a *Supernatural* way, Jesus wants you to *experience for yourself* His marvelous **Love** for you. Your Lord wants you to *know* that there is a place in His heart no one else can fill ... *but* **you**. It is your "Special Place" that Jesus has reserved for just the two of you. Jesus calls it *"The Divine Honeymoon Suite"* for the Bridegroom and His Bride. To meet with Jesus there, your *spirit-man* must steal away into Jesus' Spiritual World by *Divinely* stepping into His peaceful heart. Once there, you discover that Jesus' heart is full to overflowing with His *Great Love – for you!* Now you can experience to the utmost *Jesus' Glorious Love!* Jesus calls it "Your Master's Key" to His *Divine Honeymoon Suite.* Jesus' Awesome Spiritual Presence is intimately close to you right now, and He is just waiting for you to enter His embrace ... within the inner *Holy Chamber* of His heart.

So, calm your mind, open your heart and *receive* **Jesus' Love** – a **Love** so deep, so *Divine* and so peaceful that it gently flows into every crevice of your being. Jesus' Love comes softly. Come softly to Jesus. Step into His heart and take your rightful place there. Your Heavenly Bridegroom says, **"Come!"** Let His Betrothed Bride say, **"I come!"** Take His nail-pierced hand of Love in your frail hand of Faith and begin a New Journey through life together – Spirit to spirit.

This is the secret to witnessing – surrendering yourself to Jesus, your Heavenly Bridegroom, and giving yourself completely over to Him as a wife does to her husband. Now that the two of you have become "One," you will truly go out witnessing *with* **Jesus!** **"I in you, and you in Me."** *"That Christ may dwell in your hearts by Faith that ye being rooted and grounded in Love, may be able to comprehend with all saints what*

is the breath and length and depth and height, and to know the Love of Christ which passeth knowledge, that ye might be filled with all the Fullness of God" (Ephesians 3:17-19). *Even so, Come, Lord Jesus!!*

This book is "Jesus" inviting you to fellowship with *Him* above everyone else. Jesus knows that *when you do*, you will joyously "spend" your life (time, *same thing*) intentionally *investing* it in "God's Spiritual Eternal Kingdom" … instead of wasting it on this doomed temporal world. *"People living for this world are in the junk business"* (Adrian Rogers). Those poor Wall-Street-Wizard-Billionaires are just in the junk business; so we don't need to pay them big bucks to tell **us** how to make wise investments. We Christians could tell *them* how to make the wisest "Investment" of all! Make up *your Mind of Christ* to choose **Jesus** (and His Kingdom) over *whatever* "the world" has to offer. I can promise you that when you choose Jesus, your Lord will choose to reward you with *Spiritual Blessings* on this Earth you were never expecting and *Eternal Blessings* awaiting you in Heaven that will be your great **Joy** *forever! You can't take it with you, so send it on ahead!! "By faith, Moses forsook Egypt, not fearing the wrath of the king, for he endured, as seeing Him who is unseen"* (Hebrews 11:27).

"And straightway (Jesus) constrained His disciples to get into the ship, and to go to the other side before unto Bethsaida, while He sent the people away. And when He had sent them away, He departed into a mountain to pray" (Mark 6:45-46). As I was reading those verses one day, something like a flash of light leapt from deep within my spirit and landed in my mind. Now, I'm not trying to "add to the Scriptures" here, but a thought came into my "sanctified imagination" that I would like to share with you. I couldn't help but wonder why Jesus would "constrain" His disciples to get into that ship and sail away while *He* sent the crowd away in order to go up on a mountain *alone* to pray. As I pondered the answer, I knew that *I* definitely wasn't alone, and in a split-second, my "Spiritual Eyes" caught a glimmer of something only my "Jesus Glasses" could have revealed.

John the Baptist (Jesus' cousin) had just been murdered in the first part of the chapter. John loved Jesus, and Jesus deeply loved John. Therefore, John's beheading had been a very sad, traumatic experience for Jesus (and we know for sure it was for John). With that in mind, let me suggest to you that Jesus (the God of all compassion) could have

wanted to be alone on that mountain so that He could meet with John on their own intimate "Mount of Transfiguration" the same way He would meet with Moses and Elijah later on. It seems reasonable to me that Jesus would want to share John's joy of having a body that was "whole" again. Jesus would also have the joy of saying, *"See, John, I AM the Messiah!"* Only they know for sure, but I had often wondered why it took Jesus *so long* to go to the rescue of His terrified disciples out in the middle of the Sea of Galilee in a storm. Unbeknownst to the Terrified Twelve, our Lord had *something else* very important to do.

(Side-note: I can just see Jesus motioning to John and saying, *"Hey John, come over here and see this. Look at those seasoned-sailors struggling out there in the middle of that storm. Can you see Peter trying to convince everyone he's got everything under control? I AM just teaching them the lesson of how badly they need **Me** – always. Wait 'til you see how Peter learns that. Well, gotta run. You stay here and watch while I go have some fun. But first, we'd better pray, John; those guys sure need it ... more than they know."*)

Now granted, I can't prove a single word of what I have just shared with you, but if I know my Lord, that's exactly what He did. The point I'm making is this: Jesus loves each and every one of **us** the very same way. If you will just "go up to the mountain" in Jesus' World to meet with Him, I can guarantee you, He will definitely *be there* to faithfully meet with *you* – and reveal to you **His Glory!** Your gracious Lord Jesus will give you as much of Himself as you want. He wants more of **you** than you could ever possibly imagine – **and He's waiting for you right now.** *"Father, I will that they also, whom Thou hast given Me, be with Me where I am; that they may behold My Glory, which Thou hast given Me"* Signed: Jesus (John 17:24).

"The mountains are calling, and I must go" (John Muir). If you listen closely, you will hear Jesus "calling" to **you** from the "Mount of Transformation" within your spirit ... and your spirit-man *must* answer His "Call" and go forth to intimately meet with your Heavenly Bridegroom in the glorious solitude of your *spiritual soul*. There, in loving fellowship with Jesus, He shows you *His Glory* and the *Eternal Glory* He has for *you* – His Beloved Bride. Your Lord's *Glorious Love* always transforms you ... filling you with Joy unspeakable and Glory immeasurable. *"Did not our heart burn within us, while He talked*

with us by the way, and while He opened to us the Scriptures?" (Luke 24:32). *YES!!*

My Friend, you may have been a Born-Again Christian for many years and everything is just hunky dory in your life right now ... but *you still need **Jesus**.* You really do. And until you realize how much you need Him, you won't spend much time seeking Him. Don't make Jesus come get you. *You* go after *Him* ... in the sweet stillness of your *soul* in a solitary place ... just Jesus and you. Deep in the heart of every person whom God has created is a deeper-still **Eternal** longing for *Him* ... because **God** *has* put it there. Don't wait 'til this world has chewed you up and spit you out to start seeking **The One** Who loves you more than you could ever imagine ... and will *be there* when the stars all burn away. Your Lord dwells within the inner-sanctuary of your soul every moment of every day, and He so *longs* for you to acknowledge His Presence there ... by touching Him with your love. There is Romance at the Heart of God's Universe because there is Romance in the Heart of God. That is why your Heavenly Bridegroom is ever calling to you. Better still, Jesus is singing a Love Song just to you (Zephaniah 3:17). Make it a Duet. Sing *your* Love Song back to **Jesus!** Forget trying to make that girl (guy) fall in love with you. Jesus Christ is already madly in love with you! Wake up and smell His Heavenly Fragrance. *"My Song will silence never! I'll worship Him forever! And praise Him for His Glorious Love!"* (1970 John W. Peterson Music Co. Used by permission).

Now, I know what you're thinking, *"I would love to get alone with Jesus, but I've got a houseful of noisy kids, and I never get a minute to myself, for pity's sake!"* OK. Jesus can work with that. Don't despair ... because this is your chance to "be Jesus" to your little "arrows" – who just need to be placed into their Lord's Mighty Hands. They need to meet **Jesus**, *The Transformer God*, Who is able to turn them into His *Witnessing Warriors.* Yes siree, **Jesus** is a Saviour Who **ever** has **A Plan!** And here it is: Gather your "little Blessings" around you and tell them to listen closely; then softly tell them that instead of playing war-games, they will be joining you in a meeting with the **Lord Jesus Himself** – Who is *right there* meeting with all of **you** ... in the invisible "Spiritual Realm."

If *that* doesn't get their attention, they didn't hear what you said. So, let them know you're quite serious by telling them that *you* talk with Jesus all during the day (just don't tell them it's because of *them*). Then,

let each one initiate a personal conversation (prayer) with Jesus. Teach them to "talk with Jesus," "sing to Jesus" *and* "listen for His Voice" while "looking for His answers." Teach them how *they* can enter into "Jesus' World" through that narrow gate Jesus told us about. Tell them it's sorta like Jesus is hiding in His "Invisible Word," and it's up to *them* to seek Him – *and find Him* – by means of their invisible soul (heart). They will soon learn that Jesus loves "fellowshipping" with as many as will fellowship with *Him*. *"Parents, you can raise your kids to live in a zoo, or you can train your children to survive in the jungle"* (Tim Kimmel).

There are so many wonderful ways for the Lord to build *Faith* in His future "Witnessing Warriors." Tell them the intriguing story of Jehovah Jesus showing up as a "Mighty Warrior" on Mt. Carmel and revealing to *everyone* His Awesome Power and Great Glory by defeating satan and *his* followers. Teach them how **King Jesus** intends to use *them* in the very *real* "Spiritual War" against evil in the *Spiritual Realm*. Parents, don't let ungodly movies and TV shows teach your precious children only about the *dark demonic* side of the "Spiritual World." *You* teach them that **Jesus is God!** **He** is "The King" of both the seen *and* unseen worlds … and **He** is with them *always*. *"Be of good cheer! It is I; be not afraid"* Signed: *Jesus* (Mark 6:50).

You have probably been in a Church service when a toddler starts crying. That toddler's world is only as big as himself and his mother; he doesn't *even hear* the Preacher. There are also adults in the congregation who aren't Christians. They may be listening, but *their* world is only as big as this material world and the people in it; so they hear the Preacher, but the *Preacher* is the *only one* they hear. There are also Born-Again Christians in the congregation who have been made "Spiritually Alive!" by the **Living Christ.** *Their* world consists of this material world, the people in it *and* God's Eternal Spiritual World. They hear the Preacher, and they also hear the **Living Christ** speaking to them *through the Preacher.* *"Welcome to My World!"*

"A fellow went to a company to apply for a job during the Great Depression, but when he got there, the waiting room was already packed with people; so he took a seat. As he waited, he heard a tapping sound coming from the inner-office. He listened closely; then got up and went into the office. He came back out a little while later and said, *'I got the job!'* The others said, *'How could you get it – we were here first!'* He

replied, *'That tapping sound was Morse-code for: If you can understand this message, come on in – you have the job!'"* (Adrian Rogers). Do you have *your* "Spiritual Ears" on, and are *you* closely listening for God's Messages coming to you from *Jesus' World?* This world can't hear them, and even many Christians aren't listening for them; they don't realize that Earth is the "waiting room" for **Eternity**. So, they let the background music of the "waiting room" drown-out the *Beautiful Music* of Heaven while letting the noise drown-out *God's Eternal Messages* being sent to them from "Jesus World." As they sit there chattering away, all those clueless people in the waiting room think they are *way* ahead of you – but if **you** will turn your *Spiritual Ears* on, you will hear your Lord's still small Voice … *and* you will understand His Message to you: *"I have a job of Eternal importance to be done – and I AM giving the job to you!!"* *Mercy Me!*

Sometimes, your Lord may lead you to do things that seem "crazy" to the spiritually blind people around you. When people in your life reject and shun you, it hurts deeply, and I'm here to tell you that the only true cure for your deep pain is the deep, deep *Love of Jesus*. Only **Jesus' Love** can go as deep as your pain goes. On those dark days full of trials, heartaches, headaches, lonely moments and needs (when you don't know what to do or where to turn, *and you need answers and direction*), you have a Strong Saviour Who is also full … of *Love for you!* Jesus *delights* to see you running to Him and crying out to Him … because He is *for you*. Only **Jesus** can comfort you with everything you need. Your Good Shepherd knows you so well … He knows that **He** is everything you need. When your brook dries up, **Jesus** Himself is your Living Water. **"Come unto Me, all ye that labour and are heavy laden, and I will give you rest"** **Signed: Jesus, Our Strong Saviour** (Matthew 11:28).

When this world is too much with you, there is *Another World* you can go to. You enter Jesus' World through a heart of *"Love* for Jesus" and *"Worship* of Jesus" as your soul flies to its **Divine Source.** When you're feeling down and alone, go into your Saviour's World … and you won't come back alone. Many times, I have limped to my Jesus in *His World*, and my Strong Saviour didn't just come back with me … *He carried me back.* Yep, and my Lord didn't carry me back empty either. No siree, every time you go spend time with Jesus, He turns it into a party and loads you down with *gifts*. So, if your soul is empty and hungry today, go

through the "Jesus Door" of your soul and enter into *Jesus' World*. There, you can feast upon the "Bread of Life" to your heart's content.

When there was a lack of bread in the House of Bread (Bethlehem), Naomi and her family fled to Moab. When she returned to Bethlehem a motherless widow, Naomi told everyone she came back empty. Poor Naomi – she just didn't have her "Jesus Glasses" on. If you are a Born-Again Christian, you can never say that ... no matter what *your circumstances* are saying. You are *never* empty. Jesus fills your hungry soul and satisfies your hurting heart with His *Eternal Blessings*. The deepest hunger in the human heart is for **Jesus Himself. "My Precious Child, I AM right here with you, and I AM what you need ... more than anything else!" Signed: Jesus.**

If you are a sad, depressed Christian today, you can **"Praise!"** your way out of that. Instead of being grumbly hateful, be humbly grateful and thankfully **Praise** your Lord in your spirit as you go through your day. Jesus will see you **trusting** Him – no matter what – and He will give you more **Joy** than your heart can contain! Belonging to **King Jesus** gives you such **Joy** that it flows out of your heart in "Love Songs" to Him all day long. As you are singing a glorious hymn to your Lord, you suddenly realize that it's not just coming out of your mouth ... it's coming out of your *heart of love!! Praise* infuses your very soul with the *Supernatural Energy of God*. When satan hears you **"Praising God!"** he can't stand it. The devil hates to hear anyone praising **Jesus** instead of *him* (*he* wants to be God), so he takes off like Moody's goose.

You can be assured that you are in **Jesus'** heart and on *His* mind all the time. So, why not just return the favor? **Divine Love** is the "Key." In the ole days, America was filled with Christians who loved the Lord Jesus with all of their heart. Many of those ole-timers would sometimes set an extra place at the dinner table for "The Lord." Today, people think that's silly. Back then, they didn't think it was silly; they *knew* that the "Unseen Person" was really and truly *there*, and **He** was the *Most Important One* at the table! This book is my attempt to express the inexpressible and describe the indescribable so that you can see the unseeable, fathom the unfathomable, believe the unbelievable, understand the understandable, receive the *Spiritually* receivable and speak forth the unspeakable Gift of God – **Jesus Christ!**

This chapter began with your Lord saying to you, *"We are beginning a Journey together, you and I – that will never end!"* Your journey with Jesus is always a journey of the heart. My challenge in writing this book has been trying to figure out a way to take the "love for Jesus" I have in *my* heart and put it into *yours*. I know that I can't – **but God** can. Only **God** can ignite words on paper to start a **Holy Fire** in your **soul**. Many times, letters (and books) are sent on missions even armies couldn't hope to accomplish. This book is no different. And yet, this book *is* different. The secret is "Prayer." Prayers are sent on missions even armies couldn't hope to accomplish. **But God** can! All things are possible *with God* – He is in the *Miracle-Working Business. "Welcome To My World!"*

My Lord worked many *Miracles* in the writing of this book, and I would like to tell you about one. I know beyond a doubt that there is *Romance* at the Heart of our Universe. There is also *Laughter* at the Heart of our Universe, and yes, there is *Music* at the Heart of our Universe. After all, God tells us that He sings over us with great **"Joy!"** Do you remember the song made popular by Jim Reeves back in 1962, "Welcome To My World"? After all these years, it was a *Miracle* that *I* could. **But Jesus** is a Saviour Who *ever* has a *Miracle* for the one He is aiming at something He wants to get done. *Boing!* So, back came the memory of that ole song, but I couldn't remember the words – only the first line: *"Welcome to my world; won't you come on in?"* Neither could I understand why it just kept popping up in my mind at the oddest times. Finally, I got suspicious that my Lord might have something to do with it. In fact, I could sense Jesus saying, *"Go on-line and listen to it."* Well sir, when your Lord tells you to do something, He has a reason; there are no accidents in the Kingdom of God.

When I found it on-line and listened … I was amazed! I suddenly found myself in *Another World* – **Jesus' World!** And instead of hearing the voice of Jim Reeves, my spirit-man recognized the familiar voice of *my Saviour!* From *Another World* deep within my spirit, came the voice of **Jesus**, singing me a Love Song. I have been a widow for many years, and my dear husband's departure left a lingering sadness within my soul. But as I listened, it was as if that ole song was coming straight as an arrow from Jesus' Heart to my heart – *On the Wings of a Snow-White Dove. What a Blessing!* I knew immediately why Jesus had been bugging me

to listen to it; He wanted me to include it in this book He was bugging me to write. The fit was just perfect … just like Jesus.

The song echoed in my heart as I wrote, and I *just knew* that when my Lord Jesus inspired the writing of that song, He had this book in mind. You say, *"That's impossible."* But I say, *"Entirely Possible!!"* I tell the people I witness to that when the Lord Jesus was hanging on the Cross dying for the sins of the whole world … He was thinking about *them*. They probably think the same thing, *"That's impossible!"* But they are wrong. They just don't know Who Jesus is. **Jesus is God!** He has been thinking about **all** of us for a long, long time. So, if 2,000 years ago, Jesus could have been thinking about a person He was going to *Save* today, could He not also have been thinking many years ago about a book He was going to inspire *me* to write today? Of course, He could … because "what is impossible with man is possible with God!" *"Welcome To My World!"*

The writers of that song, Ray Winkler and John Hathcock, were just writing a nice song so that they could make a living as song writers. **But God** knew better. Our Lord had plans for their song all these years later they would never know anything about (on this Earth). In the same way, I don't know all that my Lord has planned for this book. I'm praying that fifty or a hundred years from now a copy will "just happen" to fall into the hands of someone of the Lord's choosing and change their life and their *Destiny*. We serve a **Big God**. He does **Big Things**. We call them **Miracles**. He gives them to those who **trust Him** for them. Be it unto you according to **your Faith**. *"Welcome To My World!"*

It's true, all things really *do* work together for good to those who love God and are His "Called-Out Ones" according to His purpose. You will never know this side of Heaven all the *good* your "little things" have done. One of the "Ways of God" is that He uses little things to do *Big Things*. This book is just a little thing, **but God** could use it to do *Big Things*. He could. Will He? Pray, and we'll see. One day in Heaven, we *will* see … all the answers to all the prayers we prayed while here on Earth.

Sometimes, when I'm witnessing to a young man, I will be silently praying, *"Lord, he could be the next Billy Graham!"* I may even tell the young man the same thing. I just figure that I shouldn't be the *only one* on Planet Earth with *Big Dreams*. Do you ever expect God to do *Big*

Miracles with the little things *you* do? You should, you know. Nothing is ever wasted in the Kingdom of God. Even the time you're spending reading this book won't be wasted; you'll see. As Doug Oldham sang, *"I just feel like Something Good is about to happen" (the young folks are saying, "Who?").*

With God, *Something Miraculous* is always happening. Christ Jesus is standing before you (unseen by your physical eyes but very *Present* and *Divinely visible* to your "Spiritual Eyes") inviting **you** to come into His World of **"I in you and you in Me."** This "Bigger-than-Life Relationship" is what Jesus gave His Life to have with you. *"Enter ye in at the strait gate"* (Matthew 7:13). Jesus is revealing to you "The Way" into His *Unseen World.* Your Lord is describing a gate so narrow that only you and He can go through it together. *But you* must make the choice. You can choose the wide gate – through which you find yourself in "all this world has to offer," *or* you can choose the narrow gate – through which you find yourself in a World where Jesus offers you only … *Himself.* Once you step through that narrow gate, you find yourself in Jesus' Heart – and you are amazed to discover that you have finally found the "True Path of Life." At last you understand, the *Abundant Life* Jesus promises isn't "out there" somewhere … but *here* … along this narrow path with *Jesus Himself.* It's like holding hands with **the Love of your life** as you walk along together. **Love** streams out of Jesus' eyes, and as you gaze into His eyes of **Love**, while holding His strong hand, He keeps your soul warm and secure … even on your coldest, darkest day. Since Jesus no longer has a physical hand on this Earth for you to hold, you hold Him in your heart. As you *embrace Jesus* with your "heart of love," you keep *your* heart touching **Jesus'** heart, and He sweetly abides in your soul. **"Abide in Me, and I in you" Signed: Jesus (John 15:4).**

Now, I know what you're thinking, *"I've got this big family and this busy job, see – so I don't have the time nor the opportunity to go through strait gates and walk down narrow paths … just Jesus and me."* Well cheer up, Dear Heart, because your chances of having an "Abundant Life" with Jesus just got a whole lot better. The song says: *"Ask and you'll be given the Key to this World of Mine."* Jesus has already given you the "Key" to enter His World: His Precious Blood which He shed for you on the Cross. Jesus' Blood washed you clean of all your sins; God sealed you "in Christ," and Jesus was *miraculously* Born-Again "in

85

you." Now, no matter where you are, what you are doing or who you are with, you are with Jesus in His Spiritual World, *and* Jesus is with you in your physical world.

I know it sounds like a science-fiction movie, but it is *Supernaturally True!* When you are playing with your kids, "**Jesus** in you" is playing with your kids. When you are talking with your wife, "**Jesus** in you" is talking with your wife. When you are leading that committee at work, "**Jesus** in you" is leading that committee at work. When you are coaching your son's football team, "**Jesus** in you" is coaching your son's football team. When you are visiting your sick friend, "**Jesus** in you" is visiting your sick friend. When you are serving food, "**Jesus** in you" is serving food. Jesus is always with you in your world – *in you*. Jesus' Abundant Life fills you *so full* that He spills over and out of you onto all the people around you. "**Jesus** in you" loves *Blessing* folks – through *you*. *"Even when I don't get my Miracle, I can still be 'A Miracle' for someone else"* (Nick Vuyicic).

I most appreciate my *Abundant Life* with Jesus when I am witnessing. As I stand there in front of a lost person and tell them about my Lord, I am spiritually, mentally and emotionally connected to "Jesus in me" in my mind and in my heart. Therefore, I consciously realize that it's not *just me* standing there but the **Spirit of Christ** *within me* also present and conversing with this person. I am in this physical world allowing **"Jesus"** to speak *through me* from His Unseen Spiritual World to this lost soul on Planet Earth. A*mazing!* (The more *you* do this, the more you will relate to everyone in your life this way. And I can assure you, your wife (husband) will be ever so thankful for *that*.)

Now I know what you're thinking, *"Does witnessing in this manner guarantee that every lost person I witness to will accept Jesus as their Saviour?"* I wish it did, but one of the many occupational hazards of being a Witnessing Christian is that many people will *reject* Jesus and His Salvation. The preaching of the Cross is foolishness to them who are perishing. But don't let it get you down. Either you're talking to a "tare" *or* you're talking to a "wheat" who isn't ready to be harvested yet. Just keep on keeping on – *for Jesus!* One thing that *will* happen is that you will be more at ease and confident as you talk with people. Knowing that your Lord is right there *with you* and *in you* will take a lot of the fear out of witnessing for Him.

Simply stated, the *Abundant Life* is living a life "full of **Jesus**" – Who once gave us a clue as to how we can. A crowd of people were touching Jesus when He stopped and said, *"Who touched Me? Somebody hath touched me, for I perceive that virtue is gone out of Me"* (Luke 8:45-46). Many people were touching Jesus, but **only one** received something from Him. Jesus wants **you** to be *that* person. So, when you go into Jesus' World to spend some of your life (time, *same thing*) with Him, make sure you're going there to get something. Humbly and thankfully, **receive** everything Jesus is just sitting on ready to give you: Love, Joy, Peace, Wisdom, Patience, Kindness, Courage, Knowledge, Companionship, Perseverance, Illumination and much more. Then, come back to *your* world and give it all away … *for Jesus' sake. "Cast thy bread upon the waters, for thou shalt find it after many days"* (Ecclesiastes 11:1).

"But whosoever drinketh of the Water that I shall give him shall never thirst; but the Water that I shall give him shall be in him a Well of Water springing up into Everlasting Life!" Signed: Jesus (John 4:14). *Wow!* Just think, Jesus promises *you*, my Christian Friend, that He has placed a Well in you that *never runs dry*. And I know what you're thinking, *"So, what's in Jesus' Well?"* Answer: **Jesus Himself** – in the Person of His Spirit. Jesus has sent *His Spirit* into *your spirit* from His Throne on High. The result: **"Jesus in you."** Jesus' Spirit in *your spirit* links you to the *Divine Source* of your every *Spiritual* need. Flowing out of Jesus' Well are: Living Words (the Bible) and Living Water (the Spiritual Person Who opens up the Scriptures to you as you read His Word). *Ah yes,* the "Spiritual Person" – **The Lord Jesus** is "The One" I need most of all. You are probably a lot like me, and more than anything else, you just need to know how very much *Jesus loves you*. Right? Yep, so take a really big bucket with you and go into Jesus' World. There, you will find Jesus standing by His Well. Hand Him your bucket, and He will fill it full to overflowing with His Love. Then, come back to *your* world and give it all away … to that lost person who needs **Jesus** and **His Love.** *"Love one another, as I have loved you!!"*

Your Lord's Well in you never runs dry, *but* (and all God's People said, *but*) *your soul* will be dry … *until* … you go into Jesus' World and spend some time at His *Spiritually Deep Well*. Just drop your bucket down it and draw out all your Lord has for you that will empower you to do what He has "called" you to do. Your fancy-phone can't give you

what your **Lord Jesus** will give you from His *Divinely Deep Well* in His Spiritual World. *So*, allow me to ask you a few personal questions: How often do you go into Jesus' World and draw out of His Spiritual Well? How big of a bucket do you take? On the other hand, how much time do you spend at the wells of *this* world ... drawing out of *them*? How big of a bucket do you take *then*? (You aren't required to answer out loud.)

I can guarantee you, ole slewfoot will deviously throw up every obstacle imaginable between you and Jesus' Well because he wants you to keep coming to *his* wells instead. Ole slick wins the day when he gets you drinking his cleverly disguised witch's-brew (devil's de-lite) out of the wells of this world instead of **Jesus' Living Water** out of Jesus' Eternal Well. Yep, that shifty devil has the perfect recipe for a "monster drink" that will turn you into a walking Christian Zombie. "Jesus in me" is here to warn you that you will *never* quench that thirst deep within your soul drinking the devil's "down-and-dirty" water. Only **Jesus** (The Living Word/The Living Water/The Bread of Life) can fill that empty void in your soul. You will *never* satisfy the hunger of your heart eating from satan's tree of "forbidden fruit." Just ask Eve. She found out the hard way that seven days on the devil's diet makes one weak. *Mercy Me!*

My Christian Friend, Jesus is always waiting for you in His World to give you many other things as well. If you will just go to Him with your empty bucket, Jesus will fill it up with whatever you need. And when He does, you will look into your bucket and shriek, *"Lord!! This isn't what I came to You to get, (for pity's sake)!"* And your Lord will lovingly reply, *"My Dear Child, I gave you what I know you need (to Glorify Me) – not what you think you want (to satisfy yourself). Trust Me always, for our Heavenly Father's sake."*

Our problem as Christians is that we are completely focused on this material world ... and totally oblivious to what is going on in the unseen *Spiritual World*; it's out of sight and out of mind. But it's not out of **Jesus'** mind. Oh no, Jesus is constantly thinking about **Eternal Things**. And now, He wants *you* to see "The Light" and start thinking about Eternal Things with Him. Your Lord will do whatever it takes to get your attention. He may even use this book. It came from Jesus' World to this world to get Christians in this world to live for Jesus' World instead of their own little world ... and there's a world of difference. My prayer is that *this* is the day your Lord turns "The Light" on in *your* soul so that

you can "see" this incredible **Supernatural Person** "living within you" Who is *so* longing to *do* some things. Actually, Jesus wants to do *a lot* of things … but you don't realize it … so you don't let Him. *Mercy Me!*

Wake up, my Christian Friend! Your Lord Jesus is already wide awake – **in you!** And I can promise you this: He's got plenty to say and do in our world today – *but* He can't do *anything* until **you let Him.** As your ole Timex ticks and the minutes slip away, your *life* slips away with them. Your time is so precious because your life is so precious, and your life equals the time God gives you to live on Planet Earth. Therefore, your *life* and your *time* are the *same thing!* So, get your *Spiritual Eyes* focused clearly on what really matters – for **Eternity!** Jesus' last words to us just before His ascension into Heaven are very direct and plain. Jesus has left us here to tell all those folks out there who *don't* know Him how they *can* know Him. When you obediently do *that*, Jesus Himself will add to His Church – using **you!** *That* is what matters for all **Eternity**. *Life is more than meat or drink or entertainment or sex or money or fame or … !*

Christian, you can start living a "Jesus in me" life *today* because the Kingdom of God is nigh unto thee – in your heart: *"Christ in you."* The Kingdom of God is nigh unto thee – in your mouth: *"The Gospel of Jesus Christ."* When Christ *reigns* within your heart, His Gospel will be upon your lips, and when it is, the Kingdom of God will come. Simple, isn't it? Try getting out in this world and doing it. It's simple but not always easy. However, our Lord doesn't call us to the easiest path; He calls us to the "Best Path" – His Path – the *Eternal Path.* I have discovered that the more I let Jesus tell people about Himself using *me*, the easier it gets. That's what I want for *you*, and that's what *your Lord* wants for you. May this book "be Jesus" to you, drawing you into "God's Supernatural, Spiritual World of Witnessing." As a Born-Again Christian, you not only have "The Answer," you *are The Answer!* Even though this world doesn't know the question … *they will when* **you** *show up!!* *"God hasn't 'called' you to a life of ease but to a life of VICTORY!!"* (Adrian Rogers).

While writing this book, I have had to ask myself the question: What could possibly qualify me to be writing a book when I've never written *anything* for publication before in my life? I've never been to College (you've already figured that out), never been to Seminary, never read a commentary and never had any literary training (my Publisher can vouch for *that*). Well, the truth of the matter is, my qualifications don't

come from this world ... but from Another World – *Jesus' World!* The day my **Lord Jesus** gloriously *Saved* me was the day He qualified me. Since that life-transforming day, I have had **Jesus' Spirit** in my spirit, **Jesus' Love** in my heart, **Jesus' Joy** in my soul, **Jesus' Word** in my mind, **Jesus' Gospel** on my lips and **Jesus' Sword of The Spirit** in my hand. Much like the Apostle Paul, I can say that I didn't receive my *Spiritual Power* from man but from the Lord Jesus Himself. And *you*, my Christian Friend, possess *that same Spiritual Power* – which qualifies **you** to witness to those lost folks you see every day. Christ Jesus is "living" within your inner spirit-man ... **put Him to work** ... **today!**

Here's a thought I'll throw in for free. I have discovered that the more I fellowship with my Lord during the day, the more *He* fellowships with *me* at night while I'm asleep. Now, I know what you're thinking, *"She musta fell outta her rockin' chair and hit her head. You can't possibly fellowship with someone while you're asleep, for pity's sake."* Well, give me a chance to explain. First, let me say that I'm not alone in my belief in this phenomenon. Adrian Rogers once said that he studied God's Word so much when he was awake that he would preach sermons all night long while he was asleep. Here's why. Your amazing invisible "mind" exists within your soul which dwells in your spirit – all three of which reside in the *Spiritual Realm*. Your *unseen spirit-man* is able to get his thoughts *through you* into this world by putting those thoughts into your *invisible mind* which then downloads them into your *physical brain* (don't tell the evolutionists but the entire process is a *Supernatural Miracle* of God!). Your brain is the hard-drive; your mind is the software (think: "Wireless Fiber-optics"). Your physical brain needs sleep, but your unseen spiritual mind doesn't. Since your mind is in the same "Spiritual World" as Jesus, He can continue fellowshipping with you all night long. *Jesus' Sheep don't need to count sheep!*

When I first wake up in the morning, I try to retrieve those thoughts Jesus put into my mind while I was asleep. As I linger between "two worlds," I can almost hear my hyper-mind telling my sleepy-brain, *"Wake up, already!! I've been busy all night long while you've been unconscious. And now, I can hardly wait to download all this 'stuff' into you, sleepy-head."* You would be surprised at how much of this book came to me in that way. In fact, I would sometimes awake in the middle of the night and have to get up and write something down lest

I forget it (and you probably wouldn't be surprised at how much I *didn't* write down – and it never made it into my book). If you decide to try this and just "draw a blank," don't get discouraged; every morning isn't a red-letter morning for me either. Sometimes, I have the most *fantastic dreams!* And I want to remember them – *forever*. But, just a little while into my day, I find myself in the same boat with Ole King Nebbie, *"The thing is gone from me!"* – *forever*. Why is this so? Because my brain was asleep and not fully engaged in all the shenanigans my overly active mind was up to in *Another World*. Scientists put electrodes on the heads of sleeping people to try and figure out what their brain is doing while they're asleep. Little do they know that if they could get those electrodes attached to someone's *"mind"* … it would blow their machines sky high!

When *you* have a fantastic dream that *doesn't* go away, it may be because your Lord sent it to you. Instead of letting those guys put electrodes on your brain to find out, just pray and ask **Jesus** about it. If He reveals to you that it was indeed from Him, feel free to go ahead and dream His Dream with Him. *Become Jesus' Dream!*

Do you ever wonder why some of your dreams are **"so real"**? I dream so much that I often feel like there is another *very real World* I go visit when I'm asleep. The most precious dreams I have are about loved ones who have been dead for years. And yet, we Christians know that they *aren't* dead – they have just changed locations and are now in the *Spiritual Realm* (where our *minds* exist). When they appear in my dreams, they are so **"Alive!"** that I wake up feeling like they have actually come *themselves* to pay me a visit. We talk, laugh and do all kinds of amazing things together in my dream – in the *Spiritual Realm*. They usually look younger than the last time I saw them, and our love for each other is *stronger* than ever. In his poem, *Footsteps of Angels*, Henry W. Longfellow describes such a "visit" from his deceased wife. So, how do we explain such vivid dreams? I don't think the guys with the electrodes could help us out here. Even though we no longer have free access to our loved ones in Heaven, could our loving Lord Jesus arrange a "special visit" from time to time? Makes you wonder, doesn't it? Yep, the *Veil* between God's World and our world just got a little thinner. **"Behold, I AM The Lord, the God of all flesh: Is there anything too hard for Me?" Signed: Jehovah Jesus** (Jeremiah 32:27).

Thomas Edison once observed, *"The chief function of the body is to carry around the brain."* With my "Jesus Glasses" on, *my* vision goes even deeper. The chief function of your body is to not only carry around your physical brain but to also carry around your *invisible* spirit, soul and mind. The chief function of your spirit, soul and mind is to *receive* the Lord Jesus as your personal Lord and Saviour; then love Him, thank Him, praise Him and obey Him as you fulfill His purposes for sending you to this Planet. God doesn't send us here to just "think" ... but to "love" ... *Him!*

When you live your life *in* the world and *for* the world (like most movie stars and rock stars), and you come to the end of your life ... you are in a desperately sad situation. You have spent (wasted) your time (life, *same thing*) drawing big crowds, drawing big checks, drawing your breath and drawing closer to the end of it *all*. Now your life is over, and it's curtains for you – literally. *Everything* you lived for has come to a bitter end. **But Jesus** can even now give you a *New Beginning!* You don't *have to* live and die like that ... *if* you will just let the Lord give you a "Spiritual Life" in *Jesus' World!* Jesus promises that when you live your life believing in **Him**, you will never die (John 11:26). Believest thou this? I do. When I die, I'm just shedding this Earthsuit so that I can be free to go to my Heavenly Home – and so can you. Just don't be like those worldly people who come to a tragic end. Let *your* end be your *Beginning*. Step into Jesus' Heart. Step into Jesus' World. And when you die, you will step into Jesus' Heaven! *"This may seem to be the end of me, but it is just the beginning!"* (Dietrich Bonhoeffer).

"Life is a short and fevered rehearsal for a concert we cannot stay to give. Just when we appear to have gained some proficiency, we are forced to lay our instruments down" (A. W. Tozer). The older I get the more I sense the *un-realness* of this world and the *True Realness* of Jesus' World. With each passing day, I can feel a little stronger tug on me from Jesus in *His* World ... and I'm ready for my Lord to send His Angels and take this exile *Home*. When I close my eyes and gaze at Jesus, my heart runs to Him – like a half-forgotten dream *so beautiful* and *so wonderful* that I wish so badly I could remember it and go back there. Well, not very long from now, I *will be* going to Jesus' World ... and not coming back to this one. I've seen too many sunrises and sunsets, and my earthly journey will soon be over. But don't feel sorry for me;

I will be experiencing the *most beautiful* "Son Rise" of all! I will finally be *Home* where I belong, seeing the Glorious Brilliance of Heaven, my Lord Jesus – *Whose Glory makes the Heavens shine!*

The moment my Lord *Saved* me all those years ago, I started crying. I cried for a long time, and I couldn't stop. If you had asked me why I was crying, I couldn't have told you … but after all these years, I think I have finally figured it out. When someone you dearly love has been gone for a very long time and they are finally coming home, you go to the airport (in the ole days, you went to the train station or boat dock) to welcome them home. Once you spot them, you run up to them and hug them and hug them. Then, you just start crying and crying, uncontrollable tears of *pure joy!* That's what happened the moment my Lord *Saved* me; I was reunited *Spiritually* with the Lord I dearly love after years of separation. All those tears were tears of *Pure Joy.*

"In the end, coming to Faith remains for all a sense of homecoming,
of picking up the threads of a lost life,
of responding to a bell that had long been ringing,
of taking a place at a table that had long been vacant"
(Malcolm Muggeridge).

When I take my final "flight" to Heaven, many will be there to greet me when I arrive. But the One I will want to see most of all is **Jesus**. The moment I see Jesus, my first reaction will be instant, full and complete *Supernatural* recognition as my heart explodes with Joy, *"Oh, Jesus!! I'm so glad to be Home … with You. I've missed You so very much!"* And with *Divine Love* in His eyes, my Heavenly Bridegroom will lovingly reach out His nail-pierced hand to me and say,

"WELCOME TO MY WORLD!"

GOD ON TRIAL
"Whom say ye that I AM?"
Signed: Jesus (Matthew 16:15).

J esus made an intriguing statement when He was on trial for His Life that only Born-Again Christians can truly comprehend and celebrate. Our Lord knew that His physical death was just hours away, so He lifted up His Voice and proclaimed: *"My Kingdom is not of this world!"* (John 18:36). Jesus didn't want His followers fighting for Him to be King of Planet Earth; it's living under the curse of God and heading for ultimate destruction – along with its evil prince and his demons. Why would Jesus want to be King of such a wicked, cursed place? And besides, Jesus didn't need for man to make Him King; He was *already* **King**! *Still is!* Jesus' Kingdom is of Another World – an **Eternal World** of *Heavenly Blessings*! Born-Again Christians have been granted *Spiritual Eyes* to *see* the Kingdom of our God and our **King** upon His Throne. *That* is the Kingdom **we** are living for – and *Divinely* fighting for. Only God's Redeemed can "see" this *Other World*. Lost people are blinded by the evil enemy of all mankind, satan, who wants to keep everyone trapped in *his* dismal, doomed world. **But God** had "a Plan," a *Divine Plan*, and "Jesus on trial" was part of God's Plan … and Jesus knew it. So, when those soldiers came for Jesus in the Garden of Gethsemane, He *allowed* them to arrest Him and take Him prisoner. Jesus surrendered to those soldiers on Earth because He had already surrendered to His Father in Heaven. *"Lo, I come to do Thy Will, O God!"* (Hebrews 10:9).

"All ye shall be offended because of Me this night, for it is written, I will smite the Shepherd, and the sheep of the flock shall be scattered abroad." (Matthew 26:31). As satan marched his demon-inspired,

hate-crazed mob toward Gethsemane, Jesus prayed ... *all alone* ... while everyone else slept. Then moments later, Jesus was left to face the mob ... *all alone* ... as His disciples deserted Him and fled. Jesus was roughly bound as a criminal and taken away to endure the cruel torture of His enemies ... *all alone*. My Friend, if **you** ever have to face a dark day when *you* are rejected and deserted by all the people around you ... draw up close to **The One** Who knows so well how it feels. *"And they all forsook Him and fled!"* **But Jesus** knew that His Father hadn't forsaken Him – and never would. You can be sure that your Saviour hasn't forsaken *you* – and never will. Jesus walks *with you* when the rest of the world *walks away*. *"I AM Alpha and Omega; the First and the Last"*

Every dog has his day. I wonder if that's what Jesus was thinking as He looked around at those evil people and said, *"This is your hour and the power of darkness"* (Luke 22:53). That dreadful night when Jesus was hastily arrested and falsely tried was a dark night indeed, but just remember ... **Sunday's Comin'!!** Our Lord could submit to the unfair trial, the beatings and the crucifixion because He was looking past the *immediate* into the *Eternal*. Jesus could see *through* this physical world into His Father's unseen *Spiritual World*. *"In the year that King Uzziah died, I saw The Lord sitting upon His Throne, high and lifted up"* (Isaiah 6:1). On the day that King Jesus was crucified, He saw *The Lord* sitting upon His Throne – and Jesus knew His Father's Plan. He also knew His part in it. Now, what about you? Do you know your Father's Plan? Do you know *your* part in it? Are you willing to let "Jesus in you" submit to God's Plan for *you* today ... the same way Jesus did then?

As the soldiers were taking Jesus prisoner, He said that He could pray to His Father and He would send more than twelve legions of Angels – but Jesus *didn't* pray to be delivered. He *knew* what had to be done. So, He drank the bitter Cup (*all* of it) ... all alone. But that was then, and this is now. Today, Jesus promises to send His Angels to His Servants when we *pray* and *ask Him*. I'm pretty sure I don't send up nearly enough prayers asking for Angels – but I should. Satan has *his* demon-angels helping *him*, so *we* had better have Jesus' Angels helping *us* as we go out to engage ole slewfoot in the *Battle of the Ages* over the souls of lost mankind. And always remember, for every demon-angel helping satan, we have *two* of God's Angels helping **us!**

Our Lord Jesus could endure the horrors, humiliation and pain of His brutal trial and crucifixion because He knew Who He was *in His Father's Eyes* – and that's what mattered to *Him*. Now, what about you, Christian? Do you know who *you* are in your Father's Eyes? Does it matter to you that the **Eternal Son of God** is living *in you* ... and longing to *Supernaturally* work *through you*? I know beyond a doubt that it is the *Power* of my Lord Jesus that works through *my* weakness. **"Thou art My Servant; I have chosen thee. Fear thou not, for I AM with thee. Be not dismayed, for I AM thy God; I Will strengthen thee; yea, I Will help thee" Signed: Jehovah Jesus** (Isaiah 41:9-10).

Those wicked people who crucified Jesus didn't know who *they* were in God's Eyes, and they sure didn't know Who **Jesus** was. Sadly, this world hasn't changed much since Jesus' day – they *still* cry, *"Crucify Him!"* They just don't know Who Jesus is. Satan has hardened their hearts and blinded their eyes. All they can see is darkness and gloom ... a hopeless, wretched, tormented world with no rhyme or reason, no purpose nor plan. **But God** had "a Plan." **He** is a Saviour Who **ever** has **A Plan!** Even though it looked bleak for Jesus at His trial, God had a *Divine Plan* for His Son. And God has a *Divine Plan* His Children – including *you* (no matter how bleak your life looks today). God's Plan for you involves that *Other World* where Jesus is **King** and on His Throne. Can you see that World? Hint: It's a *Spiritual World* more *Real* and more *Wonderful* than the one you are presently passing through. **Jesus** is there – thinking about **you**! Jesus is also here – *living in you* (in the Person of His Spirit). Jesus bravely endured His trial and crucifixion so that He could be "Spiritually Alive" on this Earth today ... *in you*. And now, Jesus is looking for some evidence that *you* are "Spiritually Alive" on this Earth today ... in *Him*. So, instead of just waiting on Jesus to speak to *you* ... **you** start speaking to **Him**. Instead of just waiting on Jesus to do something for *you* ... **you** start doing something for **Him**. Instead of just waiting on Jesus to be faithful to *you* ... **you** start being faithful to **Him**. Instead of just waiting on Jesus to do a Miracle for *you* ... **you** start *being* a "Miracle" for **Him**! And when you do, you will see the *Miracle* of Jesus' Resurrection all over again ... when He *comes to Life* as **"Jesus in you!"**

Jesus' trial was grossly unfair. Jesus just stood there with no one to defend Him while satan's crowd brought in one false witness after

another to accuse Him and lie about Him. Do you ever read that and feel your heart breaking for Jesus? Have you ever wished that *you* could have been there to defend Jesus? Well take heart, Dear Heart, **you still can!** Satan's crowd is *still* being grossly unfair to our Lord Jesus today. They tell lies about Him every day in every possible way. They don't care what kind of low-down dirty tricks they have to use to try and nullify His Reign as King, *they'll do it* – because "satan in them" hates God *and* His Son Jesus. So, as you walk through this world, you will have *plenty* of opportunities to defend your Lord Jesus. Truth is, all you have to do is just open your mouth, let the *Lion of Judah* out, and **Jesus Himself** will put everyone else on the defense.

Now is a good time for me to remind you that God exiled satan and his demon-angels to Planet Earth *before* He placed Adam and Eve here. Yep, and I know what you're thinking, *"What?!! Why would God ever put Adam and Eve in the middle of a bunch of demons, for pity's sake?!"* Answer: **To defeat them!!** And *today*, God puts **you** into the middle of a bunch of satan-followers so that "Jesus in you" can show them Who's God! The reason your Lord gives you **His Power** is because He knows you have an enemy to use it against. Just as America sends her soldiers into battle to win a war over *her* enemy, God sends *us Soldiers of The Cross* into battles with "the god of this world" in order to win the war over *His* enemy – **satan.** When you are out in this world witnessing for Jesus and you're the only Christian in the middle of a crowd of not-so-friendly unbelievers … remember Jesus at His trial. And when you do, also remember: **Jesus wasn't alone.** Oh no, His Father was right there with Him. And as *you* stand there "alone" in the midst of the enemy's camp, your **Beloved Saviour** is standing right there *with you*. When you stand up for Jesus, He *never* lets you stand alone. You're in "the eye of the storm" with **The One** Who calms the storm. So, take a deep *Spiritual Breath* and remind yourself: *"The Power of God's Words flowing out of 'Jesus in me' is stronger that any opposition coming against me from people with 'satan in them'."* **"Jesus didn't die on the Cross just to keep us safe; He died to make us dangerous!"** (Mark Batterson). *"When thou passeth through the waters, I Will be with thee; and through the rivers, they shall not overflow thee; when thou walkest through the fire, thou shalt not be burned, neither shall the flame kindle upon thee. For I AM the Lord*

thy God, the Holy One of Israel, thy Saviour!" Signed: *Jehovah Jesus* (Isaiah 43:2-3).

Since I mostly witness to people out in public places, there are usually other people close enough around us to hear what I'm saying to the person in front of me. *I love it!* As I tell them about *"Jesus!"* and His Plan of Salvation, I am well aware of the fact that I'm not just witnessing to *one person* but to everyone else around us! *Yes!!* When you start *thinking* like Jesus, you start *living* like Jesus. In football, the team with the ball is the team on *offense.* *You*, Christian, are on **The Team** with *"Jesus!"* – and you're a Player with *"Jesus in you"* – therefore, the Game Plan is for you to allow *Jesus* to be "on offense" in this world *through you.* Not offensive – just bold and confident as *"Jesus in you"* proclaims **God's Glorious Gospel** to a lost world that doesn't know "The Way" to the End Zone (Heaven). *"If our Lord Jesus is real, and He is here, we need to put Him to work!"* (Kamal Saleem).

Right on, Kamal. The Lord is risen *indeed* and hath appeared unto *us!* Jesus *is* here (in us Christians), and He is quite *ready* to go to work. His problem is finding Christians who are ready to "go to work with Him." Sadly, Jesus is getting plenty of rest in most of us. *But Jesus* is looking for some fired-up *Players* who are tired of just being "bench-warmers" and are ready to join *Team Jesus* and get into *The Game!* Coach Jesus is calling *your* number – and it's crunch time! It's time to put on your *Helmet of Salvation*, suit up in your *Armour of Christ* and put "Jesus in you" to work by allowing "Jesus in you" to put *you* to work. Listen up, Christian Friend, if you have ever wanted to be a "Missionary for Jesus" but didn't want to have to go through a Missions' Board and travel halfway around the world, you're in the right place at the right time – just *wake up and look around, for pity's sake!* *You* can be a "Missionary for Jesus" *right here, right now* – in the **Good Ole USA!!** Yes siree, the President of the *Divine Missions' Board* is now giving you *His* Official Permission! This is your chance to let "Jesus in you" take the football *(His Gospel)* and score a touchdown *(Salvation of a soul)* for **Team Jesus** *(God's Kingdom)* as all the Cheerleaders *(Angels)* celebrate! *Glory to God!!* *"None are so old as those who have outlived enthusiasm"* (Henry David Thoreau).

Jehovah Jesus reigns today in His Spiritual World while dwelling within your inner *spirit-man* in the Person of His Spirit. That makes

you the "not-so-missing-link" to many of the things your Lord wants to get done on this Earth. **You** are Jesus' MIA *(Missionary In Action!)*; therefore, *you* are "the one" who makes it possible for Jesus to be able to come into this world – through *your body* and *your mouth!* It's time you *"let Him."* *Now* is Jesus' chance to defend Himself – through **you**, His faithful Witness – and through **me**, His faithful Witness. Thanks to my Lord Jesus, my life has purpose, *God-ordained, Eternal Purpose* – so does *yours*. My Lord wakes me up every morning because I am here *on Assignment* for **Him –** so are *you*. My Assignment is to let **Jesus** live His life all over again *through me* – so is *yours*. The Lord wants to seek and to *Save* many souls who are enslaved to evil satan using **me** *(of all people)* – using **you** *(of all people)*. This very moment, your Lord is drawing you into *your God-ordained, Eternal Purpose* for being here on Planet Earth. "Jesus in you" wants to give *Eternal Life* to people you encounter every day – but **you** must make the decision to **let Him**. *"The two most important days of your life are the day you were born and the day you find out 'why'"* (Mark Twain).

God always chooses whom He uses, and He has chosen **you**… to be a "Mighty Witness" for His Son Jesus! Now, I know what you're thinking, *"How do you know God has chosen me?"* Because you're reading this book … and **God** is forever in control of *everything*. Do you believe that? You **will** believe it … when God starts working *through* **you** to bring lost folks to His Son Jesus. *Yes!!* *"**Believe** and ye shall receive!"* When you go out witnessing *(praying and believing)* the folks you witness to are going to see "The Light" of the *Glory of God* in the face of *"**Jesus in you!**"* *"God loves His Son Jesus so much that He wants lots of other sons just like Him!"* (Jeff Wickwire).

God "called" both Moses and David when they were just shepherds tending sheep. So, no matter *what* you may be doing at the moment, you're in the perfect position for God to "promote you" in His Kingdom. Your Lord has been watching you faithfully "tending your sheep," and now, He has decided to give you a "Ministry" to the *True Sheep* – the **souls** of men and women, boys and girls. The same God Who "called" you to Salvation is now "calling" you to do some **Eternally Important Work** for Him. The time has come for you to *accept* your promotion and start living in *God's Perfect Will* for you. So, take off your sandals, put on your Army boots, lift up your Rod of God *(Jesus in you)*, gather up some

stones for your sling *(The Gospel of Jesus Christ)* and start **living** your "New Life in Christ." **Jehovah Jesus** is *taking over* your life – *for good!* God is going to bring **Revival** to America through **you** … any day now. *It's up to **you** when He begins.*

When our Lord Jesus came to Planet Earth, He split all of time! He also splits all of mankind. Years ago, Jesus split *my life* wide open as well … and *He meant to! Thank You, Lord!* If *you* belong to the Saviour, He wants to split *your world* wide open and drop His **Divine Agenda** right-smack-dab into the middle of it. That breath you're taking right now is a gift from your Lord to keep you alive long enough to get you around a lost person so that He can **use** that breath to tell them about His **So Great Salvation.** *Embrace* Christ's Agenda for you and *commit* your life to proclaiming His Gospel in your workaday world – and He will replace your spiritual indifference with His **Supernatural Enthusiasm!** Jesus doesn't want you just marking time. *No siree*, He wants **you** marking **Eternity!** And when you do, you won't have to wait until you die and enter the *Pearly Gates* to hear Jesus speak to you. Oh no, **you** will hear Jesus speaking to *you* throughout your day right here *on Planet Earth.* Every time you tell someone about your Lord and Saviour Jesus Christ, you will hear Him say, **"Well done, thou Good and Faithful Servant!!"** (Matthew 25:21).

My Salvation was the result of a *total stranger* walking up to me in a *public place* and "trying" to tell this not-interested-in-God, wandering-around-lost, living-for-the-devil worldling about **Jesus** and His **So Great Salvation.** Even though I didn't have a clue what he was talking about, God was *still* working *His Plan.* The Lord used that stranger's witness to lead me to the place where He met with me and *Saved* my *Eternal Soul!* Today, Jesus says to me, *"Freely you have received … now freely give!"* Therefore, I witness to folks much the same way as that "daring Servant" of the Lord did. I offer a good Gospel Tract to a total stranger in a public place as I tell them about my Lord and Saviour Jesus Christ. Offering the person a tract about "Jesus" gets the conversation immediately on *Jesus* – so I can just keep talking to them about **"Jesus!"** Let me take a minute and give you a heads-up about what you're heading into if you decide to start witnessing to the lost the way I do. You will sometimes feel like the ole fellow who was on his way to the store for some things his wife needed … when his cell phone rang.

"Lo."

"Sweetheart, are you OK?"

"Sure, I'm OK. Why do you wanna know?"

"Because I just heard on the News that some **nut** is driving the wrong way on I10 and causing a major *traffic hazard*!!"

"Well, I'm on I10 right now, and I'm here to tell ya, there ain't just *one nut* going the wrong way ... no siree, thar's *a whole bunch* of nuts going the wrong way!! Yep, and not only that, but they're so all-fired proud of it, they're all *ahonking their horns!*"

Just like that ole fellow, the guy who first told me about Jesus probably got "honked" at by some folks in his life because of the way he witnessed to total strangers out in public places. They probably told him, *"That doesn't do any good."* In the same way, folks will "honk" at *you* and tell you the same thing (been there). But when they do, just smile and think of me ... all these years later, doing the same thing for *others* he did for *me* and laughing at all those "honkers" who told him, *"That doesn't do any good."* You will also get "honked" at by some of the folks you're trying to lead to Jesus. That's to be expected; you're "going against the grain" of this ungodly society by actually talking *publicly* about *"Jesus!!"* (*The Name* satan hates above all names). But, once again, just smile and think of me – God's "Called-Out Ones" *will hear* God's "Call!" So, don't get discouraged by all the "honkers." God *is* leading you to one of His "Called-Out Ones" who *will hear* God's "Call." God knows who that person is and when He's going to bring that precious soul across your path. God is more concerned with timing than time. *"Come ye after Me, and I Will make you fishers of men!" Signed: Jesus* (Mark 1:17).

You can't out-give God. Most Christians have said that at one time or another, and they are always referring to $. *But Jesus* gave *me* a very different perspective on the matter one day when He said to me, *"Molly, if you will turn off 'the world' and give that time to Me – in My World and in My Word – I will repay you in ways you can't even imagine!"* Maybe you've heard it this way: Waste time with Jesus and He will give it back to you. The same is true when you go out witnessing; what you may *think* is just a big "waste of time," Jesus will faithfully repay you for. Lavishing your love, time, money and life on your Precious Jesus is *never* a waste. When you invest your life (time, *same thing*) in giving others

the Gospel of Christ, He gives it back to you in the lives of Brothers and Sisters "in Christ" you will celebrate with *forever* in Heaven! I tell the folks I witness to, *"I'll see ya in Glory!!"* I'm telling **you**, my Christian Friend: **Waste time witnessing for Jesus NOW, and He will reward you for ALL ETERNITY!!**

Jesus didn't say a whole lot at His trial; He knew that being Almighty God and the Best Defense Attorney in the whole Universe, He could have easily talked them all out of it. Jesus could have twisted every one of them into a pretzel with His Hands tied behind His back. He *could* have – but He didn't. Jesus knew that He *had* to be falsely condemned and crucified in order to pay the penalty for all my (your) **sins**. The reason Jesus was as silent as a Lamb before His shearers was because He came to accomplish the Work His Father had given Him to do. But that was then, and this is now. Today, the crucifixion is behind Him, our Salvation has been secured, and *now*, Jesus is in a talking mood. Why do I say that? Because I was once a very quiet introvert before my Lord *Saved* me. But *Save me*, He did! Jesus came and made His abode in my spirit, in my heart and in my soul. *Heaven came down and Glory filled my soul!* And today, satan can't shut me up from talking about my **Lord Jesus!** *Glory Be Unto His Name!* Now, what about you? Has Jesus used *your* mouth to say anything about Himself to anyone lately? Jesus may have been silent during His trial, but that doesn't mean His Followers should commit "the sin of silence" today. No siree, our Lord Jesus is listening intently for *anyone* who will proclaim the *Good News* of the **Gospel of Jesus Christ!** *"Blessed is that servant, whom his Lord when He cometh shall find so doing"* Signed: *King Jesus* (Matthew 24:46).

Jesus told His disciples that He would not partake of the Passover meal again until it be fulfilled and the Kingdom of God is come (Luke 22:15-18). Well, Passover *has* been fulfilled (at Calvary), and the Kingdom of God *has* come (in us Christians)! So, Jesus is ready to commune with us around the Communion Table at Church *and* wherever or whenever *we* are ready to commune with *Him* in His "Spiritual World." It's true that we will one day eat and drink with our Lord Jesus in Heaven, but how "Blessed" are those who have already started on the hors d'oeuvres of Jesus' Banquet by sweetly abiding in His *Divine Presence* while here on Planet Earth during dress rehearsal. Come and dine ... for all things are

now ready! *Hallelujah to The Lamb!!* When you are "fellowshipping" with Jesus, you are drinking in His "New Life" into your soul afresh. Every little talk with Jesus connects you to His Spiritual Kingdom – where Jesus and you have a "Glorious Celebration" of **His Resurrection!** But in order to enter into Jesus' World, you must leave *this* world behind. The Lord is a Rewarder of those who *seek Him.* If you think it's amazing that you can converse with a person anywhere in this world on your smarty-pants phone, just think how *miraculous* it is to be able to converse with **Jesus** in "Another World" through your Spirit-Phone. So, leave *this* ole world behind and go to Jesus in *His.* There, you will hear Him say to you, *"Welcome to My World! I AM so glad you have chosen to join Me here."*

Now, I know what you're thinking, *"That sounds so nice, but I just can't do that – I may miss something important" (Hmmm).* So, how do I know what you're thinking? Because I hate to admit it, but the one holding this pen has the very same thoughts sometimes. And when I do, my Lord hears me and just gives me that same "look" He gave Peter during His trial – and I feel the same shame and remorse. The Lord Jesus is: *The Great I AM!! The Sovereign King of the Universe!! The Saviour of my Eternal Soul!!* **He** is more important than anyone or anything else in my life, for pity's sake!! I just don't always give Him that "Honor." Love not the world neither the things that are in the world. *Oh, to learn that lesson!* Loving the world produces a bored, unhappy, discontent Christian. If that's you, it's because you are only living for *this* world instead of the *Spiritual World* you will live in *forever* and the *Supernatural Saviour* you will live *with forever.* **But Jesus** is a Saviour Who *ever* has **A Plan.** He even has one to get you out of the doldrums. Your Lord has some "Greater Works" on Planet Earth He wants to do, and He needs *somebody, somebody* to do them through – so He picked out two *Somebodies*: Jesus and you *(Jesus in you!).* It's time to get crackin', Christian, and wake up each morning with a prayer such as this in your heart: *"Good Morning, Lord! Welcome to my world! You have a place here, You know – in me! You and I have some Eternal Work to do here today – together! I am Yours ... and You are mine – forever!!"*

As I look around America, I see a landscape littered with myriads of sin-wrecked souls. "Jesus in me" says, *"I have compassion on them.*

They are like sheep without a Shepherd." I would like to submit to you that our Country is ripe for the harvesting of satan's victims who need **The Great Shepherd of the Sheep** to bring them into His Fold. *"Them also I must bring, and they shall hear My Voice; and there shall be One Fold and One Shepherd" Signed: Jesus* (John 10:16). Only the *Great Shepherd's Voice* (spoken through *our mouth*) can *miraculously* "call" America back to Himself. There are "Miracles of Salvation" all around us – just waiting for **believing** Christians to be *brave enough* and *wise enough* to go out there and *claim* through *Jesus' Love* and *Gospel*. I don't know about you, my Friend, but I want to press hard to lay hold of that for which **Christ Jesus** laid hold of *me!* Our Lord is like the Marines … all He needs are "a few **Good Men**." I want to be one of *Jesus' Good Men*. Jesus told His disciples, *"He that hath seen Me hath seen The Father"* (John 14:9). When people see you, do they see "Jesus in you"? *"That the Father may be glorified in the Son."*

Any nation is just one generation away from becoming a pagan nation, but I like to think that **we** are just one generation away from reclaiming America for our **Great God**! Even though America is deserving of **God's Judgment,** we Christians can humbly fall to our knees and pray for **God's Mercy** and **Grace** instead. *"When thou art in tribulation, and all these things are come upon thee, even in the latter days, if thou turn to The LORD thy God, and shalt be obedient unto His Voice: (for The LORD thy God is a Merciful God), He will not forsake thee, neither destroy thee, nor forget the Covenant of thy Fathers which He sware unto them"* (Deuteronomy 4:30-31). *Praise God!!*

Then, we must rise to our feet and be obedient unto our Lord's Voice, *"As you are going through your world, share ME with everyone you can!"* Don't sit around waiting on God to move. *No! God* is waiting on **you** to move. Don't make this harder than what it is. Just give yourself over to **The One** Who gave Himself for *you* on the Cross. Let the **Love of Jesus** *fill you* and *flow through you* to all those around you who need **Jesus' Love.** Instead of waiting for God to push you out the door to go tell some lost folks about Jesus, you open that door *yourself* and skip out of it with a pocket full of "Miracles" and a heart full of **love for Jesus!** Go tell those lost Sheep, *"A **Saviour** has died! Your Good Shepherd has faithfully provided **The Lamb!**" "And, lo, I AM with (in) you always, even unto the end of the world!" Signed: Jesus* (Matthew 28:20).

It was during Jesus' trial that Peter denied even knowing Him. What was Peter thinking?! We say, *"Peter!! How could you ever deny your Lord Jesus, for pity's sake?!!"* But what about us today in the Good Ole US of A? Do *we*? I certainly can't throw stones at Peter because I have vivid memories of something I did years ago that I have regretted and grieved over more times than I can count. Charlie and I were very poor, so I worked at a Bed and Breakfast to help out. I was the only full-time employee of the couple who ran the B&B, and we had a good relationship even though they weren't Christians. I witnessed to them regularly, so they knew where I stood with my Lord Jesus.

Well, one day they told me they were going to be hosting a homosexual "wedding" and that *I* was naturally going to be their "right-hand-man." I am so ashamed to report to you today that I caved-in to their expectations of me (and my own financial needs) and served at that ungodly "wedding" – and through it all, I felt so dirty. I could deeply *feel* my Lord's broken Heart the whole time … just like Peter did when he heard that rooster crow. Even sadder is the fact that I didn't get to witness to anyone about my Lord Jesus (my employers would **not** have appreciated me starting a riot at their lovely "wedding"). So, I don't know of any good that came out of my being there … *unless* … it was so that I could warn my Fellow-Christians of the deep grief and regret *you* will experience (just like Peter and me) when you deny your Lord in the midst of the unbelievers' camp.

I can't tell you how many times I have wished that I could get into a "time-machine," push a button, go back to that day and boldly stand with my Lord Jesus – no matter the consequences. However, He could have allowed me to do what I did (without striking me dead) so that He can now use my story of "moral failure" for good – *somehow*. Those judges who are *forcing* Christians to "embrace" the *sinful* homosexual lifestyle are forcing us to *forsake* and *grieve* **"The God we love"** in order to serve the demon-god of this world – **satan**. *No Christian* should ever be *forced* to take part in an *evil abomination* that defiles **"God's Sacred Marriage."** Justice McCoy has decided that the Government (or Supreme Court) shall **not** have the authority to *force* business-owners to hire homosexuals and transgenders. (If only our *Godly Grandparents* could come back!! **They**

wouldn't stand for this ungodliness one second!) *Stand up, stand up for Jesus, ye Soldiers of The Cross!* *"When people tell you that what you're doing or saying isn't politically correct, you tell them that you aren't a politician ... you're a **Christian!!**"* (Zig Ziglar).

(*Breaking News*: I just heard that the Hallmark Channel is very excited and pleased to announce that they will be including homosexuals in their movies from now on. *Satan* is also very pleased with their decision. So much for Hallmark's "family entertainment." They are showing us which way *they* want the family to go – *satan's* way (and we know where *that* leads). In the name of "fairness," they will probably also be making movies about men living as women "marrying" women living as men. I'm sure Hallmark is defending their actions by saying, *"Well, homosexual 'marriage' is legal now, you know."* **But God** had *nothing* to do with legalizing homosexual "marriage" – period. *Hey Christians*, it's time for a **Christian** Movie Channel!! I will never again buy any Hallmark products. I refuse to fund satan's agenda. *"If God doesn't judge **America**, He will owe Sodom and Gomorrah an apology!"* {Ruth Graham}.)

Now, what about you? Are you just climbing the ladder of success with your very life denying that you even know Jesus? Have you confessed to anyone lately that the **Holy One** called **Jesus,** Who was crucified on Calvary's Cross, is actually the **Son of God** ... and He is *your* **Lord** and **Saviour?** If *you* were on trial for being a Christian, would there be enough evidence to convict you, *or* ... would you be found innocent of all charges? Don't *you* be like "someone we all know and love" who let the same people who had heard her claim to be a Christian see her serving at a homosexual "wedding," for pity's sake! Don't *you* betray your Saviour by failing to stand up and defend Him before an evil world that constantly crucifies Him. **No!** Jesus deserves better. Our Lord deserves committed Members of "The Fellowship of The Unashamed!" *Don't let the cock crow and find you crying.*

Thanks to the *Mercy* and *Grace* of my faithful Lord, He loved me, forgave me and restored me – the same way He did Peter. Jesus graciously allowed Peter to preach powerful sermons, bring many lost folks to "Faith in Christ," write two Epistles in the Bible plus ghost-write the Gospel of Mark. *All Praise to our Great Saviour!* Jonah isn't the only one who gets a second chance. Our Lord gave Peter and me

another chance to do it right, and every morning Jesus allows *you* to awake to a new day, He's giving **you** another chance to do it right as well. In every sunrise, see **The Son** rise. His *Mercies* are new every morning. *Praise be to the God of all Hope! "Who then is willing to consecrate his service this day unto The Lord?"* (I Chronicles 29:5).

When Jesus said to satan's crowd, *"This is your hour, and the power of darkness,"* He was telling them the truth. Satan had to be *allowed* the power to crucify Jesus, or else we would all still be dead in our trespasses and sins. So, it really *was* satan's hour and the time of his power over our Lord – or so it seemed. But that was then, and this is now. Today, things are *way* different. *Almighty God* worked "His Plan" (using satan as a pawn in His hand) and *now*, it's **Jesus'** hour and the *Power* of **His Kingdom!** Yes!! The *Power* of *Love* and *Light* are always victorious over hate and darkness. The prince of darkness grim; we tremble not for him ... because he could **not** extinguish "The Light of the World!" And today, **Jesus** is shining *brighter* than ever! God *never* leaves Himself without a Witness. Can I get a witness? Can **Jesus** get a Witness? *Yes! You and I can testify!!* **"I think I can say, I have never risen a morning without thinking how I could bring more souls to Christ"** (Robert Murray McCheyne).

If you had been in that crowd at Jesus' trial, would *you* have been shouting, *"Crucify Him! Crucify Him!"*? Of course, not. So, don't crucify Him *today* as He seeks to live His Life *again* on this Earth – in **you**! The easiest way for you to crucify Jesus is to just ignore Him. Honor "Christ in you" and give *Him* pre-eminence in your life. To do that, you have to go to *Jesus* in His *Spiritual World*, where He's waiting for you. Jesus is always waiting for you. He patiently waits for you to come to Him and share your heart with Him. That requires your time, your attention and your devotion. The more you love your Saviour, the more you will want to spend time with "Jesus in you." Any child will tell you: Love is spelled: "T-i-m-e." Even when you're spending time with others, keep spending time with Jesus, and He will just naturally be a part of the conversation. Your Lord will always find a way to jump in there – one way or another. The day you start treating Jesus like He is really *Alive* "in you" is the day you start experiencing *Real Life* – **Jesus' Resurrected Life!!** You also start knowing what an *Intimate Relationship* with Jesus really is. Now that you know "Who" Jesus really is, you want

to tell the world … like Jesus did during His trial. Jesus didn't say much at His trial, but one thing He *did* confess was: "**I AM** 'The **I AM** God!'" (Mark 14:62). Our Lord Jesus is Almighty God, and He has unveiled His Eternal Plan.

"I AM building My Church!"

To the hungry heart, Jesus offers, "I AM The Bread of Life!"

To the thirsty soul, Jesus promises, "I AM The Living Water!"

To the dark spirit, Jesus reveals, "I AM The Light of the World!"

To the little lost Lamb, Jesus calls out, "I AM The Good Shepherd!"

To the wounded heart, Jesus promises, "I AM Faithful and True!"

To the Born-Again Christian, Jesus says, "I AM abiding in you!"

To the unredeemed, Jesus reveals, "I AM The Lamb of God!"

To the lost world, Jesus proclaims, "I AM The Way!

To the sorrowing soul, Jesus assures, "I AM
The Resurrection and The Life!"

Signed: Jesus, The Great I AM.

My Christian Friend, your Lord Jesus longs to live His Life *through you* so that He can tell this lost world: "**I AM GOD!**" They *must* believe that in order for Jesus to *Save* them. They *won't* believe it … unless **Jesus** tells them. They won't hear Jesus tell them … *unless* … "somebody" *lets* Jesus use *their mouth* to do it through. If **you** will be that *somebody*, Jesus and His Holy Spirit will show up and show you what a *Real Christian* looks like. **"Jesus in you"** wants to become *physically visible* and *powerfully active* on this Earth *today* – in and through **you!** Lost folks will believe that Jesus is *indeed alive* when they *see* Him "Alive!" – *in* **you!** *Then*, they will say, *"Wow! Jesus really is God!!"*

Jesus Christ is **God the Son** Who is ruling His Universe and building His Church while "dwelling" in **me** and in **you!** *Amazing!* And yet, true. Your Lord Jesus wants you to catch a glimpse of *Who* He is and *where* He is. Jesus knows that when you *see* **The Spirit of Christ Jesus** "in you," all

the demons of hell won't be able to keep you from daring to **"be Jesus"** to this spiritually needy world! Those "Greater Works" Jesus promised we would do **He** is doing – *through* **us!** **Jehovah Jesus** worked through Elijah in *his* day, and Jehovah Jesus is **"Alive!"** in America today ... in *you!* These truly *are* the days of Elijah – and *you*, my Christian Friend, are "Elijah!" There's no God like Jehovah Jesus, and *He* can give "Spiritual Life" to this dark and dying world ... through *you!* Yes indeed, your *earthly life* is part of *Something Bigger* than you could ever imagine and will last *longer* than you could ever comprehend! **"If God can use a man without arms and legs to be His hands and feet, then He will certainly use any willing heart"** (Nick Vujicic).

I know you – you want to do something "Great!" with your life. You want to make a lasting "Mark" on this world. Well, let me tell you how. Spend more of your life (time, *same thing*) with Jesus. Spend your days loving Jesus and letting **Him love you.** When you do, *Jesus* gives you a *Joy* you can't explain and a *Wisdom* you can't deny as He shows you that the **Greatest Thing** you can ever do is really just a "small thing." Telling a lost soul how they can know the **Lord Jesus** as *their* Saviour may seem like just a "small thing" ... but in *God's Eyes*, it is a *"Great Thing!"* You are making a lasting "Mark" on **Eternity** ... not just this passing world. So, give your heart to the **Eternal Son of God**, take His *Spiritual Hand* in yours, humble yourself like He did and do "small things" for God – and you will be truly "Great" in *His Eyes*. *"For who hath despised the day of small things?"* (Zechariah 4:10).

One of Jesus' own followers betrayed Him for thirty pieces of silver – the price of a slave. But Judas discovered when it was too late that 'tainted money' taint enough. Let **us** purpose in *our* hearts that *we* won't ever betray our Lord for *any* amount of silver (or American Greenbacks). Make up your *Mind of Christ* that *you* won't take that job at a bar (or serve at a homosexual "wedding") just because you need the money. If you do, it's as tainted as Judas' thirty pieces of silver. All these years later, I am still haunted by what I did *("the ghost of memories past")*. Instead, make a Covenant with your Lord that you won't take *any* job that helps satan build *his* wicked kingdom. That's getting harder and harder to do in "modern America," but pray and ask your Lord to lead you to a job that brings Glory to *Him*. He will help you. *Satan* is the cruel taskmaster who forces you to make bricks without straw.

But Jesus supplies everything you need to help Him build *His* Eternal Kingdom. *What God orders, He pays for.* Your Lord is pleased when you have Daniel's uncompromising heart … and He grieves when you sell-out to the devil. Jesus willingly came and gave His Life for *you*. Now, willingly give your life *to Him* and *for Him*. Crucify *yourself* and let Jesus "live" again – *through you!*

Being a witness of Jesus Christ is *Spiritual Warfare* with the devil, his demons and his followers. When you dare to let Jesus proclaim His Gospel to lost folks through you, satan will make sure that, at times, *you* are treated the same way he treated *Jesus* when He was on trial for His Life. During Jesus' trial, He was mocked, threatened, ridiculed, cursed, physically abused, laughed at, lied about and spit upon. As you share Jesus' Gospel with the lost, if they do similar things to *you*, just remember: You're in very good Company. *"If the world hate you, ye know that it hated Me before it hated you."* Signed: Jesus (John 15:18). Jesus doesn't ask you to endure something that He didn't first endure. The Good Shepherd *leads* His Sheep – sometimes through the valley of the shadow. The Lord knows that there are times when He must bruise a man before He can use that man. More often than not, Jesus has to *humble* the man He plans to use. My Lord has had to remind me of that on many occasions. Nevertheless, it is a glorious "Honor" to be counted worthy to share in the sufferings of **Jesus Christ**. *"Peter preached and got four thousand converts. Steven preached and got four thousand rocks!"* (Tommy Nelson).

Are you a faithful Christian who is having to go through a very difficult trial right now – and you're wondering why God would ever let something like *this* happen to *you*? Don't feel alone; we *all* have to endure the hassles of life. Now is the time to turn your *Spiritual Eyes* upon **Jesus** *(Whom having not seen, you love)*. Maybe your Lord hasn't delivered you out of your trial (yet), but I can guarantee you this: *Jesus is right there with you in the midst of your trial!* Your circumstances may be bad, **but Jesus** and **His Love** are still with you. His Word is still true … *and* it's still true *for you*. Jesus knows how to tie a strong love-knot in the end of your rope so that you can hang on … *to His Love.* Your Lord is teaching you that you can *trust Him* … even in your darkest valley. In order for you to really *know* Jesus, you have to be in a situation that requires Him to show up and show you

that He really *is* your *Strong Saviour*. When Jesus brings you *through this* to a better place, you are going to know Him and His Love like never before. Truth be told, *Jesus* knows how it feels to have a really bad day – and now, He feels compassion for **you**. So, have no fear; your faithful **Good Shepherd** is near. Jesus is always on duty, and He is just leading you to … *something*. You don't have to know where you're going because you know **The One** Who is leading you – and **He** knows where you're going. *Time is on His side! "He shall feed His Flock like a Shepherd; He shall gather the Lambs with His arm and carry them in His bosom, and shall gently lead those who are with young"* (Isaiah 40:11).

(Side-note: *"To him who overcometh I will give a white stone, and in the stone a new name written, which no man knoweth saving he that receiveth it"* Signed: Jesus (Revelation 2:17). Any idea of what Jesus is talking about here? Well, I have one that is near and dear to my heart. In the family I grew up in, my Daddy showed you he loved you by calling you a "nickname" – and the more he loved you, the "nuttier" your nickname was. So, as you might guess, he gave me a pretty "unusual" one when I was a little girl and called me by it the rest of his life. My Daddy was the only person who ever called me my nickname, and I actually loved hearing him do so because I knew it was his ole-timey way of letting me know how much he loved me (can anyone relate?). When he died, I was heart-broken that I would never hear him call me "my special nickname" ever again. **But God!** In Heaven, I believe that **Jesus** will have His own special "Nickname" for His Little Lamb that He alone will call me for all *Eternity* to let me know how near and dear I am to *His* heart. And *that* is what's on my White Stone … perhaps.)

In the meantime, just know that you have been sent to Earth on a "Rescue Mission" by King Jesus – Whose "Mission" was to hang on a Cross and give *His Life* for you. Jesus will sometimes allow *your* mission to lead *you* into a trial … so that you can discover that *one +* *God = a Miracle!* One thing your Lord doesn't want you to do is give in to discouragement. I've heard it said that discouragement is the dark room in which the negatives of failure are developed. If the devil ever locks *you* up in a dark room, just remember, he can't *lock out* the "Light of the World" – **Jesus!** *"Fear not, for I have redeemed thee, I*

have called thee by thy name; thou art Mine!" Signed: Jehovah Jesus (Isaiah 43:1).

When you start making a difference for your Lord and His Kingdom, ole slewfoot will come against you to silence you anyway he can (hello, *Lord of The Rings*). Sure it's a dangerous life being an "Active Member" of the Lord's Army, *but* when you were on *satan's* side, you lived close to the edge *all the time* – remember? You weren't just a follower of satan ... you were *a General in his army, for pity's sake! Now* it's time for you to work as hard *against* the devil as you used to work *for* him. Bravely infiltrate the enemy lines, fearlessly distribute plenty of propaganda *(The Gospel of Jesus Christ)* and bring back *lots* of captives into **King Jesus' Camp!** Be willing to be a casualty if you must; just don't go down without a fight to the finish – *of satan.* And when satan and his minions are having board meetings in hell discussing **you** ... you can smile, knowing that you're making a real dent in his evil kingdom. *Praise The Lord! "When your name is known in Heaven, that's wonderful – but when your name is known in hell, that's even better!"* (Matt Fox).

Legalized abortion, legalized homosexual "marriage," legalized public nudity, legalized pornography, legalized teaching of homosexuality/transgenderism/evolution in all Public Schools and Colleges, legalized deadly addictive drugs for recreation, legalized drag-queen-story-hour for children in Public Libraries, election of ungodly politicians, Court-ordered removal of Jesus' Cross and Bible Scriptures from public view all across our Country and the escalation of full-blown hate, anger, rage and lawless behavior in her Citizens are all signs of the manifestation of **satan** in America – *taking over America.* God Blessed America is now godless America. *"And God saw that the wickedness of man was great in the Earth, and that every imagination of the thoughts of his heart was only evil continually"* (Genesis 6:5).

*"America no longer leads the world in righteousness but leads the world in sin. Americans are living in a fantasy world, not only calling good evil and evil good, but also celebrating evil! Let's face it; we've become a degenerate, hedonistic culture obsessed with materialism, sin and pleasure, leading to destruction and death. We are overdue for judgment. America is on a collision course with **God**!"* (Bob Boyd).

Folks, I fear for my Country. *Someone* needs to stand up and warn America that the **God** Who sent destruction upon His People Israel (who were sacrificing their children to pagan gods) *and* destroyed the Sodomites (who were proudly living in ungodly, perverted sexual **sin**) is *the same* **God** Who is watching **us** today to see what **we** are going to do about legalized **sin** in **our** Country. What do you suppose **God** is thinking when He sees homosexual parades marching *proudly* down streets in cities all over America – right past *magnificent* old **Churches** built to **His Glory**? How angry does **God** get at ungodly judges who "rule from the bench" and legalize **sin** in our **One Nation under God**? I truly believe that the intercessory **prayers** of **Christians** (who are pleading with God to *Save* those lost folks who shamelessly **sin** against Him … and couldn't care less) are the *unseen power* that holds back the wrath of God upon America during her rebellious teenage-years. Only dedicated, mature **Christians** can help America become a "Christian Adult" when she grows up. And *that* is going to require quite a "Christian Awakening" because satan has *every* Country conforming to his wicked agenda. **Jesus** is on trial in our world once again, and the cry goes up from the entire Planet: ***"Crucify Him! Crucify Him! We will not have this Man (God) to rule over us!"***

People hate Jesus because He tells them the *Truth* about their **sin** (which they love). What they don't realize is that the joke's on them … because **Jesus** isn't the One Who is on trial … **they are!** And here's the punch line to the joke: *"**Jesus** is their Judge!!"* Mercy Me! *"We have evicted the Father Who created us, and the whole world is now an orphan!"* (Ravi Zacharias).

Folks, I fear for this satan-saturated, sin-loving world. Someone needs to warn them that by rejecting the Lord Jesus, they are literally playing with **fire**. **Jehovah Jesus** created Planet Earth with His Word, and He is well able to *destroy* it with His Word. The Lord just may decide to crash this ungodly party going on down here on Earth and give those folks who are having such a blast a "Real Blast!" Little do they know that their prideful laughter could actually be their last hurrah. The people of Noah's day had never seen water fall from the sky, and the people of today (like the people of Sodom) have never seen **fire** fall from the sky … but they may live to. It wouldn't surprise me one bit to learn that God has spoken a huge **"fire-ball"**

into existence somewhere out in our Universe and is aiming it right at Planet Earth ... in order to fulfill II Peter 3:7. And before *you* laugh, remember: Lot's sons-in-law also laughed ... just before *the fire fell*. You don't mock God and get away with it – *forever*. At the time of His choosing, God looked down from His Holy Heaven and said, *"Hey, Sodom! Your number's up ... and you're toast!!"* On Feb. 14, 2020, an asteroid large enough to cause planet-wide devastation *just missed* Planet Earth. Can you say, **"WAKE-UP CALL!!"**? *"Let all the Earth fear the Lord: Let all the inhabitants of the world stand in awe of Him. For He spake, and it was done; He commanded, and it stood fast."* (Psalm 33:8-9). *"Likewise also, as it was in the days of Lot ... even thus shall it be in The Day when The Son of Man is revealed!"* Signed: *King Jesus* (Luke 17:28,30).

America is very prosperous *materially* but poor and needy *spiritually* because so many of her Citizens are sorely lacking one thing: **Love for God.** A Nation that throws **God** out and turns its back on Him doesn't become neutral. Nope, *satan* takes it over. Just take a good look around America and tell me what you think. When a person or a Nation follows satan, they become proud and arrogant – just like satan. This proud Nation struts its wickedness in God's Face with no fear of His Judgment. Not a good idea. God meant what He said – and said what He meant. Our God is *faithful* one hundred percent. God's great *Mercy* is holding back the floodgates of His great wrath upon America right now. *We are so at God's Mercy every moment.*

America isn't mentioned in the book of "The Revelation" in the Bible (unless she is one of the Nations that come against Israel). So, why isn't America mentioned? I can think of two reasons. One is that so many Americans had become Born-Again Christians that most of them were "snatched away" to be with their Lord at the Rapture. The other is that God has unleashed His wrath upon America in some catastrophic way and most have been annihilated. I hope it's not *that* one – but only time will tell. The more I hear the staggering statistics on abortion, drug addiction, pornography addiction, murders, etc. and see the sodomites proudly marching down the main streets of America as they control our Government, Courts, Schools, Colleges, Libraries, TV, movies, the corporate world

and the media world, the more I consider what **God's Judgment** on our Nation is going to be. I know that ungodly America breaks the heart of our loving Heavenly Father Who founded her "One Nation under **God**." *"Lo, the smoke of the Country went up as the smoke of a furnace!"* (Genesis 19:28).

Christian Friend, stand with the **God you love** and **Pray** for our drifting Nation. Sadly, more and more Americans are rejecting God in favor of following *satan* into deeper and deeper levels of sin and depravity. Have the *majority* of Americans abandoned God? I don't know, but I do know this: We Christians need to pray that America hasn't yet been abandoned *by God* ... to the path that she has chosen. If the *majority* of Americans ever abandon God, He just may decide to return the favor. And we may live to see it ... because judging from the way people vote, America is rapidly approaching the tipping point. When ungodly people are the vast majority in America, they will vote for and elect only ungodly leaders – and our *One Nation under God* will no longer exist. *Mercy Me!*

Americans proudly proclaim, *"We're free!"* (What many really mean is: *"We're free to sin all we want!"*). Yep, they're free alright, but what they forget is that God is also free – free to exercise "tough Love" and hand America over to the "god" she has decided to follow – who will devastatingly destroy her with all the degrading *sins* she has foolishly chosen. Every day on the news, I hear of liberal judges ruling *in favor* of things that our Godly Grandparents would call **"Insane!"** The more **God** is rejected in America, the more *morality* is rejected in America.

"Because I live, ye shall live also." Signed: Jesus (John 14:19). *At this very moment,* Jesus is very much "Alive!" in us Christians, and we are very much "Alive!" in *Him!* I'm always saying that if our *Godly Grandparents* could come back, *they* would get this Country straightened out. *But wait a minute!!* **The Lord Jesus** is here ... in all of **us Christians!** Why aren't **we** standing up for Him and showing satan's crowd that **Jesus** really *is Alive and well* in America today ... *in* **us?!**

Folks, what did our Godly Grandparents have that **we** don't have? Let **us** start standing with our Lord on this Earth (like *they* did) so that when we die and stand before Jesus, we will have Joy unspeakable and full of Glory (like *they* do)!

Today is the day for Christians to **wake up** and smell the rat (the demon-rat); then quickly put their "Jesus Glasses" on so they can *see* what is happening here in the **Spiritual Realm** ... before it's too late. Satan is fighting hard for the *Soul* of America by gleefully filling our Country with his "freedom-from-religion" groups. The most vile, degrading sinful things imaginable are openly and freely allowed anywhere and everywhere by a society that *champions* "freedom of expression" – while it fiercely *condemns* "freedom of Religion." **But God** is looking for millions of Christians to come together and form **"The American Freedom From Satan Coalition!"** We *must* defend our *Christian Liberties* from the never-ending attacks of satan and his gang. It's time we moved this fight out into the street! Yes indeed, it's time we Christians showed up and confronted satan on his own turf – the streets, the sidewalks, the neighborhoods, the high-rise buildings, the stores, the prisons, the schools, the parks, the malls – *any* place satan is holding folks captive. Don't let that demon silence *you*, and don't waste your time being afraid of satan. *No!* Spend *your* time making sure *satan* is afraid of **you!** I'm pretty sure that my picture is on the bulletin board of the post office in hell – and yours can be too. Make up your *Mind of Christ* to be the devil's worst *nightmare!* It's time for *all* of us to man-up, stand up and stand with our Lord Jesus. *This is no time for boy*s.

We all remember "Mighty Horton the Elephant" who was willing to give his life in order to save the Whos down in Whoville. Looking through our "Jesus Glasses," we Christians can see that our **Lord Jesus** is the **Mighty God** helping **us** down here on Planet Earth. It's time for *us* to be like the Whos and let the whole world know *we* exist – *and* Who our Leader is: **King Jesus** – Who is **Undeniable Truth, Unconditional Grace, Undying Love** and **Undefeatable Power!** Our Mighty Leader is our **Servant King** Who graciously shed His own blood to *Forgive* and *Save* every lost sinner who **Believes** and **Receives.** Let's give the winds a Mighty Voice! *Our Voice!* Don't whimp-out. *Man-up!* **"The LORD liveth, and Blessed be my Rock! And let The God of my Salvation be exalted!" Signed: Every Born-Again Christian** (Psalm 18:46).

The Scribes and Pharisees were *determined* to bring about Jesus' physical death, and satan and his followers are *determined* to bring about America's *spiritual death*. The Wickersham Gang (satan's crowd)

is constantly trying to rope us Christians and force us into a cage in order to silence **God's Voice** in America today. *But* we Christians, who to Jesus for refuge hath fled, love Him enough to actually *do* what He said. So, while satan's gang shouts, *"Crucify Him!" we* are coming to our Lord's aid by proclaiming His Gospel in even *greater amounts* ... because in this crucial *Spiritual Battle* with satan *every voice counts!* The entire Nation of Whoville came very close to being boiled in beezle-nut oil because not every single one of them was working – one was shirking. And today, *someone* isn't witnessing for Jesus in America. Is that "someone" you? Has satan distracted you with trying to win "The National Yo-Yo Contest"? Well, in case you're thinking that you're just a nobody who could never do *anything* to keep satan from boiling **America** alive in beelzebul oil, let me encourage you to put your yo-yo down and go **be about your Heavenly Father's Business.** Never forget: *Whoville was saved by the smallest of all!*

When you belong to the Lord, He absolutely *loves* giving you "Big Ideas." So, let me "be Jesus" to you for a minute and give you one. Go to your Preacher and tell him that you have resolutely decided to be a bonafide Member of "The Fellowship of The Unashamed," and from this day forward, you are going to "be Jesus" to lost folks by sharing the Gospel of "Salvation in Christ" with them. Tell him that Jesus wasn't afraid or ashamed to die for you on the Cross, and now, *you're* not going to be afraid or ashamed to stand *with Jesus* and *for Jesus* in your workaday world. Then, ask him to announce to your Church that anyone who wants to join you can get in touch with you because you're starting a weekly "Bible Study" in which everyone shares their witnessing experiences – which encourages and equips the *entire group* to be all that their Lord planned for them to be ... *for Him.* *"And they entered into a Covenant to seek the Lord God of their fathers with all their heart and with all their soul" Signed: Every Member of The Fellowship of The Unashamed* (II Chronicles 15:12).

I know you need encouragement because we all do. Left to ourselves, we try doing everything in our own strength; our own way; all by ourselves. But our Lord never intended for it to be that way. Jesus had to remind me of that a few years back through a dear Sister-in-Jesus.

I was going through a tough time, and Helen was praying for me. One day, I checked my voicemail and heard her sweet voice saying,

"Molly, years ago, I was up against something so bad that I prayed, 'Fight this battle for me, Lord!!' Then, I heard His still small voice, 'I will, My Child, but you must trust Me!!'
We must trust Him, Molly.
Take one day at a time and keep your eyes on Jesus;
He is so faithful.
I'm praying for you. Jesus loves you!
Everything's gonna be alright."

That's a good prayer for all of us to pray. We have not because we ask not. Our Lord Jesus is just sitting on ready to help us … when we "call." I think you already have His *Divine Number*. Actually, it's not a number; it's a **Name** – *above all names!* *"The Name of The Lord is a strong tower; the righteous runneth into it and is safe"* (Proverbs 18:10). *"Don't worry about getting the devil's number … he's already got yours … and he'll be calling on you soon enough!"* (Ken Davis).

By the time a kid reaches 18, he's seen it all, done it all and knows it all. Just ask him. He'll tell you. Jeff Allen says, *"I truly believe that teenagers are God's revenge on mankind. It's like God says: Let's see how* **man** *likes creating someone in his own image who denies his very existence."* Jeff is pretty sure that the devil was 15 when he rebelled against the Lord. Hopefully, *your* teenager is being led by Jesus to be truly wise – instead of just a smart aleck. Our Lord is always looking for someone with the *Faith of a child* and a *teachable spirit*. So, just humble yourself under the Mighty Hand of God so that He may exalt you in due time. When we try to exalt *ourselves*, we're headed for the rocks, *but* when we humbly let *our Lord* lift us up, we're headed for the heights of Glory. On the day of Jesus' trial, He *humbled Himself* under the Mighty Hand of His Father, and today, God has exalted His Son to **The Name** above all names! *Hallelujah to The Lamb upon His Throne!!*

As Jesus stood in front of Pilate that day, Pilate asked Him, "What is Truth?" ... then walked away. Isn't that amazing! Pilate was standing in front of *Truth Himself* ... and just walked away. People do the same thing today. They stand in front of *us* knowing not that "The Truth" Himself is living right on the inside of us *speaking to them!* People don't want to hear *Jesus' Truth* because satan has them deceived into believing they already *have* the truth. Lost folks resist "The Truth" because "satan in them" is resisting *"Jesus in us."* Satan knows that Jesus can *set them free*, so he uses every trick in the book to keep them rejecting Jesus' Truth and believing his lies. *But Jesus* has *Saved you*, my Christian Friend, so that He can live *in you* and speak His Truth *through you* to those lost folks satan is deceiving. When you are speaking *Jesus' Gospel Truth* into the soul of such a person, pray that Jesus will keep them from "just walking away" into this dark world. Pray and ask your Lord to hold them there as He opens their heart, their soul and their spirit to *receive* "The Way, The Truth and The Life" – *Jesus Christ. Yes!!*

Even Christians can fall prey to satan's evil deceptions. The devil is working overtime to get you thinking that your life is of no importance at all in this vast Universe and you don't matter in the least in the Grand Scheme of things. *But Jesus* is wise to satan's tactics, so He's sending you *His Message:*

"My Dear Child, your Life is a Precious Gift
from Me, The King of All Creation! Every moment,
I AM closely watching to see what you are doing with it.
When I AM The One at the Epicenter of everything you think,
everything you say, everything you do or even think about doing,
there is no such thing as a dull, boring or unimportant day.
This glorious life you are living – made up of minutes,
days and years – is your investment in Eternity!!
Don't waste it!! Invest your life in My Eternal
Kingdom, and you will never ever regret it.
I promise." Signed: Jehovah Jesus

In the midst of Jesus' turbulent trial, there was that split-second moment-of-time when He turned and looked *intently* at Peter – and *that look* broke Peter's heart. Have you felt Jesus' gaze upon *you* lately? As this Universe swirls in the vastness of Space, our **Lord Jesus** is forever enthroned in the *Realms of Glory* as its **Majestic King**! *And yet*, this *Exalted One* is as close to you as the next beat of your heart. *Amazing!* At this very moment, Jesus is lovingly looking directly at **you** with more **Love** than you have ever felt from any human being on this Earth! **Jesus' Love** will break your heart; then His Love will fix your heart by *filling* your heart. **Jesus' Love** is a flame of **fire,** and His eyes of **Love** are penetrating your heart, turning you into a tender *Witnessing Warrior* for Him. **Jesus' Love** molds you and makes you into the person He desires you to be; you'll see. Jesus never leaves you where He finds you; He brings you into *His World* where He can love you more deeply, more purely and more passionately than you have ever been loved before. *Let Him!* Now that you belong to Jesus, you will never again be the person you used to be. You are no longer just "one somebody." You are now "two Somebodies" – who are bonded together with "God's Realla Love-Glue" and are therefore forever inseparable. Dearly Beloved, receive *Jesus' Divine Love* with great joy, and then love Him back with it. When you love your Lord Jesus with all of your heart, you find yourself doing everything you do out of love for **Him**. *"And ye shall be my Faithful Witness!"*

When Jesus Christ invades your life and *Saves* you, He promises to give you His Peace. Your Saviour desires for His Peace to be ever-present in your heart and soul. So, is it? Well, if I know you like I know me, I would guess that many things in this life cause you to "lose your Peace." So here's a tip: Start thinking like Jesus thinks. Now, I know what *you're* thinking, *"But I don't know what Jesus is thinking."* Well, a good way to find out is to just ask Him. I truly believe that when you do, Jesus will tell you He's thinking about His Father, His Father's Glory, Eternity and **you**. Jesus is looking at you walking around down here on Planet Earth and thinking, *"Eternity!"* That's why He tells you, *"Labor not for the meat which perisheth, but for that meat which endureth unto Everlasting Life!"* (John 6:27). Jesus is also thinking about the Glory of His Father and those things which bring Him Glory – such as you allowing "Christ in you" to *do* what He is in you to do. When you let Jesus "be Jesus" in *you*, God is *Glorified* – and that Glory will last for *all*

DARE to be JESUS

Eternity! So, no matter *what* falls apart in your life *today,* you can *rest in Peace* knowing that your **Eternity** is going to be … well … *out of this world! "Herein is My Father Glorified, that ye bear much fruit" Signed: Jesus* (John 15:8).

People today are absolutely obsessed with "living the Good Life." Everywhere you turn, you see billboards advertising "Top of the World Golf Communities" for the wealthy and "Paradise Vacation Cruises" for the soon-to-be-poor when they lose all their money gambling. Most folks equate "living the Good Life" with having lots of $$$$ – but I know the Truth. I know that my Lord has His eye on me every moment of every day and night, watching to see what I am doing with this life He has given me to live on Planet Earth for a very short span of time. "Living the Good Life" isn't indulging myself in everything this world has to offer. Oh no, living the *Good Life* is indulging myself in the *Great Joy* of **"Living for Jesus!"** A wise man once said that life is not a problem to be solved … but a mystery to be lived **(with Jesus).** So, won't you join me? Dare to be **Jesus' Ambassador** everywhere you go … even if it's to the "Top of the World" or a "Tropical Paradise." Be on perpetual vacation with **Jesus!** But I must warn you: *He likes to make all the stops along The Way.*

(Side-note: When you see a picture of a beautiful "Tropical Paradise," you say, *"Oh, how lovely! What a joy it would be to live there!"* But what you don't realize is that the guy taking the picture was probably sneezing uncontrollably due to the high pollen count while dripping sweat in the oppressive heat and humidity as he brushes up against some poisonous vines and … *oops!* … steps on a deadly snake slithering away from a nearby hungry alligator. When the poor guy tries to escape, large thorn bushes inflict deep lacerations upon his skin which is being bitten by swarms of disease-infected mosquitoes … *yikes!* … and scorched by intense UV rays from the sun. *Mercy Me!* Adam and Eve are probably still hiding out in Heaven today from all the people looking for them to blame them for letting Planet Earth go to the dogs … snakes, mosquitoes, wild predators, poison ivy, coronavirus, "Cains," etc.)

One of the *true joys* in life is driving down the highway doing the speed limit and passing a Highway Patrol car hiding in the bushes. You want to honk, wave at him and smile, you feel so good … because

you know he won't be chasing *you*. When the **Lord Jesus** patrols your life, you can relax and smile at whatever the day brings. Will Jesus ever allow "bad" things to come into your life? Unfortunately ... yes ... but only so that He can use them in *His Perfect Plan* for you. I'm always telling people that the Lord has a reason and a purpose for everything He does. That is probably the reason Jesus allows so many "bad" things to come into *my* life; He's testing me to see if I really believe what I say I believe. *"God will allow you to go through a storm to see if you meant what you said when you said, 'Amen!' to the sermon"* (Tony Evans). But I'm wise to Him by now, so I bow my head and my heart, and I pray,

"Lord, this thing is from You. So, I receive it as from
Your loving hand.
You and I will face this ... together. You and I
can handle this ... together.
I will do whatever You tell me to do, and You will do
what only You can do.
Through it all, I will trust You, Lord, because I know
how much You love me.
So, I rest in the Perfect Peace You alone can give as I trust
Your Wisdom, Your
Reason and Your Purpose for it all. I love You, Lord, and it is
well with my soul."

Only the Lord can give you Peace in the midst of the storm, and I am convinced that our **Great God** is busy doing *Something Big* in our Country today. Many Christians are praying for another "Great Christian Awakening," and I know that our Lord hears our fervent prayers. *"God may be silent, but He is never still"* (Charles Stanley). I firmly believe that Aslan is *ON THE MOVE!* The Lion of Judah is "Roaring!" Do you hear Him? *I do!* But I can also hear wicked satan roaring as well. Crime, violence and sins of every kind are rising rapidly in our Country; satan is definitely on the loose! It's time for you, my Christian Friend,

to join "Jesus' Safari" because *The Battle is The Lord's!* Just take the ammunition of God's Love and Christ's Gospel, walk up to that lost slave of satan, open your mouth and turn *JESUS* loose!

"Behold, the Lion of the tribe of Judah hath prevailed!"
(Revelation 5:5).

"WELCOME TO MY WORLD!"

GOD CRUCIFIED

"The Son of Man came
not to be ministered unto, but to minister,
and to give His Life a Ransom for many!"
Signed: Jesus (Matthew 20:28).

E ven though I'm no theologian, I have decided to begin this chapter with a theological discussion. There are two Schools of thought on the crucifixion of Jesus. Some Bible Scholars say that satan did *not* want Jesus to be crucified because he knew it would seal his doom. If that be true, then why did **satan** enter into Judas to betray Jesus to His enemies to be crucified? After satan entered Judas and he left, Jesus said to His Apostles, *"Hereafter I will not talk much with you; for the prince of this world cometh and hath nothing in Me"* (John 14:30). The *prince of this world* is satan; therefore, Jesus was saying that **satan** was the evil-one coming for Him. The wicked Jewish leaders, who forced the Romans to kill Jesus, belonged to satan and were controlled by him (John 8:44). So, if the devil did *not* want Jesus crucified, he would never have moved them to do so. When Jesus said to them, *"This is your hour, and the power of darkness,"* He was saying, *"This is **satan's** hour to have power over Me!"* Satan is the evil-one behind all murder. *"Satan was a murderer from the beginning!"*

The Scholars often quote Mark 8:33 in which Jesus says to Peter, *"Get thee behind Me, satan; for thou savourest not the things that be of God, but the things that be of men."* I don't think Jesus was saying satan didn't want Him crucified; Jesus was just comparing Peter to satan, who always wants things going *his* way, not *God's* way – and in this case, satan's way was to get Jesus *out* of his way so that he could continue being

"the god of this world" *(he likes the sound of that; he's finally "god")*. Satan is a corrupt, fallen-angel, ruled only by pride, greed and hate; therefore, he actually thought he could overthrow *Almighty God* in Heaven. So, it's no surprise he would have the same thoughts about *God's Son* on Earth. Satan offered Jesus all the kingdoms of this world *if* Jesus would just bow down and worship *him*. Some say this was satan's scheme to keep Jesus from going to the Cross, but it was actually satan's scheme to enthrone *himself* as "the god" of this world. Fortunately, God the Son could read the stitches on the fast ball (like Rush) as well as the "fine print" in the contract, and Jesus saw that even though satan was offering to give Him a lot of "earthly stuff," that demon would *still* have all the "power." The devil was always coming up with plots to kill Jesus – but not to keep Him from going to the Cross; the fake-god was just trying to eliminate his Competitor – *The True God.*

In I Peter 1:9-12, Peter indicates that the Holy Angels of God (and possibly the Prophets) didn't know the mystery of our Salvation. If *they* didn't know, neither did the *fallen-angels* (including satan). The Apostle Paul says that God only reveals the mystery of our Salvation to Christians through His Holy Spirit: *"But we speak the Wisdom of God in a mystery, even the hidden mystery, which God ordained before the world unto our glory; which none of the princes of this world knew; for had they known it, they would not have crucified the Lord of Glory ... but God hath revealed them unto us by His Spirit"* (I Corinthians 2:7-8,10).

Never forget that the devil is "God's devil." **The Lord** is Sovereign over all things (including satan). Known only to **God** are all His works; the devil only knows what God *wants* him to know. The following passage of Scripture confirms what Paul states above – **God** is the One in charge of revealing the mystery of Salvation: *" 'For (The Son of Man) shall be delivered unto the Gentiles, and shall be mocked, and spitefully entreated, and spit upon; and they shall scourge Him, and put Him to death; and the third day He shall rise again.' And they understood none of these things; and this saying was hid from them, neither knew they the things which were spoken"* (Luke 18:32-34). Luke clearly states that the mystery of our Salvation "was hid" from them. Since God hid it from Jesus' Apostles, He most likely hid it from satan as well. Jesus tells us that the mystery will only be revealed: *"When ye have lifted up the Son of Man, then shall ye know that I AM He!"* (John 8:28). I

think the only Scripture satan could remember was Genesis 3:15 when God said, *"Hey, you devil, listen up! The Seed of the woman is going to **crush your head!"***

I may be wrong, but it is my belief that even though satan knew Jesus was going to crush his head … he didn't know *how.* Therefore, he *actually thought* he could get rid of **Jesus** and save his neck. Many people say that satan is smart, but just how smart is someone who actually *thinks* he can overthrow **The Son of God,** for pity's sake! Incredibly, satan is always just itchin' for a fight with the very *God* of this Universe. And he never cries *"Uncle!"* and gives up either (can you say, *Wiley Coyote*?). Too bad more folks don't give *him* up. But they don't … because satan has blinded his followers to the *true identity* of their leader – a fugitive criminal in the demonic realm of the spiritual world. Those poor souls can't "see" that they belong to an evil demon that is making them *just like himself* and taking them into a very dark future. We Christians are *so* thankful that *we* belong to **King Jesus** – Who makes *us* just like *Himself* and takes us to Heavenly Glory! *Thank You, Lord.*

Getting back to ole slewfoot's plan, he had devised a "brilliant" one (at least, *he* thought so): (a) Kill Jesus; (b) Bring to nought God's Kingdom; (c) Set up *my throne* above the Throne of God; (d) Get *all* the Glory for myself. *"The devil doesn't want casualties; he wants converts. The devil wants to be worshipped"* (Adrian Rogers). Satan wants *everyone* bowing down and worshipping *him* "as god" – he's fighting for "world domination." Most of all, satan wants to be worshipped by **God *Himself,*** and since Jesus wouldn't bow down and worship him in the wilderness … well … **Jesus** had to go. Yep, that arrogant, deluded demon wants to wear the Crown and get all the Glory for himself – and *nobody's gonna stop him* (or so he thinks). Have you ever seen anyone more intoxicated with the "illusion" of their own self-importance? *Don't answer that.*

God makes rich; greed makes poor. And satan is the best example of *that* in the history of the world! But ole super-genius couldn't see it because his *pride* had convinced him that his was the best fool-proof plan ever devised. Yep, it all sounded *so good* … on paper. *But* he grossly underestimated his Opponent, and in the end, the only thing satan's plan proved was … that *he* is a fool. Unbeknownst to *him,* that "brilliant" demon had planned the execution of his own demise, proving that love isn't the only thing that's blind … so is *pride.* All satan could see was

his name in lights – not the day he would *crash and burn!* So, blinded by greed, prideful satan set out to get rid of God – *for good!* But, alas, the best laid plans of mice and men (and satan) often go awry and leave us only pain for promised joy. The devil may be "the deceiver," but when he crucified Jesus, *he* was the one who was deceived.

The *Eternal God* had an *Eternal Plan*, and unsuspecting satan was going to help Him pull it off. Truth is, God couldn't have asked for a more delusional dufus than the devil to be His adversary because that arrogant fruitcake was actually plotting to kill the **Eternal God** *(Who had created him)* so that *he (a condemned demon)* could take **Holy God's** place (yeah, right). Satan is so evil and so prideful it blinds him; therefore, the prince of darkness grim just couldn't *see* that his demonic pride would "do him in" once again. God hadn't forgotten that it was Lucifer's *pride* that caused him to lead a rebellion against Him in Heaven in Eternity past. *So*, to settle the score with His fallen-angel, God (in His wisdom) would use satan's own prideful arrogance to defeat him. *God* was setting him up … his *pride* would take him down – and all the demons of hell couldn't stop God's Plan.

Here's a tip: Don't ever follow the devil. When you do, you end up doing some of the dumbest things … and wondering how you ever got *so* duped. And don't be surprised when you hear satan laughing just around the corner. Your demonic adversary gets great devilish delight out of your pain, suffering and sorrow. There's a better way. The **Lord Jesus** offers you that better way, and you must choose *His* way or *satan's* way. Just keep in mind that *Destiny's Door* turns on very small hinges, and the way you choose has *Eternal* ramifications. Choose wisely. **"If you don't crown Jesus … you crucify Him!"** (Adrian Rogers).

Jesus' crucifixion is shrouded in mystery – *Divine Mystery*. Satan didn't see it coming and the world can't understand it, but from Jesus' death on the Cross comes *life* – *Spiritual Life* – **Eternal Life!** The crucifixion of Jesus was a very high price to have to pay, **but God** *also* had a Plan – a Bigger Plan, a Stronger Plan, a Wiser Plan "because the foolishness of God is *Wiser* than men (or satan), and the weakness of God is *Stronger* than men (or satan)" (I Corinthians 1:25). There are three ways to get something done: (a) Do it yourself; (b) Hire someone else to do it for you; (c) Tell your kids *not* to do it. If you doubt me on that last one, just ask God. It is my belief that God created our Universe (and mankind

upon Planet Earth) for the purpose of defeating His arch-enemy satan. *Really!* When the Angel Lucifer rebelled and challenged God in Eternity past, the wheels in God's mind started turning (figuratively speaking, of course). Yep, God had already planned out every single detail of everything He was going to do before He ever spoke the first Word of "Creation" – and He did it with fallen Lucifer in His crosshairs. When God told Adam and Eve *not* to eat of the forbidden fruit, it was the beginning of the end of satan once and for all … because it was all part of God's Plan (a Plan God *didn't* let satan in on because he had already rebelled). Our Great God knows how to use "problems" to bring about perfection (so don't give up on your kids just yet). **"Trust Me, My Child, I have everything under control!" Signed: Jehovah Jesus.**

"Now is the judgment of this world. Now shall the prince of this world be cast out!" Signed: King Jesus (John 12:31). *Good News* for a dark, oppressed world. Our **Lord Jesus** has crushed the head of the "serpent of ole" just like He said He would. Yes siree, that ole lying snake-in-the-grass in The Garden has been decapitated and mortally wounded by the Son of God – **King of Glory!** Today, the demonic underworld's pitiful leader is "the headless snake-demon." *Mercy Me!* Isn't it amazing how a freak that's done lost his mind can still control so many people! Satan ain't half the god he wants his followers to think he is. Nope, the joke's on him because he's *still* just a slimy snake … and he *still* doesn't have a leg to stand on. We Born-Again Christians are safe and secure "in Christ." *We're* standing on **The Rock** of our Salvation. *"For the prince of this world cometh, and he hath nothing in Me" Signed: Jesus* (John 14:30). *Praise Him! Praise Him! Jesus our Blessed Redeemer!!*

Does the evil prince of this world have power? Yep, but there's a "New King" enthroned on High Who has the devil on a leash down here below. And to add insult to injury, when Jesus conquered and subdued satan, He gave *us Christians* the spoils of the victory! *"When (Jesus) ascended up on High, He led captivity captive, and gave gifts unto men"* (Ephesians 4:8). So, what did we get? What did that rascal satan have that we would want, for pity's sake? Answer: Every God-given Gift he had taken from Adam. *Yes!!* God had given Adam "Spiritual Life," but ole slewfoot took it away and gave Adam "spiritual death." *Now,* God gives those who accept **Jesus** as their Saviour "Spiritual Life" once again. Jesus gives us His Precious Holy Spirit Who brings with Him Spiritual

Gifts and Spiritual Fruit. We Born-Again Christians can joyfully run *to* our Heavenly Father instead of running away from Him … because all of our sins have been wiped away, thanks to Jesus our Lord. We can truly *love* our Heavenly Father once again because we *know* how very much **He loves us.** Our Lord restores our status as Sons and Daughters of God and gives us *Dominion* over the devil. We can once again walk and talk with our Lord in the sweet Fellowship of **The Spirit** in the cool of the evening … *and* in the heat of the battle … with satan. *Mercy Me!*

God gave Adam the authority to name all the animals. Since the animals have all been named, we Christians can name other things. For instance, we can name *Jesus* the same Name God calls Him: **"The Mighty God!"** We can name *America* the same name God calls her: **"One Nation under God."** We can name *Christians* the same name God calls us: **"Mighty Witnesses for Jesus!"** We can name *satan* the same name God calls him: "ↄ ↄ⬡⬡ↄ⓿⬡ↄ ⬡⑥⬡" *(a defeated foe).* Yep, the lord of the flies may bug us, but our Lord Jesus has some strong "Pesticide" that works real well on him – *the Blood of Jesus Christ!* There's not a person or a situation in this whole world that our Lord Jesus can't cast satan out of. *Hallelujah!*

David Berkowitz, who is in prison in New York State, has *miraculously* become a Born-Again Christian. You may know his story. It's a powerful one, and you can go to his website (ariseandshine.org) and get acquainted with him. Sometimes, when I offer his tract (Son of Hope) to a person, they will refuse it and say, *"He's not going to Heaven; he killed people!"* I ask them if they think the Apostle Paul will be there. Before his Salvation, Paul the Apostle was Saul the Destroyer who had many Christians killed. After Jesus appeared to him and *Saved* him, Paul wrote, *"By God's Grace you are Saved!"* If you are a Born-Again Christian today, it is purely because of the *merciful* **Grace of God.** David knows that. Do you? I do; I have my own B.C. (Before Christ) story. Some of our B.C. stories are worse than others (at least, in man's eyes), but it still takes the Precious Blood of Jesus Christ *(the Most Powerful Cleansing Agent in the Universe)* to cleanse us *all.* You may ask, *"Why would God ever Save someone like David Berkowitz?"* Answer: To show this doubting world the *Supernatural Power* of His Son's Blood – shed on Calvary's Cross for the Salvation of *any* lost soul who will *receive Him.* Jesus' Blood makes the foulest clean. His Blood avails for me.

Does His Blood avail for you? Our Lord Jesus has cleansed David's soul with His Precious Blood, and even though David is in a high-security prison, he is a free-man "in Christ." So, if you know someone who is nothing but bad, Bad, BAD, introduce them to **The One** Who has the *Divine Power* to *Save* them and transform them into a Christian who (by God's Grace) is capable of being good, Good, GOOD!

A person who claims to be a Born-Again Christian *but* can't rejoice in the Salvation of a lost soul (*any* lost soul) is a mystery to me. I personally rejoice in *every* soul our Lord *Saves*, no matter their background, skin color, race, former religious affiliation and so forth. I never forget that God *Saved this* lost soul in spite of *my* terrible background. *Grace, Grace, God's Grace!!* Jesus forgave the criminal on the cross, the Apostle Paul, David Berkowitz and even the ones who murdered *Him*, and yet, some Christians say, *"I don't care if Jesus did forgive all those murderers, I'm not forgiving David Berkowitz."* What they are blind to is the fact that, in God's eyes, we are *all* murderers – we killed **Jesus!** So, *they* were just as much a criminal as David was … before God *Saved* them. David humbled himself, asked God for forgiveness and received His *So Great Salvation*. But *they* are so proud they don't think they *need* God's forgiveness – for anything. *"Pride forged on the anvil of a hard heart will escort you to hell!"* (Adrian Rogers).

Don't *you* be like those pious people who think they will be in Heaven because *they* haven't lived such a bad life. Listen Folks, before God *Saves* us, we are *all* in satan's cauldron of sin … and ole stewfoot loves stirring us and stirring us at will. So, don't be a Pharisee who looks down on some guy below you in satan's pot. With just one stir, *he* could rise to the top, and you, Sir, could sink to the bottom. *Mercy Me! "The Pharisees knew everything there was to know about religion. They could dot every 'i' and cross every 't' … but they couldn't spell 'Love'"* (Adrian Rogers).

Self-righteous people have forgotten the *Mercy* and *Grace* of God in *Saving* them. They don't spend much time at the foot of Jesus' Cross. If they did, they would see unmerciful satan pouring out his hate and cruelty upon the innocent Son of God – Who is humbly, lovingly and willingly taking *their* place there. On Calvary's Hill, demons poured out satanic hate, **but Jesus** poured out *God's Love*. Love always wins over hate, and on the day Jesus was crucified … *God won over satan!* The evil prince of darkness wickedly tried to extinguish The Light of the World,

but darkness has no power over our Lord's Glorious Light. So, take your *Holy Spirit Candle* and run to the darkness. God will use you to start a **Holy Fire** in *someone* ... you'll see. *Jesus' Love is the Victory that overcomes satan's evil world! Oh, to love like Jesus!*

The next time you feel like you're having a really bad day, take a moment and reflect on all the pain Jesus endured the day He was crucified. After the merciless beatings and the scourging, Jesus was forced to carry His Cross to Calvary ... until He collapsed. I've heard it said that if you go to Israel today, you can walk on some of those same stones Jesus walked on as He struggled to carry His Cross (my Cross) down the Via Dolorosa (The Way of Suffering). Whether that be true or not, I don't know, but I do know this: Even though I've never been to Israel and walked where Jesus walked, Jesus is here in the USA *today* ... walking *with me* everywhere *I* walk. Since Jesus willingly walked down "The Way of Suffering" for *me*, I have no trouble a'tall walking with *Jesus* up to someone else and letting Jesus tell them what He did for *them*. Jesus would love for **you** to join Him down the Via Dolorosa as you and He stop from time to time along *The Way* to tell some onlooker that He is going to Calvary ... for *them*. Tell them that Jesus is passing by, and when **Jesus** passes by ... *everything changes.* Then, when you and Jesus finally reach Calvary, and Jesus is hanging there on the Cross (that you helped Him carry), He will be thanking you for making it worth all of His suffering – down the Via Dolorosa all the way to Calvary. *You are never closer to Jesus than when you are with Him on His Cross.*

That day you came to the foot of Jesus' Cross and gave Him all of your sin (which He washed away with His Precious Blood), did you also give Him your heart? Did you? Did you fall deeply in love with **The One** Who fell and fell and fell carrying *your* Cross to Calvary? Did you fall in love with **Jesus** – the Saviour Who deeply loves *you* with an *Everlasting Love*? This could be the day you did. Give your heart to Jesus. When you do, He *fills it* with **His Love** – a **Love** so sweet, so deep, so warm, so strong, so real, so beautiful and so joyous that it's as if Jesus is sitting *right there beside you* holding your hand. Jesus is so close to you that you can even feel His heart beating – *for you, His Favorite Child.* In this moment of pure bliss, you realize that the *Wonderful Love* you feel for Jesus is actually coming from *Him!* As your two hearts beat together, Jesus softly whispers, "*I love you so much that I have sealed you in Me*

with My Spirit – Who is in **Me** *and in* **you** *at the very same time.* **I AM** *forever yours ... and* **you** *are forever Mine."* **"We love Him, because He first loved us"** (I John 4:19).

When you watch movies of Jesus' crucifixion, does your heart ache as you watch Him struggling to carry His Cross (your Cross) to Golgotha's Hill? Do you ever wish that *you* could have been there to help Jesus? Do you wish that *you* could have been Simon of Cyrene to Jesus in His moment of great need? Well cheer up, my Friend, you still can. Our Lord Jesus suffered greatly for the opportunity to live "another Life" on Planet Earth. Nailed to a rough wooden Cross and suspended between Heaven and Earth, Jesus spent His last moments thinking about that *glorious day* He would be able to live His Life *again* on this Earth – in **YOU**. And *today* is that day! God doesn't waste His Son's Blood, and Jesus' death has made your "New Life in Christ" a living, breathing "Reality." And now, *He needs you – not* to carry His Cross up Calvary's Hill – but to carry **Him** and **His Gospel** to all those lost folks everywhere you look. Jesus showed you how much He loves you by dying for you on the Cross. Now *you* show Jesus how much you love *Him* by dying to yourself and telling others how much Jesus loves *them*. I'm no Bible Scholar for sure, but that doesn't stop me from telling people about my Saviour ... because *nothing* could stop my Saviour from dying for *me*. *Jesus' Marvelous Love* sent Him to that cruel Roman Cross to die for us sinners. Jesus so loves us; now let's so live for **Him**. *Oh, to love like Jesus!*

Just before the soldiers nailed Jesus to the Cross, they offered Him "wine mingled with myrrh – but He received it not" (Mark 15:23). That mixture was given to dull the senses and ease the pain, but Jesus didn't drink it. He knew that He *still* had to be about His Father's Business, and He needed for His mind to be as sharp, clear and alert as it possibly could during those last excruciatingly painful moments of His physical life. Jesus drank "the Cup" by *not* drinking the cup of wine mingled with myrrh. *Oh, to be like Jesus!*

Without a doubt, the crucifixion of God's Son was the crime of all time. It was satan at his worst. However, when satan was at his worst, God was at His Best. On the day Jesus was crucified, He was at His Best at being courageous. When I think about what a big baby I am over the least little pain, I am awed by Jesus' great *Courage* ... for me ... and for you. I don't know about you, my Friend, but I want my life

to be one continuous *"Thank You!"* to my Saviour for all the pain He suffered for *me*. Jesus' Love for His Father (and for us) far out-weighed all of His fear. *Oh, to be like Jesus!*

On the day of Jesus' crucifixion, satan was at his *worst* at being an arrogant, prideful executioner. If you want to see what pride looks like, just look at satan. That demon prefers to spend all of *Eternity* in hell rather than *humble himself* and bow before the Lord Jesus. That's pride on steroids. Do you know someone who is so proud that they prefer to spend Eternity in hell rather than *humble themselves* and bow before the Lord Jesus for His forgiveness? If so, you can "be Jesus" to them *today* ... before proud satan takes them into a sad tomorrow. *The Way of Jesus' Cross leads Home.*

Jesus, on the other hand, was at *His Best* at being the humble, sacrificial Lamb of God ... silent before His shearers. To illustrate the contrast, let me ask you this: Have you ever heard of a Christian pointing a gun at an unbeliever and demanding, *"Deny satan – **or die!!"?*** No, and you won't. So, why do demonic people kill *Christians* who refuse to deny **Jesus**? I'll tell you why. Satan is the "god" of **hate** – mixed in with **pride**. He will do whatever it takes to get whatever he wants. He wants to be "top dog" – always has. Therefore, he hates *anyone* who is more important than *him*. In Heaven in Eternity past, Lucifer (like a rebellious teenager) said to God, *"Hey, Ole God, I'm **way** more important than You are – so You'd better 'Gimme, gimme, gimme'!"* (So *that's* who we get that from.) But look what it *got'em, got'em, got'em* – and he can't *standit, standit, standit!*

"And ye shall be hated of all men for My Name's sake" Signed: *Jesus* (Luke 21:17). Many of the lost people in this world don't just ignore Jesus ... *they hate Him!* That's because their *evil master* hates Jesus. "Calvary Love" is unknown to those who belong to that prideful, hateful devil. **But Jesus** is the **God of Love** – mixed in with **humility. Jesus** is willing to do whatever it takes to give **Eternal Life** to whosoever will accept Him ... *even* if it means being the "Sacrificial Lamb of God" from the foundation of the World! Jesus knows that *True Love* always sacrifices for the good of others ... even though it may lead you to a Cross ... because it ultimately leads to *Great Joy. Jesus first. Others second. You third.* **"The God I find in Christ is a God Who overcomes evil with good, hate by love and the world by a Cross"** (E. Stanley Jones). *Oh, to love like Jesus!*

Some Christians will tell you that if you can just convince lost folks that they are *sinners*, they will accept Jesus as their Saviour. Not so. They already *know* they're sinners – and they don't care. Many even sin and are proud of it; just like satan. Their problem is that "the deceiver" has blinded them to the *very real, extremely horrific* **eternal damnation** awaiting those who follow him to their death. Satan has them enslaved in his "religion" of atheism, in which death is the end of them and there is nothing more to their life. It is my belief that if you want to get the attention of a lost sinner, you must persuasively present him with God's Truth: He is *not* just a physical body; he is, in fact, a "spiritual soul" who will live on *after* his body dies … *somewhere*. Next, he needs to know that because of **sin**, his **soul** is *controlled by* **satan** (yep, there is an **enemy**) and is therefore *condemned by* **God** (yep, there **is** a **God**) to **hell** (yep, there *is* a **hell**) *forever* when his physical body dies … *but* there *is* a way of escape: The Way, **Jesus Christ** (yep, there *is* a **Saviour!**). Tell him that *without Christ* as the Saviour of his **soul**, he is indeed "a sinner in the hands of an evil devil … as well as an angry God." If he still doesn't care, strike a match and hold his hand over the flame for a few seconds. That should do it. If not, you may be talking to a "tare," or you could be talking to a "wheat" who just isn't ripe for harvest yet. *The good seed are the Children of the Kingdom, but the tares are the children of the wicked one!*

"*Father, forgive them; for they know not what they do.*" Signed: *Jesus* (Luke 23:34). Beaten and bloodied, Jesus hung on that Cross in agony and great pain – but it didn't stop Him from praying to His Father in Heaven to forgive those who were responsible for His crucifixion (like us). Jesus was at His Best at showing God's Grace and undying Compassion. Satan only knows how to hate and kill. Our Lord Jesus knows how to *Love* and *Forgive* … even His enemies. *Oh, to forgive like Jesus!*

Jesus asked His Father to forgive the people who were crucifying Him because they didn't know what they were doing. They didn't realize that they were crucifying **God**! However, they didn't succeed in *killing God*. I know … because I (and millions of other Christians) live in *His Presence* each day. When I witness to lost folks, I will sometimes ask, "*What happened three days after they placed Jesus' body in that tomb?*" They all say, "*He arose*" (even the lost know about Easter). Then, I ask,

135

"So, what does that mean?" They just stand there giving me a blank stare because they don't really believe what they just said. So, *I* say, *"HE'S ALIVE TODAY!! Right Here!! Right Now!!"* It's true, Jesus walks with me and talks with me and tells me I am His own. God is *never* out of Business. *"They flung Him outside the gates to die, not knowing that in that very moment they were lifting up all the gates of the Universe to let The King of Glory come in!"* (James Stewart).

If the sandals and garments taken off of Jesus before His crucifixion were suddenly discovered today, they would be worth an unimaginable fortune – but the soldiers at the foot of His Cross callously gambled for them. The "spirit" of those soldiers lives on in many people today who view a Man shamefully crucified on a Cross centuries ago as worthless. It's all foolishness to them … just as it was to people back then. The crowd around the Cross mocked, jeered, cursed and shouted, *"He saved others; Himself He cannot save!"* If they had only known the truth of their words! Jesus couldn't *Save* both Himself *and* us … so … He humbly and lovingly chose to *Save us*. Not even the cruelest hecklers in the crowd could make even a dent in the Passion of our Lord Jesus, Who is forever *Saving others* … no matter how badly they may have treated *Him*. *"Thank You, Lord!"* That was the day our Lord was at His Personal Best at being a Sacrificial Servant. *"Christ demonstrated His Love for us and died for us while we were getting on His last nerve!"* (Tony Evans). *Oh, to be like Jesus!*

In our modern evil world, nothing much has changed – satan is *still* at his worst. And yet, something *has* changed. Today, *Jesus* is here – *in you!* And He is *still* God's Best Man to destroy the wicked works of the devil. So, "Jesus in you" has His work cut out for Him. Are you ready? Jesus is. Are you willing? Jesus is. Are you His – *all* His? Jesus is yours – *all* yours. The Bridegroom and His Spirit say "Come!" What does His Bride say? *"It doesn't take much of a man to be a Christian. It just takes all of him!"* (Adrian Rogers). *Oh, to work like Jesus!*

"Thou shalt daily prepare a burnt offering unto the Lord of a lamb of the first year without blemish; thou shalt prepare it every morning" (Ezekiel 46:13). Jesus, the Lamb of God, has been sacrificed for you. Now *you*, my Christian Friend, have a purpose in life – a God-ordained Purpose – an *Eternal Purpose*! As your Good Shepherd's Little Lamb, you are to offer *yourself* and *your life* up to Him every morning … *for*

His use. Present yourself a "living sacrifice" unto your Lord and make His desires *your* desires. Jesus has given you a *Purpose* to live out and a *Destiny* to fulfill. Never forget: All that is necessary for evil to triumph is for good men to do *nothing* (Edmund Burke). If you remain silent at such a time as this, deliverance *will come* for God's People ... but *you* will suffer loss. If you can *Supernaturally* hear your Lord Jesus *personally* and *passionately* "calling" to you to come help Him build His Eternal Kingdom here on Planet Earth, and *not* respond with renewed commitment and enthusiasm ... you're already dead ... we just haven't buried you yet. **Jesus has "Called" you!** Are you ready to come back from the dead and answer Jesus' "Call"? **"If you're not dead ... you're not done" (Craig Groeschel).** *Oh, to "live!" like Jesus!*

When Jesus was on the Cross, He was at His Best at remembering Scripture and pointing us to a Psalm that describes His crucifixion. Centuries earlier, Jesus had written this Psalm through King David about His own birth and crucifixion. The life and death of our Lord Jesus were the ultimate fulfillment of the Prophecy of Psalm 22, and amazingly, it was written centuries before crucifixion was used as a means of execution! Who knew ... **but God?** Most folks say that Jesus' "My God, My God" quote from Psalm 22 indicates that God the Father abandoned Him while He was on the Cross ... but did He? I believe that our Heavenly Father *separated* Himself from His Son (somehow) while Jesus was bearing our sin (Holy God the Father must stay pure from sin) but I don't think God *abandoned* His Son. When a young man has to go to prison for a crime, he is separated from his father – not *abandoned* by him. When a father has to punish his son, he still loves him; and during those hours of darkness, when the wrath of God (that *we* deserved) was poured out upon Jesus, He still *knew* that God was His Father ... Who still loved Him ... because in Luke 23:34 and 23:46, Jesus prayed to God and addressed Him as **His Father.** In my opinion, Jesus' *"My God, My God"* words sound more like a statement than a prayer and are intended to point us to this prophetic Psalm. However, in His humanity, Jesus probably *felt* the temporary separation from His Father on the Cross that day – which would qualify Him to be able to say to *us* today, *"When you feel forsaken and all alone, you're in Good Company – so did I. But now, I AM here to tell you, Cheer up, My Child! Sunday's Comin'!!"* *Oh, to encourage like Jesus!*

If you are an unbeliever reading this who has never read the Bible, let me encourage you to find one and read Psalm 22; then read the New Testament Gospel accounts of Jesus' crucifixion (which occurred centuries after that Psalm was written). The writer of Psalm 22 had never seen a crucifixion, but he described the events which took place at Jesus' Cross. Then, ask yourself, *"How could this be?"* You are now on the horns of a dilemma – either the Bible is just a bunch of concocted lies and myths, *or* ... **Jesus is Lord!** I know that **Jesus is LORD**!! Since you *don't*, you need to start facing your future: Death is coming – *for sure!* What's going to happen to you *then*? Are you going to suffer the same fate as those people in the Old Testament who refused to heed God's Word? When God says, *"Build an Ark!"* it won't be just another rainy day. And when God says, *"Come to My Son's Cross, receive His death for you and enter into the Ark of My Kingdom!"* it won't be just another rainy day. *Oh no*, it will be a **fiery day** ... that only the *Precious Blood* of **Jesus Christ** can deliver you from. *Mercy Me!*

So, before you have to die and face God's Judgment, pray and ask the Lord to open your *Spiritual Eyes*, soften your *heart*, enter your dead *spirit*, wash your *soul* clean with *Jesus' Precious Blood*, break satan's chains and set you free – *today!* You cannot escape your meeting with the Lord Jesus Christ. Meet Him in this world ... or meet Him in the next. Meet Him now ... or meet Him later ... but meet Him *you will!* Jesus is dying to meet *you* ... *right now*. **"Verily, verily, I say unto you, he that heareth My Word and believeth on Him Who sent Me, hath Everlasting Life, and shall not come into condemnation, but is passed from death unto Life!!" Signed: Jesus** (John 5:24).

Now, maybe you're a Born-Again Christian, my Friend, but you're in a dreadfully dark place in your life right now. The circumstances of life have beaten you down to the ground, and you're beginning to feel like you're living in the "Valley of Achor (Trouble)." You're convinced that God is surely far off from you. You feel abandoned, deserted and forsaken by the very God you once trusted. Like the disciples on the day Jesus was crucified, you feel like *hope* has packed up and left *your life* for good. But you are wrong. **Jesus** hasn't packed up and gone *anywhere*. And He never will. Your faithful Saviour is in the *same place* He was the moment He *Saved* you and came to "live" in you. Yea, though He lead you through the valley of the shadow, your Good Shepherd never leaves you alone. *He is with you* ... even in the worst situations of your

life (when all seems lost and you *feel* totally forsaken). *Listen*, weary Christian, Jesus is whispering *your name*, **"My Precious Child, I AM right here with you, and I AM giving you a future and a hope. Your end is going to be so much better than your beginning. You'll see. I AM simper fi. I love you with an Everlasting Love ... you can trust Me. I AM the Rock of your Salvation! Just give Me your troubled, fearful heart, and I will give you My Peace that passeth understanding." Signed: Jesus.**

Jesus and I could write another whole book about *that!* So, let "Jesus in me" tell you what you don't know. You don't know what **Jesus** knows ... because you can't see what **Jesus** sees. But you **will** – all in your Lord's good time. In the meantime, be thankful for all your Lord has done, all He is doing and all He is going to do. Just don't murmur in your tent. If you do, you'll find out that the more you complain, the longer God lets you live ... in the wilderness. Try praying instead. Miracles happen when people pray. Without a doubt, your Mighty God hears the sound of your cry – music to His ears. Then, you hear *His* cry, *"O Little Lamb, look up! Your Redeemer draweth nigh!! Here I come to Save the day!!"* *Miraculously,* your loving Saviour parts the dark clouds of depression and floods your soul with the "Brilliant Light" of His *Glorious Presence.* **Joy** fills your heart! **The Love of your life** *is with you. Hallelujah! "Why art thou cast down, O my soul? And why art thou disquieted within me? Hope thou in God, for I shall yet praise Him!"* (Psalm 42:11). *Oh, to bring Joy like Jesus!*

While on the Cross, Jesus wasn't having a pity party and lamenting, *"Father, this is so unfair! Why Me? Why this? Why now?"* Nope, while on the Cross, Jesus was at His Best at thinking about *others.* He provided for His Dear Mother's care by entrusting her to His Beloved Apostle John (such a tender moment in His time of great pain). Jesus was also asking His Father to forgive all of *us sinners* responsible for His crucifixion. Then, He gave Salvation to the criminal at His side. While satan was at his *worst* at showing his great cruelty, **Jesus** was at His *Best* at showing His Great Compassion. *Oh, to be like Jesus!*

C. T. Studd was a well-known Christian missionary to Africa who had given all of his immense wealth to God's Kingdom after becoming a Christian. In her book *Passion and Purity*, Elisabeth Elliot tells of going to hear his daughter speak who described her father's last moments on this Earth. As her father's death drew near, she and a few others were

keeping vigil at his bedside. Lying on his small cot, the aged missionary looked around at his little hut and few possessions. After a few minutes, he quietly said, *"I wish I had something to leave to each of you ... but I gave it all to **Jesus** long ago."* Oh, to be like Jesus ... and C. T. Studd.

On the day of His crucifixion, Jesus was at His Best at being submissive to His Father. God the Son personified meekness: Power under control. Jesus definitely had the Power to destroy all of His enemies that day ... but He didn't. Jesus knew His Father's Will. He also knew that the pain God allows always has a purpose – *an Eternal Purpose*. So, Jesus drank "the Cup" – *all* of it. Sometimes, my Saviour hands *me* "a cup" and asks me to join Him. Jesus has "a cross" for me to bear and "a cup" for me to share; He gives me my own personal cup – full of all the things I am to sacrifice and endure for Him and His Eternal Kingdom. *"Where did we ever get a Christianity in which Jesus is the only One Who has to suffer; in which Jesus is the only One Who has to bear a Cross; in which Jesus is the only One Who has to die?"* (Alistair Begg). *"Oh, to endure like Jesus!*

The Cross of Jesus Christ is the heart of our Christian Faith (without it, we would still be lost in our trespasses and sins), but we don't like thinking about all the *pain* our Lord had to suffer there. However, remembering the *depth of Love* Jesus had for His Father (and us) enables us to pass that Love along to the people all around us who need it. Sadly, most Born-Again Christians can't see the forest for the trees. They are looking for ways to show their Lord (Who *Saved* them and *lives in them*) how very much they love Him ... while carrying Him past lost folks every day. And all the while, Jesus is crying out from within them, *"My Child, please listen! I AM right here, longing to tell them that I love them and died for them! Please, let Me tell them!!"*

Christian, Jesus didn't let *you* down when you needed *Someone* to give His Precious Life to *Save* you from having to spend forever in hell. *Now*, can *Jesus* count on *you* to help Him *Save* others? "Love for others" is the *Spiritual Power* the Lord Jesus brings with Him when He comes to dwell within the spirit of every Born-Again Christian. A "little person" is little because his world is so little ... he is the only one in it. Out of a deep "love for others" Jesus humbled Himself and went to the Cross. Can I humble *myself* and let my Lord Jesus use *my*

body to tell a lost person (whom He died to *Save*) about His *So Great Salvation*? Jesus was willing to be nailed to a Cross for *me*; am I willing to put myself on the altar of sacrifice for *Him*? Can I find it in my heart to be a "living martyr" for my Saviour so that others can have "New Life in Christ!"? Jesus was willing to be broken and spilt-out *for me*. Am I willing to be broken and spilt-out *for Him* ... and for others? Are *you*? **True Christianity isn't for Sissies.** *"If any man desires to be first, the same shall be last of all, and servant of all"* Signed: Jesus (Mark 9:35).

"Some wish to live within the sound of Church or Chapel bell;
I want to run a Rescue Shop within a yard of hell!"
(C. T. Studd).

I was listening to my little radio the other day when I heard the news announcer get his tongue all twisted up and call the United States the "United Snakes." *Oops!!* Even as I laughed, I knew how sadly true that blooper was. That demonic serpent of ole and his followers are aggressively *united* against our Lord and His Saints in our Nation today. With each passing day, we followers of Christ feel more and more like we're within a yard of hell in America. *But* when all of us Christian Saints get "missionary hearts" and become *equally united* in our resolve to take the Gospel of Jesus Christ to as many of satan's followers as we possibly can, the United Saints will once again out-number the united snakes in America. *Oh, to be like Jesus ... and Saint Patrick.*

In Bible times, when a criminal was crucified, the Romans would nail a sign to his cross declaring his crime. Jesus' sign read: "JESUS of Nazareth THE KING of the Jews." When the chief priests of the Jews read it, they were incensed and protested to Pilate. Why? Well, according to Ezra Griffiths, when the words on that sign (recorded by John) were read in the Hebrew language, the first letter of each word appeared as the acronym: YHWH – *Jehovah* – the Jews' Holiest Name for God! *Jesus does all things well!!* *Oh, to be like Jesus!*

So, according to that sign, Jesus' crime was "being a King." If they crucified Jesus for being a King, then they killed an innocent man ... because Jesus really *is* KING! Not just of the Jews but of the Whole Universe! I live in a very modest little house, but it's a *Castle* ... because

The King lives here! Likewise, when they nailed *King Jesus* to a Cross … *He made it a Throne!* Even the thorns in the crown on Jesus' head ultimately bore a Rose – the Rose of Sharon. Thorns are the result of God's curse on this Earth due to man's sin. Unbeknownst to those Roman soldiers, they were placing on Jesus' head a symbol of the curse which Jesus Himself (the Second Person of the Godhead) had placed on this world. As Jesus hung on the Cross with that crown of thorns on His head, the message was clear: The curse was now placed upon Jesus – Who was paying for it *Himself.* When Jesus bowed His head and died, it *seemed* that all was lost – but all was finally won! God had given His Son for *the whole world* … and His Son was *enough.*

"They thought they had defeated God with His back to the wall,
pinned and helpless and defeated; they did not know that
it was God Himself Who had tracked them down!"
(James Stewart).

Using the pious religious leaders of the day, satan forced the Romans to nail Jesus to a tree of death – and when they did, that demon shouted, *"Checkmate!!"* But God!! Our Lord had the final "move," and it was one that satan couldn't counter. God's final move is still moving lost souls even today. What is it? It's another tree: *The Tree of Life.* It appears in the Garden of Eden, in John's vision of Heaven in Revelation 22:2 *and* (to those of us with our "Jesus Glasses" on) right here, right now in the *Spiritual Realm – The Cross of Jesus Christ!* Our Lord is the great *Transformer God,* and Jesus has transformed His tree of death into *The Tree of Life* for all who choose to partake of "New Life in Christ" by receiving His death on their behalf. Just as David defeated Goliath with his own sword, Jesus took satan's weapon of death and defeated him with His own *Sacrificial Death!* Jesus promised the Church of Ephesus, *"To him who overcometh will I give to eat of The Tree of Life."* Today, Jesus promises the "whosoever wills" the same thing. *"The fruit of the Righteous is a Tree of Life, and he that winneth souls is wise"* (Proverbs 11:30).

Jesus' only crime was being guilty of loving His Father in Heaven and us lost folks down here on Earth. Jesus is still guilty of the same

"crime" today – and people still crucify Him. They mock and reject the **Son of God** while embracing every false religion and wicked sin in the world. Unbelievers think they can say, *"I don't believe in Jesus,"* and they're done with Him. *Surprise! Surprise!* They aren't done with Jesus … because **Jesus** isn't done with *them*. They will meet Jesus on this Earth at the foot of His Eternal Cross, *or* … they will meet Him after death at the foot of His Judgment Throne. If they continue running from Jesus, refusing to acknowledge Him as King and refusing to bow their knee to Him, they are going to run into **death** one day, and then … *Philippians 2:9-11.*

In my book *Ole Slewfoot*, I include my testimony of how my Lord Jesus *Saved* me by revealing Himself to me in a *Supernatural, Spiritual Vision* of Him on the Cross. One day, I was sharing that with someone when she suddenly interrupted with, *"Oh no, that wasn't God; that was **satan**!" (Hmmm)*. I responded by asking her a couple of questions: *"Why would satan use that vision to bring me to Jesus' Cross where the Lord forgave my sins, gloriously Saved me and made me His Child … forever! Why would satan turn me into a Born-Again Christian who spends her life telling lost folks how they can be set free from him and his evil kingdom of death?"* Now, you're a thinking person; would satan do such a thing? Of course, not; not even the devil is *that* stupid. I can't help but wonder what she does with Acts 26:12-20 and II Corinthians 12:1-5 in the Bible. Were *those* the manifestation of satan in the Apostle Paul's life? Of course, not; and neither was my Lord's vision to *me*. Jesus Christ, the same yesterday, today and forever. For almost half a century I have refrained from making my Salvation experience known because I knew the reaction it would get from people who insist on denying the *Supernatural Power* of God at work on Earth today.

Next, this person said that my vision of the Lord Jesus could not possibly have been from God because Jesus is no longer on the Cross; therefore, the whole thing was definitely from *satan!* I agree that Jesus is no longer on the Cross *physically*, but there is a "Spiritual Realm" in which *our God Reigns!* The last time I checked, Jesus is still **God**, and He still has the *Power* to do whatever He wants to do. I don't know about her, but I serve *The Living Lord Jesus – The Great I AM –* Who knew exactly what He was doing the day He *Saved* me, and He did it exactly the way He wanted to do it. *God's Ways* are not our ways; God's

Ways are way higher than our ways, and I'm living proof of one of *His* many ways. I'm like the ole-timer who was asked how he knew he was *really Saved*. With a big smile, he replied, *"Well Sir, I was there when it happened, so I guess I oughta know."*

I often hear Preachers invite lost folks to come to the foot of Jesus' Cross for Salvation. When a lost person comes to the Cross, they need a *Saviour* on that Cross, giving His *Divine Life* to pay the penalty for all their sins – and Jesus can only be on His Cross *today* in the "Spiritual Realm." In my case, I didn't go to Jesus' Cross to be *Saved*; I was so lost I could never have found my way there. *So*, in His Love and Mercy, Jesus brought His Cross to *me!* I joyously accepted Jesus' death as payment for my sins and received His Spirit into mine, and today, Jesus is no longer on the Cross for *me* – He doesn't need to be; His Supernatural Work of Salvation for *me* has been accomplished.

That being said, I know there are lots of folks who just can't get their mind around the fact that Jesus could *possibly* still be on the Cross in the *Spiritual Realm* for lost people who need Him to *Save* them. But I have *my mind* well wrapped around the fact that Jesus is "The I AM God" – He is whatever I need at the moment, and if I need a Saviour dying on a Cross to *Save* me from an *Eternity* in hell, then *that* is what He will be. The Son of God showed up in the fiery furnace with Shadrach, Meshach and Abednego when *they* needed a Saviour, and Jesus showed up in the fiery furnace of my soul when *I* needed a Saviour. Nearly half-a-century ago, I stood before Jesus in His *Spiritual World* as He hung upon His Cross, and He *Saved* me there. If Jesus was there for *me*, He will surely be there for *anyone* who comes to Him in sincere "Faith" and "Repentance." Even though I can't explain how my Lord did it, He arranged for me to meet Him at the Cross, at the Cross, where I first saw "The Light" and, like Pilgrim, the burden of my heart just rolled away (along with the burden of my **sins**). Do you remember where *you* met Jesus? (I love the ole hymn that says: *I remember passing Calvary*. Whatever happened to all those great ole hymns?)

Now, I know what you're thinking, *"But how can Jesus be on His Throne in Heaven, dwelling in the spirits of Christians and on His Cross all at the same time?"* Answer: No problem a'tall for "The I AM God." Our Lord Jesus is **The King** of the *Supernatural Realm*; nothing is too

hard for *Him!* Some two thousand years ago, our King came and died *physically* on the Cross to redeem lost mankind. *Today,* Jesus is in the "Spiritual Business" of tracking down us lost Sheep and applying His *Spiritual Blood* to our soul. Our Lord is able to accomplish that through His Holy Spirit – *Who is limitless!!* Only "The Great **I AM**" can pull off such a *Supernatural Miracle. God dwells in the Eternal Now!* The One Who created our Universe is the King of an unseen Spiritual World so far above ours that we can't even begin to imagine what it is like. *Our God is an Awesome God ... He Reigns from Heaven above!!*

So, the question every Christian *must* deal with is: *"Do I have a Supernatural God ... or not?"* Are you like the woman who quickly gives *satan* the credit for anything *Supernatural?* People who *don't* think God still does Supernatural Miracles today will find it difficult to believe that my Salvation was of Him. But let's face it Folks, *everybody's* Salvation is a Supernatural, Spiritual Miracle of God the Father, God the Son and God the Holy Spirit. My Christian Friend, on the day you were *Saved,* you didn't need a pep talk or just some good advice ... you needed a **Miracle**! It would take a **Miracle** for you to *actually believe* that a dead Man rose up from His grave and is still alive today ... but you *actually believed it.* It would take a **Miracle** for you to *absolutely know* that all of your sins had been forgiven and wiped away by His Blood ... but you *absolutely knew it.* It would take a **Miracle** for you to *deeply feel* such Love, Joy, Peace and *New Life* ... but you *deeply felt it.* It would take a **Miracle** for you to *totally give* your entire life over to *Someone* you had never met before ... but you *totally did it* ... because **Jesus** is the **Miracle-Working Saviour** Who *Saves* your *Eternal Soul* to the uttermost by His *Supernatural Power!* And now, my Friend, **you** are *Jesus' Walking Miracle* – who speaks forth "Jesus' Words of Life" that work the *same* **Miracle** in someone else. *"The road to Faith is to risk everything on the Promises of God!"* (Ken Davis).

The person rebuking me *and* my book with her "message from God" wasn't done yet; there was more. She practically demanded that I call my publisher and pull *Ole Slewfoot* off the market. According to her, God didn't want it written because it's a book about *the devil.* But she is wrong; *the devil* didn't want it written because it's a book about **Jesus** – *defeating him* on the Cross!! She accused me of glorifying satan, but she is wrong. Through the *Power* of God's Holy Spirit, my book will

expose satan, *defeat* him and bring much *Glory to God!* I talk to lots of lost folks who don't think satan exists (and they think I'm a "hay-seed" for believing that he does). The "enemy of their soul" blinds them to his deceitful way of keeping them in bondage to him. It is so sad to see people in satan's death-grip *(being squeezed to death by him)* laughing and telling you that satan doesn't even exist. While they are laughing at satan ... *satan* is laughing at *them*.

Next, this person informed me that (according to her) she had just cast a demon out of a man *that very morning (Hmmm)*. **Only God** can cast demons out of people, and He will not give His Glory to another. Therefore, *she* was taking the Glory that belongs to God ... and God alone. She was obviously trying to convince me that *I* had a demon and needed her to cast him out of *me*. So, she asked, *"Do you ever rebuke satan?"*

I answered, *"Nope. I don't talk to him."* It's true; I'm not on speaking terms with that demon. I don't get close enough to satan to *have* a conversation with him. That arrogant devil *loves* attention; it feeds his inflated ego and makes him feel important. He doesn't care *what* you're saying to him ... *you're talking to him!!* And he's lovin' it. So, don't waste your time giving that loser the time of day. I guess you've noticed that I don't honor him by capitalizing his name – and his abode will freeze over before I honor *him* with a conversation. When satan attacks *me*, I go straight to my Heavenly Father and pray, *"Lord, You know what satan is doing to me right now, so I'm asking You to take care of him. In fact, give that devil a real shock by working this for the good of Your Eternal Kingdom! Thank You, Lord, for all You do to protect me from that evil-one."* Then, I go on about my business of serving Jesus – and our Father takes care of satan. Works every time. Folks, I feel so sorry for people who go through life trying to make sense of trials, sickness, hardships, death and all the complexities of this life without the Lord being *The Great* **I AM** to them for their every need. *"My times are in Thy hands. Deliver me from the hand of mine enemies and from them that persecute me" Signed: Molly* (Psalm 31:15).

(Fake-News Alert: After writing that I never have a conversation with satan, my Lord revealed to me that's not true. Sometimes, when I'm talking with a lost person about Jesus, I can tell by what they are saying to me that it's actually "satan" speaking; it's coming from "satan

in them." So, in a way, I *am* having a conversation with satan – but fortunately, "Jesus in me" does *my* speaking {Matthew 10:20})

Now, it doesn't take a rocket-scientist to figure out what was going on here; ole slewfoot hates *Ole Slewfoot* because it contains the Gospel of Salvation in Christ Jesus – *Who defeated him!* A book that would *dare* to expose that devil to "The Light" infuriated him so much that he sent someone to unleash his anger on the one who wrote it. *Mercy Me!* She continued mocking, rebuking and condemning both me and my book until she abruptly got up and took off in a huff as she yelled back at me, *"You talk too much; you write too much, and you need to stop doing both!!"* **"I know well that when Christ is nearest, satan also is busiest"** (Robert Murray McCheyne).

Folks, that is so funny to me. Does satan *really* think I'm stupid enough to fall for his lame schemes? You would think he would know me by now. But even though he probably knew it was a long shot, he decided to try it anyway and hope I would tremble in my shoes and say to myself, *"Oh, my! This person is telling me that I should do away with my book, stop writing and stop witnessing for Jesus. She must be right, so I'd better do what she says."* My Christian Friend, you'd better keep your "Jesus glasses" on, or *you're* gonna be blind-sided by ole slewfoot – who is dogging your every step. Jesus-Vision enables you to not only spot satan but to also see right through those insidious schemes he comes up with to try to shut you up and take you out of your Service to your King.

There's another argument that I'm surprised she didn't attack me with, so I'll do it for her. In Exodus 33:20, God says that no man shall see His face and live. Jesus is God the Son, so I'm claiming that I actually saw God and lived. Yep, and so did thousands upon thousands of other folks who saw Jesus walking around on Planet Earth two thousand years ago *(Hmmm)*. So, why weren't all those folks toast? Answer: **Jesus is LORD of All!** He can do anything He wants to do. All things are possible with **God**. *"Our God is so real, and He is in charge of everything! He is involved in every detail of your life!"* (Jonathan Cahn).

So, let us hear the conclusion of the whole matter: Fear God, not satan, because greater is **"Jesus in you"** than that ole devil prowling about in the world. You'll need to keep reminding yourself of that when you get serious about letting "Jesus in you" tell lost folks how *they* can become

a Christian ... because satan is coming after *you* as well. All Born-Again Christians have a very real enemy who is hell-bent on taking them down and taking them out. *But* we also have a very real **Saviour** Who is more than able to hold us up and keep us in His Service. *"If it had not been The Lord Who was on our side, when men rose up against us, then they had swallowed us up quick, when their wrath was kindled against us"* Signed: Every Born-Again Christian (Psalm 124:2-3).

Now here's the situation; Jesus came to Planet Earth to destroy the works of the devil. Satan knows it, and it makes him *really mad;* but he doesn't just get *mad* ... he gets even. So, the devil has decided to retaliate by trying to destroy all the works of **Jesus** – and *you,* my Christian Friend, are a piece of work ... of **Jesus.** Therefore, satan has **you** in his crosshairs. Fiery missiles are on their way to **you** (like they came to me) from your number-one enemy – little rocket-man of the spiritual underworld. Time to tighten your *Belt of Truth,* strap on your *Breastplate of Righteousness,* secure your *Helmet of Salvation,* lace up your *Shoes of the Gospel of Peace* and hold up your *Shield of Faith* while whipping out your *Sword of The Spirit* – the *Perfect Weapon* to whittle that little pip-squeak down to size – and *"Pray! Pray! Pray!"* It's *Battle Time* ... between **Jesus** and satan. *Mercy Me!*

> *"And though this world, with devils filled, should threaten*
> *to undo us,*
> *We will not fear, for God hath Willed His Truth to*
> *triumph through us.*
> *The prince of darkness grim, we tremble not for him,*
> *his rage we can endure, for lo, his doom is sure,*
> *One little Word will fell him!"*
> (Martin Luther).

"JESUS!!!"

This book is "Jesus" saying to His People, *"Welcome To My World!"* Just never forget: Jesus' World on Planet Earth is a battleground ... not a playground. We are spirit-beings battling demon-spirits in the Spiritual

Realm. Jesus battled satan and won; today, His Victory over satan is *your Victory* over satan. So, strap on the *Armour of God* and go to battle for your King! This is *your* chance to *man up* for the One Who went to the Cross for *you*. Make up your *Mind of Christ* that *you* will **not** give up, shut up, let up or back up. Your Guide is reliable; your Mission clear. *You* are going to stay up, pray up, stand up and preach up for "The Cause of Christ" in *The Power of His Might*. The only failure that lacks dignity is your failure to *get back up* when ole slewfoot has knocked you down. Don't give up, *"Get up!"* You *can* win! You *will* win! You have *already* won! You are winning *now* … because you are a *"Praying Christian"* with the Supernatural Power of God working in you, with you and through you. All the darkness of satan's evil kingdom can never snuff out the light of even the smallest *Christian Candle. Jesus is Greater!!*

Knowing that death was near (and knowing the Scriptures), Jesus said, *"I thirst,"* and someone gave Him drink. Today, our Lord no longer thirsts, but He knows that this lost world is *dying* of thirst for His *Living Water*. Lost folks are really thirsting for *Jesus Himself* – they just don't know it. They need "Someone" to give them a *Spiritual Drink*. Jesus longs to pour His "Saving Message of Salvation" into their dying souls the same way He did the first time He walked this Earth – and the same way He did during His last moments on the Cross. Being brutally beaten and cruelly nailed to a wooden Cross couldn't keep our Awesome Saviour from doing His Heavenly Father's Will. As He hung on that Cross with His physical life slipping away, Jesus was at His Best at being an Evangelist. In Luke 23:43, we see Jesus giving Eternal Life to the criminal at His side. Earlier, this guy had been mocking, cursing and hurling insults at Jesus like everyone else. *But then*, the Holy Spirit touched his hard heart, and he became a *Believer in Christ Jesus.* Why would the Holy Spirit do that? Answer: Because **Jesus** was interceding for him – and Miracles happen when **Jesus Prays!** That criminal on *his* cross heard **The King** on *His* Cross ask His Heavenly Father to forgive those sinful people who were crucifying Him and cursing Him. The Holy Spirit opened that dying man's *Spiritual Eyes*, and he *saw* "Who" Jesus really was. He also saw who *he* really was – a terrible sinner whose **sins** were crucifying The Son of God. "The Light" went on in his soul, and he *knew* that *he needed* **Jesus** to be *his* Saviour. The same thing happened to the Centurion standing at the foot of Jesus' Cross. That

man was *gloriously Saved* by Evangelist Jesus' last breath of life! (Mark 15:39). How *wonderful* it would be to die while telling someone about **Jesus**! *Oh, to die like Jesus!!*

Let us linger a little longer at the foot of Jesus' Cross to see how our Lord is still being an Evangelist from it *even today*. After all, the foot of Jesus' Cross is the best place for a person to receive Jesus' death for them and enter into a "Spiritual Relationship" with Him. As I revealed earlier, that is where Jesus *Supernaturally* appeared to *me* and filled my heart with **His Glorious Love!** Then, Jesus asked if I would let Him die for me. **Yes!!** That was the wonderful day I became the Betrothed Bride of Jesus, my Heavenly Bridegroom!! Myriads of books have written and sermons preached on the words spoken by Jesus from His Cross, but I know of some words Jesus is *still* speaking from His Cross to every person who shows up on Planet Earth: **"Will you marry Me?"** *Is that Wedding Music I hear?*

"Looking unto Jesus, the Author and Finisher of our Faith; Who for the Joy that was set before Him endured the Cross" (Hebrews 12:2). I once heard a Bible teacher say that Jesus embraced the Cross with joy. That teacher was doubtless thinking of the above verse, but if you go with Jesus to the Garden of Gethsemane, you will see that He did *not* embrace the Cross with joy. The verse says that Jesus *endured* the Cross. However, in our Lord's Eternal Kingdom, pain is never wasted, and the "Joy" that Jesus *did* embrace was the *result* of His crucifixion – the Joy of spending Eternity with *you* ... as well as all of *God's Redeemed Saints. (Yes! I do hear Wedding Music!!)* Jesus also saw *our* great "Joy" – the Joy of our Salvation (which the Angels desire to look into). Even the Angels never knew the "Joy!" that our Salvation brings. *"He shall see the travail of His Soul and shall be satisfied"* (Isaiah 53:11).

According to the Apostle John, Jesus' last breathed word on the Cross was **"Tetelestai!!"** And all the folks standing around Him said, *"Yep, that guy's finished."* So, they turned, left the crime scene and went back to work. It was business as usual in Jerusalem. And so ended the life of a wonderful young man ... or so they thought. Little did they know that *at that moment* Jesus was at His Best at *completing* the Work His Father had given Him to do. Unbeknownst to those curious on-lookers, **Jesus** wasn't the one who was finished that day – *satan* was. *Hallelujah!*

When Jesus walked out of that tomb three days later, He finished-off satan; then handed-off *His* victory to you, Christian. Therefore, the devil is finished having power over *you*. *Now*, make sure *you're* finished with the devil. Don't give him *any* power over you *anymore*. When you go to pick up that cigarette, drug, whiskey, pornography or "immoral person," pause and look into the *Spiritual Realm* to see what is *really* going on. *Ah yes*, satan *himself* is the evil-one handing it to you. *Mercy Me!* Yep, and you must make a *"Spiritual Decision"* to take care of that rascal once and for all. First, construct a cross in your soul; then mercilessly nail that demon-rat *satan* to it. Trust me, all the demons of hell don't have the power to come and rescue him … only *you* do. *"Neither give place to the devil!"* (Ephesians 4:27).

"I am crucified with Christ, nevertheless I live; yet not I, but Christ liveth in me" (Galatians 2:20). The moment God *Saved* you, He terminated the "ole you." God knew that the only way to keep satan from bossing you around, controlling you and using you to further *his* evil kingdom on Earth was to kill you – in Christ at Calvary (it's hard to boss a dead man). *But* until you *forsake* that "ole dead-man" (you *used to be*) and *start living* your "New Life in Christ" (you *received at Salvation*), you won't have the power you need to live your Christian life. That's because God isn't going to empower your "ole dead-man" to do *anything*. God wants him **dead**, for pity's sake! That's why He crucified him (Romans 6:6-8).

So now we're back to where we've always been. The only way to live a powerful, joyful Christian life is to do the same thing to your "ole dead-man" that you did to satan … and have his funeral. After the demise of your ole dead-man, the *only One* left "Alive" in you is **Jesus**. *Now*, Jesus' passionate, intimate, close *Love Relationship* with you works a *Miracle:* **The two of you become "One!"** *Yes*, you become a "New Creation in Christ Jesus," and you're ready for your "New Life" of letting your "New Lord" actually "live" His *Resurrected Life* in you … and *through* you.

Jesus' One Solitary Life (lived for God) had an *Eternal Impact* on the *Destiny* of this world. And *now*, so can **"Jesus in you!"** Your Lord Jesus may only have an *Eternal Impact* on just *one person* "through you," but who knows *what* God may explode through that *one person! God knows.* That one Ethiopian eunuch Philip evangelized went back to northern Africa and started more Churches than any other place on Earth at the

time! Your Lord only gives you *one chance* to do *His Will* on this Earth. *Don't blow it. Be like Jesus!*

"For God so loved the world, that He gave His only begotten Son" (John 3:16). I was reading that verse one day when it dawned on me that just as God gave His Son Jesus to the world for the Salvation of lost souls, *now* He is giving "Jesus in me" to the world for the same reason. I call myself "Jesus' Little Lamb," and the Bible calls Jesus "The Lamb of God." God doesn't ask this Little Lamb to be "The Sacrifice" for the *sins* of mankind (Jesus already did that at Calvary), but He does ask me to *sacrifice myself* for the *souls* of mankind. So, am I as willing as Jesus was to sacrifice myself for the sake of other people's Salvation? Are you? If you are, you will be the fragrance of Jesus to His (your) Father. *Oh, to be like Jesus!*

"But all their works they do for to be seen of men" Signed: Jesus (Matthew 23:5). When you see a Christian with a bunch of bright, flashing neon-sign lights all pointing to himself saying, *"Look at me! Look at me! Look at me!"* you can rest assured that he isn't all that interested in people seeing **Jesus** – only *him*. But just keep watching him. The higher he flies, the closer he gets to the sun (but the farther he gets from The Son of God), and the quicker his wings of wax are going to melt – and the quicker he's going to fall. The bigger they are (in their own eyes) the harder they fall. *Mercy Me!* Don't *you* be like *that* person. No, *you* be the person who loves **Jesus** with all your heart and gives *all* of the Glory to **God**. *"Now unto Him Who is able to keep you from falling."* Humble yourself like Jesus did and let *Jesus* exalt you – in His own time; in His own way. *"But by the Grace of God, I am what I am."* Oh, to be humble like Jesus.

On the day of Jesus' crucifixion, there was one man in particular who benefited from His death. Except for the Providence of God, the man who *should* have been crucified on that center Cross was the leader of the rebels, Barabbas. Have you ever wondered if Barabbas hung around long enough to watch the crucifixion of the Man Who was taking *his* place on that Cross? My guess is that he took off like Moody's goose. He probably couldn't have cared less about the death of Jesus. The way Barabbas had it figured, it was just Jesus' bad luck and *his* good luck. There was most likely not one speck of gratitude in his hard heart; not a single: *"Thank God!"* But we just don't know.

The people you witness to will be one "Barabbas" or the other. They will either be so enslaved to their rebellious life-of-sin that they will have absolutely no interest in a Saviour paying the Price *they* owe God for all their sins, *or* ... they will be strangely drawn to this Holy Man of God, dying on a Cross ... in *their* place. *"Thank God!!"* Your job is to interrupt their life with "The Truth" (Who is also "The Way" and "The Life"). For just *one moment* in all of *Time* and *Eternity*, you have the privilege of turning their eyes upon **Jesus** – Who is able to open their blind eyes, melt their hard heart, free their satan-controlled mind and *Save* their Eternal soul. *Praise to The Lamb! "Our Lord Jesus turned death into a door!"* (Charles Stanley).

Lost people don't believe that *Jesus is God*, and *that* is their bottom-line problem. When I talk with them, I tell them, *"When Jesus was on the Cross, that wasn't just a man hanging there dying. Not at all; Jesus is God's Son Who came from Heaven to this Earth to die on that Cross for* ***you.*** *Therefore, His Blood wasn't just man's blood. Oh no, that was God's Holy Precious Blood ... being spilled out for you! More precious still, that was God's Love being poured out for you! Jesus dying on the Cross was God loving you."* When you tell a person, *"Jesus loves you,"* if they believe that Jesus was just a man, it won't matter to them one whit ... because Jesus died some 2,000 years ago, and a dead man can no longer love anyone. Therefore, the typical attitude of the average lost person on the street toward Jesus is: *Who knows and who cares.* So, how can they believe that Jesus loves them? Answer: When Jesus tells them *Himself.* They will know that Jesus is "Alive!" when His Spirit *Divinely* sends *God's Love* into their heart (the Witness of The Spirit). Now, I know what you're thinking, *"God only does that to Christians."* Well, all I can tell you is that Jesus flooded *my* heart with His Great Love *before* I had my "moment of Salvation." Pray for *God's Love* to enter into the hearts of the people you witness to as you are speaking. Your job is to let "Jesus in you" ***love*** that person in front of you. In a *Supernatural way*, they will sense *Jesus' Love* coming to them from you – because *it is!* Pray for them as you let *The Lion of Judah* out. Turn **Jesus** loose, and His **Love** will find a home in *someone.*

Chuck Missler has an interesting theory about Jesus' crucifixion that allows us to *lessen* Jesus' suffering on the Cross *even today.* Chuck believes that Jesus pays the penalty for our sins by dying for

each sin *individually* and *specifically*. Therefore, each and every one of our sins has the capacity to increase Jesus' suffering on His Cross some 2,000 years ago (Chuck also believes in the Eternality of Jesus' Cross). The sins of our past have already been placed upon Jesus on His Cross (causing Him the pain of dying for them), *but* the sins we will commit in the future haven't. So, the fewer sins we commit from this day forward will diminish the suffering Jesus must endure to pay for them. That gives us a new motivation to live a life as free from sin as possible. If Chuck is right, our conduct going forward can either increase or diminish Jesus' pain on the Cross. So, you can *still* help Jesus ... by choosing to sin less; thereby lessening His agony on Calvary. Simply stated, it's time you started *seriously* considering every little (and big) thing you do. From this day forward, start thinking about the *ultimate outcome* of your actions – like the guy in the following story.

"Times were bad and life was hard for a little Don Knotts-type fellow who had lost his job. He couldn't pay the rent or feed his family. He had always been a 'good guy,' but things got so bad and he got so desperate that he decided his only option was to rob a bank. He knew it was wrong, and he was so nervous he didn't know if he could pull it off, or not ... but he just *had* to do it; his kids were hungry. So, he found an old gun and a pouch, put a handkerchief on his face and ran into a nearby bank. He nervously approached one of the tellers behind the counter, pointed his shaking gun at her and in a trembling voice said, *'Don't stick with me, this is a mess-up!'* He thought about it for a second; then blurted out, *'No! No! Don't mess with me, this is a stick-up!!'* He quickly threw his empty pouch down on the counter. The teller took it, put some money in it and passed it on to the next teller who did the same. When all the tellers had put some money in it, they put it back down on the counter.

Our little thief – the shakiest gun in the mess – nervously crept up, grabbed the pouch, turned and ran out the door. The tellers looked around at each other as if to say, 'OK, who's calling the cops this time?' when ... *Oliver Sutton*, the front door flew open again, and who should run back in but our little friend the thief! With

his gun now tucked in his belt, he runs up to the counter, plops the bag of money down, yells, 'IT AIN'T WORTH IT!!' ... and runs back out the door!"

Don't you just love it? We so applaud that little guy who saw "The Light" before it was too late. God's message to every young person (and every other person) out there is, *"It ain't worth it!"* When the Lord saw our little friend make his God-honoring choice, He probably opened the windows of Heaven and provided for him in *miraculous* ways – and that's when he discovered that obeying God is *always* worth it! So, I beg you, *please*, don't let the enemy of God (and the enemy of your soul) convince you that you just *have to* do those sinful things that will only wreck your life and add to Jesus' suffering on the Cross. *"It jest ain't worth it!"* Don't ruin your witness for your Lord. *No! He needs you* to be His Faithful Witness in a world that crucifies Him constantly. Every day and in a thousand ways, they find new ways afresh to crucify the Son of God. When those ungodly judges voted to legalize the destruction of little babies in their mothers' wombs, Jesus was crucified afresh. When they voted to legalize the abomination of homosexual "marriage," Jesus was crucified afresh. When they voted to legalize pornography and dangerously destructive drugs, Jesus was crucified afresh. Christians are also "crucified" because satan hates *"Jesus in us"* the same as he hates *Jesus*. But fear not and stand strong because "Jesus in us" has the *Power* to withstand the attacks coming from ungodly people with "satan in them."

"Whosoever liveth and believeth in Me shall never die. Believest thou this?" Signed: Jesus (John 11:26). Do *you* believe it? I do. We're going to depart our Earthsuit one day, but we won't be *Spiritually* dead (or even asleep, you'll see). And what is true of us is also true of our Lord. Satan killed Jesus' body of flesh, but that only freed *His Spirit* to do abundantly more. This world thinks that Jesus' death on the Cross was His shameful defeat, *but God* knows that it was His Glorious Triumph! Satan took Jesus down with sin (our sin), *but God* raised Jesus up in Righteousness (His Righteousness)! It wasn't possible for death to defeat the Lord of Life! So, spiritually speaking, Jesus didn't die; He just started moving around like never before – in the Person of His Spirit! *Now*, Jesus is able to get those "Greater Works" done He told us

about. Are you His disciple? Good; then get ready to get into the yoke with Jesus and do those Greater Works – *with Him*. To do so, you'll need some Keys. *"And I will give unto thee the Keys of The Kingdom of Heaven: and whatsoever thou shalt bind on Earth shall be bound in Heaven: and whatsoever thou shalt loose on Earth shall be loosed in Heaven." Signed: Jesus* (Matthew 16:19).

The Keys Jesus is referring to are most likely the *Right* and *Authority* to use God's Power on Earth. The Lord gives you *His Authority* so that He can use *you* to get done what He wants done. Jesus wants God's Will done on Earth as it is in Heaven – and the Key to doing *that* is being connected to Heaven through *Prayer*. Spirit-inspired prayer is more than mere words; it is the *living energy* of your spirit being sent to God through *His Spirit*, Who draws the *Powerful Energy* of God back into *your spirit*. Prayer quickens your spirit to God's Presence within you, and you become more "Alive!" to "Jesus in you." The more you include Jesus in your plans, the more Jesus includes you in *His Plans*. Your Lord also reveals to you what His Plans are. They always include "Jesus in you" making Himself known to those around you.

A life lived in *Spiritual Communion* with your Lord empowers you to live the "Abiding Life." Spending time with Jesus in Prayer, Fellowship and His Word makes you privy to His *Desires, Purposes* and *Will*. This gets Jesus' attention, and He watches you very carefully. When Jesus sees you using *His Faith* to act on *His Word*, He looses *His Spiritual Power* from *His Heavenly World* to accomplish *His Word (Work)* through *you* on Earth – and that brings "Glory" to His (your) Father in Heaven. Jesus watches over His Word to perform it because only **He** has the Power to do so – which makes **Jesus Himself** the "Key" to loosing and binding on this Earth. Therefore, what Jesus *really* wants us to loose on this Earth is … **Him!!** **"Jesus in you"** is the One Who does His *Greater Works* on Earth using *your* yielded body! *My meat is to do the Will of Him Who sent Me, and to finish His Work!*

So, don't keep Jesus all bound-up in Heaven. *No!* Let Jesus loose on this Earth – through **you**. Become a physical outlet for God's Spiritual Power! Those friends of the paralyzed man in Mark 2 knew that if they could just get him to **Jesus**, Jesus would heal him. And they were right! If *you*, Christian Friend, can just get those lost folks (paralyzed by sin) to **"Jesus in you,"** He will *Save* them! Be willing to *overcome all obstacles*

in order to get them to the Lord, and you will start seeing *Miracles of Salvation.* But you don't have to tear the roof off the house to do so. Not at all; just tear the doubt out of your mind, the fear out of your soul and the muzzle off of your mouth; then let *"Jesus in you"* tell them, "*I AM here – right here, right now – and I AM Mighty to Save ... even you!*

You may have heard the amazing story of the Police Officer who chased down and stopped a speeding car ... only to end up delivering a healthy baby girl! *Happy ending!* That's a good picture of what our Lord Jesus wants to do to sinners racing down the road to hell. He wants to chase them down, stop their mad rush to destruction and deliver them into His Eternal Kingdom as His Child. *So ...* the Sheriff of the Universe, *aka the Hound of Heaven,* relentlessly pursues them until they **crash** their get-away-car. Ever so gently, Jesus reaches in and grabs them by the heart, rescuing them from their wrecked-life. Then, Jesus puts them into His Police Cruiser, takes them down to the Courthouse, listens to their pathetic "lame excuses," declares them guilty of all charges, brings down His gavel and sentences them to *Eternity* in hell. *Mercy Me!* They stand there trembling in fear before the Supreme Judge of the Universe as their heart cries out, *"Lord, have Mercy!"* That's when Jesus smiles; then hands them their sentence with the word *"Tetelestai"* written all across it ... in **His own Blood.** *Happy ending!! "The Angel of The Lord encampeth round about them that fear Him, and delivereth them!"* (Psalm 34:7).

I was talking with my Lord one time about something that looked to me like it was going to be more than I could handle. So, I decided to use my "get out of jail free" card and prayed, *"Lord! I need You to work a Miracle in my life – right now!!"* I shall never forget His reply: *"Yep, and I AM giving you one ... a do-it-yourself Miracle" Signed: Jesus.* I was hoping He was just kidding – but He wasn't. It was one of those times when I *had to do* what I *had to do.* **But Jesus** walked with me through it all and taught me that some of God's *Greatest Blessings* come disguised as "a lot of hard work." Looking back, I'm convinced that Jesus and my Daddy were in cahoots when I was a little girl ... because both of them have the same theory about hard work: *It's good for you!* My Daddy was always saying, *"Hard work never killed anyone."* He's dead now, of course. That's why we children didn't believe it then, and we adults don't believe it now ... but it's true. *And Jesus knows it.*

God gave His Son the "Miracle" of *Redeeming* fallen-man, and it was definitely a "do-it-yourself Miracle." Our Saviour came to this Earth, worked tirelessly hard and suffered more than we could ever imagine in order to pay the *Price* for our Salvation. Crucifixion caused excruciating pain. The word "excruciating" means: Unbearable pain, out-of-the-cross, extreme agony. God's wrath was poured out upon Jesus – the full, fiery *eternal* punishment for all our sins was compressed upon Him on that Cross. Jesus literally endured hell for us there. Hell is spiritual death; so how could **God** die *spiritually*? I don't know (and neither do the Bible Scholars). All I know is that only a Supernatural God of *Infinite Power* could endure such suffering and still survive. Only **King Jesus** could – and only **King Jesus** did – *for us.* Jesus knew that the "Work of Redemption" was a God-given task only **He** could accomplish. Jesus *had to do* what He *had to do* – and *He did it! Thank You, Jesus!* **"I have glorified Thee on the Earth; I have finished the Work which Thou gavest Me to do!" Signed: Jesus, Lord and Saviour** (John 17:4).

When God instituted the first Passover in Exodus 12, He told the people that the blood of a lamb applied to their door posts would cause the Death Angel to pass over their home. Today, we Born-Again Christians call **Jesus** our "Passover" because His Holy Precious Blood applied to our inner spirit-man causes God's Eternal Death Angel to pass over *our* **Eternal Soul!** *"Thank You, Lord!"* Jesus was crucified on the day of preparation for Passover when the sacrificial lambs were slain (John 19:14,31). Normally, the priests would start killing them before three o'clock in the afternoon – but on **this** day, **God** was intervening by sending darkness over the land from noon until three (the time of Jesus' physical death) so that the priests couldn't see how to kill any lambs ... because the "True Sacrificial Lamb of God" was being sacrificed *first.* Once *that* was accomplished, those priests could have all just gone home – **Tetelestai!!** **"Behold the Lamb of God, Who taketh away the sin of the world"** (John 1:29).

"Take now thy son, thine only son Isaac, whom thou loveth, and get thee into the land of Moriah; and offer him (lift him up) there for a burnt offering upon one of the mountains which I will tell thee of" (Genesis 22:2). When God spoke those words to Abraham, he rose up early, took his son Isaac and traveled to Moriah. As they approached the place God had told Abraham of, Isaac asked where the sacrificial lamb was, and Abraham replied, *"My son, God will provide Himself a lamb."* I truly

believe that two thousand years later, a Cross was placed on the very spot Abraham laid his son Isaac, and Jehovah Jireh fulfilled that prophesy by hanging *His* Son Jesus on it, providing the **True Lamb of God** – sacrificed to God for the sins of the world. You may have your doubts about that, but I don't. Our Lord *loves* doing amazing *Miracles* like that just to show us **He's God!!** The Bible Scholars tell us that Solomon's Temple was built on that spot, but in my humble opinion, God was more interested in honoring the Sacrifice of His Son Jesus on Calvary than the sacrifice of animals in the Temple. *And in Abraham's Seed (Jesus) shall all Nations of the Earth be blessed.*

We thank God for sacrificing His Son for us on the Cross; we thank Jesus for having the courage to endure the horrors of the crucifixion for us, and we can even thank satan for pulling the whole thing off (give satan enough rope and he'll hang himself every time). The best way to thank *Jesus* is by telling the lost folks He came to seek and to *Save* that He died on that Cross for *them.* Tell them He engraved *their name* on the palms of His hands – at Calvary. *"If you cannot preach like Peter, if you cannot pray like Paul, you can tell the Love of Jesus and say, 'He died for all!'"* (Ole Spiritual Hymn).

Earlier, I mentioned that none of us can avoid our meeting with the Lord Jesus Christ. I am so thankful to Jesus for allowing *me* to meet Him *already* on this Earth and stand before Him in judgment. I thank Jesus for His Grace that opened my blind eyes and showed me my sinful self; I could *see* that I was guilty as charged. And **Jesus** could see something else – my great need of His Faith to believe. I gladly received it and let Him die for me. Jesus hung on a cruel Cross on a dark day so that He could "live again" in me *today* as my Glorious Lord and Saviour! I praise Him that the battle is over and I can now *joyously* join all the rest of you Born-Again Christians in proclaiming:

"Tetelestai!
It Is Finished!
JESUS CHRIST is LORD of All
to the Glory of God the Father!"

"WELCOME TO MY WORLD!"

GOD VICTORIOUS

"Be of good cheer!
I have overcome the world!"
Signed: Jehovah Jesus (John 16:33).

I n the first couple chapters of God's Holy Bible, He reveals to us the *"Supernatural Beginning"* of our world. God shows us a virtual video of the *Creation* of His Beautiful Planet, His Beautiful Garden and the two Beautiful People He places there to walk and talk with Him in Perfect Fellowship. *(Wouldn't it be glorious if today all people everywhere could experience the same Joy and Thankfulness that our Salvation brings?!) Ah*, the sun is shining, the birds are singing, the flowers are blooming, the couple is healthy (all the fruit is organic), God is smiling and all is well in God's Wonderful World ... *until* ... we turn the page and, alas, there is trouble in Paradise. Yep, and trouble's name is Lucifer, the rebel-angel who just hates it when the Crown of God's Creation is peacefully and joyfully living in *Divine* harmony with his Creator – *thanking Him in endless Praise.*

With malice on his mind, that ole serpent slithers into The Garden ... and there goes the neighborhood. Satan loves to corrupt innocence and defile purity (just look around). So, true to form, he manages to corrupt God's Perfect Creation by offering sweet Eve the fruit of sin – lies. She swallows them (fruit, lies and sink her), and all y'all know "The Paul Harvey Rest of The Story." No one can make a mess like satan can make a mess. *"In the beginning was the **Lie**. And the **Lie** was made News and dwelt among us, graceless and false"* (Malcolm Muggeridge).

(Side-note: There are those who claim that the Bible couldn't possibly be true because everybody *knows* snakes can't talk to people. It's true

snakes can't talk to people *today*, but what about in God's amazing Garden of Eden? I wasn't there, but I do know how *Supernatural* God is. So, could Adam and Eve have been able to talk with **all** of the animals in the Garden of Eden? They talked with God; why not the animals also? I know, I know ... I made that silly joke about "the talking snake" in "Ole Slewfoot." I should have known that joke would come back to bite me. But seriously, Folks, only **God** knows what it was really like in His Awesome Garden *or* what it is like in Heaven today (does Saint Peter *really* meet you at the Gate?) *or* what the "New Earth" will be like in the future. All we can do is surmise (and make silly jokes). With that being said, there is another consideration. The Hebrew word translated *serpent* is "nachash" which also means "the shining one" *(Hmmm)*. Now, who is it again that appears to us as an "angel of light"? This is getting stranger by the minute. Alice would say, *"Things are getting curioser and curioser."* God didn't choose to give us all the details *(the secret things belong unto the Lord our God)*, but it is entirely possible that satan didn't appear to Eve as a garden-variety snake at all. In my book, however, I will bow to tradition and refer to satan as the snake-in-the-grass he is.)

I look around at my beloved Country today and see that the crown has fallen from our head. Don't let anyone tell you that we were *not* a Christian Nation at birth. We were. I know there are those who say we couldn't have been a Christian Nation because some people here owned slaves. Truth is, the vast majority of Colonists *didn't* own slaves, and they weren't hindered by those who did from living out their Christian Faith. Even though I didn't really come over on the Mayflower, I can *still* remember an America that was a whole lot closer to God and His Laws than she is today. When I was coming along, we had laws *against* **sins** that are legalized today. Most everybody *knew* that the "True and Living God" was the **God of the Bible**, and o*h*, what a different Country we had back then! But hang onto your hat (and your Bible), Folks, because our ole fiend satan couldn't stand it. So, in he slithers once again ... and there goes the *entire Country!* Yep, ole slewfoot took the Bible out of Schools and replaced it with non-Christian secular books. Then, he threw a monkey-wrench into the Truth that **God created** man in *His Image* and started teaching everyone his concocted **lie** he calls "evolution" – which *brainwashes* them into believing that they really came from

monkeys. Satan has managed to convince people that "believing in a **Great Creator God**" is just a silly notion ... while he makes dead-sure liberal TV channels indoctrinate them with plenty of his ungodly "evolution is proven science" programs. A writer of one such show quoted a "famous scientist" as saying: *"Evolution is the story of life on Earth."* And he is so right – it's all just "a story" ... made up by *satan* himself!

God-centered Prayer, Bible reading and America's Godly Heritage have all been ripped out of our Schools and replaced with Evolution (the religion of the lost), Buddhism, Islamic teachings and even the Occult (where are the separation-of-Church-and-State groups when you need 'em?). Ungodly people make sure our Schools have *plenty* of sex-ed classes and homosexual indoctrination – and satan *loves* it! **But God hates it!** It is a **sin** to teach children to engage in homosexual sex (or any other kind). *That* is depraved *child abuse*, and the Lord is taking notes on *everyone* who is allowing it to happen. *"I AM HE ... I WILL give unto everyone of you according to your works!!" Signed: Jehovah Jesus* (Revelation 2:23).

In *modern* America, people are no longer allowed to mention our Great God at School, sports events or graduation ceremonies; satan doesn't want us offending any atheists that might be there – and we bow to him and let him have his way, for pity's sake! Do you know of any other Nation that has quit practicing its religion openly just because some *Christians* have moved there and they don't want to offend the Christians? Of course, not! Muslim and Communist Countries (like ours is becoming) "get rid" of Christians. In America, every religion is smiled upon ... *except* Christianity. Why? It's our **LORD JESUS** satan hates. So, our Christian Faith is sacrificed on the altar of the devil's "political correctness." Yep, satan is doing a jig to the tune of the heartbreaking sound of "God's Moral Laws" being thrown out and hitting the concrete down below. America is a wide-open society today and just about *anything goes.* **"Katie, bar the door!!"** The Bible has been discarded as an ole out-dated book; therefore, most people don't care *what* **God's Laws** have to say about *anything*. Today, man has set *himself* up as "god," and *man* says, *"Anything you want to do, just do it"* – *unless* you are a Christian who wants to follow **God's Laws.** *Then*, no can do, because the liberal left tolerates *anything* and *anyone* ... *except* **Christians** who stand up for **God** and **His Truth.**

According to a recent poll, America is split on abortion; fifty-five percent of all people say that abortion is just fine. All New York State legislators stood, applauded and cheered their passage of a law legalizing the murder of a baby right up to birth (they were applauding *themselves* for sending our Patriot-President Donald Trump the message: "Take *that!*"). Virginia is very proud of its law that allows the negligent murder of a baby *after* it is born! I never thought I'd live to see the day. When I was coming along, if you had asked people, *"Do you think it's OK to kill a baby inside or outside of its mother's womb?"* I guarantee you, not a single person would have said, *"Of course!"* Everybody back then *just knew* that a pregnant woman is carrying a "baby" – and *murdering* that baby is a SIN!! What a difference a devil makes. I feel like Rip Van Winkle. I went to sleep with the sun shining and the birds singing. I woke up to an evil darkness and wailing so eerie and foreboding that only "the god of hate and death" could have possibly conjured them up! Now granted, there have always been ungodly, devilish people amongst us, *but* it's a scary day when those *demonic people* have been voted into office, are making the "Laws of the Land" and have their ungodly judges in place to enforce their evil laws. *Lord, have Mercy!*

Abortion is a terrible sin, it's true, but we need to look beyond abortion and see "why" it is so off-the-charts in America today. *Roe vs. Wade* doesn't force *any* woman to have an abortion. Women have abortions because ... they *want to*. Without **The Lord** in their lives, they are "free" to do anything they want to do. Yes!! They can finally *"Just do it!"* And **that** is America's *real problem* – all the **SEXUAL IMMORALITY** that is *causing* all the unwanted babies in the first place! *(Duh)*. In **God's Holy Eyes**, *sexual immorality* is just as sinful as abortion (check out **God's Bible**), *but* how many times have you ever seen people rise up in anger and march through our streets protesting against all the *sexual immorality* that has totally taken over America? Right. I constantly hear about *all the people* all over the place trying so hard to convince women *not* to abort their babies – *but* I don't hear *a word* about anyone trying to convince those women **not to commit sexual immorality** in the first place!! People everywhere are fighting for the "sanctity of God-given life" – *but* where are the people fighting for the "sanctity of God-given sex" *within* the sanctity of *"God-given Marriage"*? Preachers preach sermons on abortion in which they say, *"Abortion is sinful; we need to eliminate it!"* But they

don't say a word about eliminating the sinful lifestyles of the **sexually immoral** people causing the abortions! America is like the inmate in an insane asylum who is put in a room to mop up the water coming from an overflowing sink – but he never goes over and turns off the faucet. So, he just keeps on moping and moping and moping. That's America. People protest abortion … while all the unwanted babies (products of *sexual immorality*) just keep coming and coming and coming.

Recently, a governing official made this statement concerning abortion: *"You can kill 'em now, or you can kill 'em later."* As terrible as that sounds, it was just an honest assessment of the sad state of affairs in our morally bankrupt Nation. In the ole days, young folks were taught that "making love" was for husbands and wives in marriage. In this *new* day, people don't have **God** (*or* His Love) in their lives, so they say, *"What's love got to do with anything?"* In this modern "hook-up generation" people just "have sex" because they are taught that evolution is true and they are merely evolved-animals; so they live like animals. Unbelievers (blinded by satan) think that all they are is just … a body. All they have is just … a body. All they have to give to another person is just … their body. Since they don't have *God's Love* within their soul to give to another person, they give them the only thing they *do* have to give them – their body. So, that governing official was just stating the obvious – millions of babies are conceived each year out of **sexual immorality** between sinful people who have no intention of getting married and raising the child in a loving home. Nope, they love themselves and their sin … but *not* the child. Therefore, the child would only live to be abused by unloving adults who would neglect him and cast him out into the world to make it on his own. Such a child usually ends up wounded and hardened – a hating, raging, angry young man who joins a gang and becomes a threat to all of society. An abused girl usually gets hooked on drugs and ends up having to sell her body just to support her drug addiction (have I been reading anyone's mail?). *By God's Grace, there **are** exceptions*

I don't have a TV, but I do have a little squawk-radio, and I sometimes leave my Christian station in search of National News. That's when I run across those advertisements for male sex-enhancement pills featuring young girls describing their "sex life" with their *boyfriends*. These girls either swoon over or ditch their boyfriends depending on their "sexual

performance." Yep, *sex* is the most powerful force in the Universe. Never mind the fact that the **God** of all Creation says it's **"Love."** Nope, forget God and chase after the *best sex* you can possibly find. Forget about the fact that the day *is* coming when that sexy body of yours is going to **die** ... and you're going to face **God** ... *and* **Eternity**. *Mercy Me!*

Sir, if your wife is hanging onto you because of your sexual performance, you've got a weak, shaky marriage. *But* ... if your soul is anchored to **The Rock** of God's Son and His Precious Word, your wife most likely thinks you hung the moon and loves you for "who you are" and "what you are." *Then*, you have a rock-solid marriage that cannot be shaken. **Love** makes the world go 'round, and sex is **God's Gift** to loving husbands and wives to *celebrate it.*

The sophisticated free-spirit moderns of today are proud of being the "liberated-generation." They have no sexual restraints on themselves whatsoever – and their parents are to blame. Ungodly adults *allowed* satan to pour all of his sexual sin and perversion into the eyes, ears, minds and souls of an entire generation of young folks growing up in America – and look what it got us. We now have a Super Bowl halftime show that has become nothing more than a *sexy, sleazy strip show* ... with nearly *all* of our children watching, for pity's sake! The most recent one was a shame and a disgrace. The girls' "performance" was so vividly *sexually stimulating* that it turned the entire stadium into one big "strip-joint" with the crowd yelling, applauding, whistling and cheering the girls on as they "did their thing." By the time they were done, everyone there and watching on TV (including children) were all "primed for sex." That was the purpose of the whole show – to get everyone in a fever-pitch for **sex**. Is it any wonder that liberal states are on the fast-track to legalize prostitution? Nope, and you will *never* be able to take abortion away from such ungodly, sexually immoral people. **They must have it. "Sin doesn't always look sinful to us; sometimes it looks beautiful. That is why we need Grace to see sin for what it really is – dark, dangerous, enslaving and destructive!"** (Paul David Tripp).

When I was growing up in America, **adults** were in charge and running the show. Today, **demons** are in charge and running the show. Satan-controlled, spoiled *children* (who *must have* whatever they want) dutifully give their "master" whatever *he* wants. That halftime show was *satan-on-display* ... being applauded, celebrated and praised by his

many fans. Evil satan was finally getting what he has always craved – to be worshipped as "god." Yes siree, *that* is what church looks like in the synagogue of satan. The demon-god of this world *demands* that his subjects dance and "perform" before him in the wickedness he so lusts after. Therefore, satan-controlled people must throw aside all *Godly* restraints in order to please their "master" – so they did. They *thought* they were being paid money for their "performance," but the wages of satan isn't money … it's **death**. *"The devil promises high wages, but he always pays off in counterfeit bills"* (R. G. Lee). If they (and those cheering them on) could have somehow *Supernaturally* seen themselves as **God saw them**, they wouldn't have been "dancing" so hard *or* cheering so loudly. They *thought* they were celebrating "life" – *but* they were actually celebrating their own *"spiritual death."* Mercy Me! *"America shall fall captive to dark circumstances beyond her control"* (Lon Woodrum).

Since I don't have a TV, I didn't actually see that halftime show. It was only after hearing such an **"outcry"** from so many people that I looked it up on-line. Decent people are describing it as "soft porn" (a degrading sex-show), *but* I haven't heard the "Me Too Movement" voicing any condemnation of *it* or *any* of the massive amounts of pornography America is drowning in. Therefore, they no longer have a leg to stand on. How can men (who are sexually stimulated *to the* **max** by pornography everywhere they turn) be blamed when they are sexually aggressive toward women *who are going along with it all?*!! Our Godly Grandmothers would *never* have let satan push *them* around. Watch "A Rare Tour of New York City – 1911" on-line and see how *they* dressed when *they* went out in public – *beautiful long dresses and ornate hats. Glory to God!! "Indecent dress is a fast-track to immoral behavior"* (Jack Graham).

Everyone who promotes and participates in all the *sexual immorality* in America today will one day die. Yep, **die** – and stand in **Judgment** before **Holy God**. Be not deceived; God is not mocked; **He** *will have* the last Word. Life isn't over when it's over. Oh no, it is *just beginning*. Do you ever wonder where all the pornographers and "sex queens" of yesteryear (who have slipped into **Eternity**) are today? I truly believe that our Godly Ancestors, who condemned *sexual immorality*, will also be at God's Judgment Throne, standing *with Him* as He banishes God-rejecting people to the place of *eternal death*.

In the unseen demonic realm, satan is courting America, and that devil is ever so cunningly winning her heart. Instead of giving her flowers and candy, he showers her with his: (d) demon-inspired, soul-corrupting pornography, (e) excessive, deadly addictive alcohol and cigarettes, (a) always-available, at-her-fingertips immoral entertainment, (t) totally degrading, disease-spreading, society-consensual "sexual freedom," (h) horror-producing, reality-escaping, mind-destroying, life-wrecking drugs – *and she's lovin' it* (without realizing that she has actually fallen in love with *satan himself*). Deep within the soul of every unsaved man (or woman) are dark, foreboding feelings of "lostness" and "emptiness" that *drive him* to try to fill that void and numb that pain with drugs, lewd entertainment and sexual immorality of *every* kind. America is just like that man; she has a deep hunger and longing for … *something.* And she *thinks* that satan's titillating *sexual entertainment* and *sexual immorality* will satisfy her – but it only satisfies **satan.** It can *never* satisfy the **Eternal** longings of the human **soul.** *But I know Who can! (His initials are:* **J.E.S.U.S.***!!)* *"Entertainment is the devil's substitute for Joy. The more Joy you have in the Lord, the less entertainment you need"* (Leonard Ravenhill).

Run with wise men, and you will end up wise. Run with fools, and you will end up a fool. America is a *fool* to run with **satan.** *"A fool is a person who lives as though God does not exist"* (Joni Eareckson Tada). I hear people saying, *"America is the greatest Nation on Earth!"* And then I see demonic "adult entertainment" (like that halftime show) being pumped into the eyes, minds and souls of nearly everyone in America, and *I* know the truth: America is ever so quickly committing "spiritual suicide!!" Satan-controlled unbelievers proclaim, *"God is dead!"* **But God** is very much **"Alive!"** It is the *unbelievers* who are **spiritually dead.** They are like the prodigal son who left his *Godly* father, went into the "far country" and squandered his life and money on whiskey, drugs, women and wild livin'! Yep, this generation has been "sexually liberated" alright, but what they don't realize is that they have only liberated *satan* to take over their *souls.* They have given him the freedom to totally destroy them … and their children right along with them. Satan gets great devilish delight out of corrupting the innocence of children and destroying whatever is left of the morality of everyone else. *"The 'far country' has a price tag that is much higher than what was originally advertised"* (Tony Evans).

(Side-note: Unbelievers say that we Christians are a bunch of silly ignoramuses to believe that there actually *is* a **devil** behind all the evil in this world. But the fact that they can walk around in a *"Supernaturally-created-living-body"* {carrying around an unseen spirit/soul/mind} and yet *still* deny that a "Supernatural God" brought *every part* of them into being ... is the work of "someone" *very evil*. They admit that there *is* "evil" in our world while denying *the very God* Who is convicting them of that evil. Ole slick has them so *spiritually blind* they can't *see* that **he** is the evil-one blinding them. But he doesn't have us Christians blinded. *We see* our God; we *love* our God; we *celebrate* our God and *sing* His Praises in the midst of this satan-infested/sin-saturated wicked world. Every moment of every day is a "Worship Service" for the True Child of God!! *"Worship is enjoying the Presence of God!"* {Adrian Rogers})

When I was coming along, everyone just seemed to *know* that there *is* a God, and **He** made the Rules, watches over us all and will judge us after we die according to *His Word*. America was indeed birthed a "God-fearing Nation." Today, America is largely a "God-rejecting Nation," and sadly, I have lived to see much of that transition take place in *my* lifetime. In so many ways, America has become a godless Country populated by godless people ... and nobody seems to care. **But God cares!!** *He* was also watching that halftime show ... and taking notes. It breaks God's heart that His Beloved America is *first* in exporting such ungodly, sexual "entertainment" to the rest of the world. I truly hope that America *isn't* Babylon the Great; however, I couldn't help but think of the following verse as I wrote this chapter: *"Babylon is fallen, is fallen, that great city, because she made all Nations drink of the wine of the wrath of her fornication"* (Revelation 14:8). Decent, *God-fearing* Americans need to push back against satan and his evil agenda by standing up to the **NFL** and holding them accountable for what they shamelessly did. They punish their players for extreme "unsportsmanlike conduct" by extracting high fines from them; *now* it's time to fine *the NFL* for the same reason. Make *them* pay the price ... *not* our precious children, for pity's sake. *Whatever happened to "censors" in America who kept her a decent Country?* **"America will be governed by God or ruled by tyrants!!"** (Peter Marshall, Sr.).

Today, satan is working overtime telling *everyone* that homosexual *sin* is normal and wonderful. Our young folks get a steady diet of his

indoctrination every day from every direction. Satan's favorite way of talking them all into being homosexuals is by teaching it to them in *all of our Public Schools,* starting in kindergarten!! Therefore, many of them start thinking they really *are* homosexuals, but when I was in School, it was quite different. We girls would have sleepovers with each other from time to time, and we would spend the night lying around in our pajamas, giggling and talking about boys. It *never once* crossed our mind to have sex with each other. And do you know *why* it never once crossed our mind to have sex with each other? *Because it had never once crossed our mind!!* That's why. We were still like innocent children who didn't *even know* about all the **wickedness** that lurked out in this evil world. I was an adult before I ever heard the word "homosexual," and I sure didn't know what it meant. When I was eventually given the sexual details, I understood why God calls it an abomination.

In *my* generation, there were wise **God-honoring** Parents and Grandparents in America, and they did a great job of protecting us from *satan's wickedness* – in movies, on TV, at School, in magazines, at football games, etc. *Great is their reward in Heaven!* The world I grew up in *just knew* that living a life of sodomy is a **sin** against Holy God, **The God of the Bible.** The world I live in today (except for Born-Again Christians) *just knows* that living a life of sodomy isn't a **sin** at all. Nope, it's perfectly fine and so wonderful that it should be embraced and even celebrated by *everyone*. Those of us who believe **God** and **His Word** are called "bigots" and "homophobes" instead of what we really are: **"Christians!"** Put your "Jesus Glasses" on, Folks, and you will clearly see that it's the age-old "Spiritual Battle" of **God vs. satan! "The Cornerstone of Civilization is Godly Morality" Signed: Every Born-Again Christian.**

Another reason it never crossed the minds of us "sleepover girls" to have sex with each other is because none of us were having sex with boys. In other words, we weren't sexually active. Our **Godly** Parents taught us that sex is for **marriage** (between a **man** and a **woman**), and we actually trusted their wisdom, feared God's punishment and took it to heart. *What a novel idea! "Our Grandparents didn't care if we were happy"* (Robert G. Lee). I'm sure this present generation has a problem with that statement, but it's true; our Godly Ancestors *didn't* care a whole lot about us being happy all the time. But they *did* care

a whole lot about us being well-disciplined, God-loving, God-fearing, law-abiding, hard-working, responsible, patriotic American Citizens all the time. They knew that their job wasn't to spoil us by making **us** the center of the known Universe. No, their job *wasn't* to make sure nothing ever hurt our feelings but rather to protect us from being totally destroyed by satan, the wicked enemy of our souls.

Today, however, people are so "enlightened" that they must bow to their master (satan) and allow him to give his pornographic "entertainment" to *everyone*. America is now "first" in producing and consuming **pornography!** No wonder our young folks are so sexually immoral. I feel so sorry for them. Where, pray tell, are all the adults?! Oh yeah, I just remembered; they're busy ... watching pornography. Yep, satan has turned more people than ever into his pitifully addicted sex-slaves. *"When I called, none did answer; when I spake, they did not hear."*

The America I grew up in was not yet as dangerous, crime-ridden or immoral as America is today. So, when I was just a little girl, I walked quite a few blocks to School and back home every day *through deep snow!* (Just kidding about the deep snow; we lived in the Deep South.) I grew up being taught that Policemen are "good guys" who would help me if I ever needed them. My Mother did her part by always warning me, *"Don't take candy from a stranger."* She drilled that into me because she was wise and knew that wicked men would offer candy to little girls like me to entice us to like them and go with them ... to sexual abuse and death! Now, *I'm* here to warn *America:* **Don't** take wicked satan's evil "candy." It's not really candy. It's actually *poisonous fruit* from his "tree of death!" *Just ask Eve.*

"A little girl came home and told her mother that she would like to give some money to an ole lady in the park who needed it. The mother was touched by her daughter's compassion and gave her a couple dollars to give the elderly lady. Then, the mother asked, 'Isn't the lady able to still work?'

'Oh, yes,' answered the little girl, 'she sells candy.'" (Ken Davis).

America is selling her soul to the devil in order to get money to hand over to him for his evil "candy." America is worse than a harlot because she *pays her* lover to commit sexual immorality with *her*. Americans are wholeheartedly paying satan to fill their minds and souls with his

pornography and sexual perversion. They are actually *purchasing* his poisonous "candy" … and they are headed for sexual abuse and death – *spiritual death* – **eternal death!** The devil must think we're the biggest pack of fools he's ever seen – and he is right. We have refused to put any restraints on satan whatsoever, and we now have a Country full of people who have no *moral* restraints on *themselves* whatsoever! Satan is controlling and corrupting an entire generation by filling their minds and souls with his ungodly **sexual sin** of every kind. Yep, it's *satan's* world … we're just ~~living~~ dying in it. *Mercy Me!*

"**Sexual immorality** *is the last step down on the way to the bottom.*" (Adrian Rogers). That is true for people *and* for Nations. I would say that America is on her last leg. Even worse, she's like a drunken man passed-out on the freeway with a whole fleet of tractor-trailer trucks bearing down on him! Is there anyone reading this who is tired of letting the devil destroy you *and* your Country with his *sexual immorality*? Only "Jesus in you" has the *Power* to say *"No!"* to satan's poisonous, deadly "candy." God is seeking some dedicated **Christian Lawmakers** in America who have "Jesus in *them*" and are tired of letting satan destroy our children and young adults with his "sex-ed" classes (provided by Planned Parenthood and the homosexuals) that teach them to have sex *and* perverted sex of *every* kind. I'm praying that God finds *plenty* who are brave enough to bring back **Godly Laws,** *for* **Jesus'** *sake.* The rest of us need to become "Christian Activists." Christians need courage today like never before because we're up against vicious attacks on our Christian Morality like never before. If your Library is having "Drag Queen Story Hour" for children, it's time for some "Peaceful **Christian** Protests." It's time to let the world **see** that **someone** is willing to stand up for **Jesus** and stand against satan in America today! *"Whosoever shall confess Me before men, him will I confess also before My Father Who is in Heaven!" Signed: Jesus* (Matthew 10:32).

Satan-followers tell us that we can't censor *anything* because America is a "free Country." Near-nude parades; nude bike rides; nudity on public beaches; obscenity, nudity and indecency in movies, on TV, on-line and in magazines are all permitted because, after all, America is a "free Country." In the ole days (when we were a God-fearing, God-honoring, moral society), we had "Public Indecency Laws" which were strictly enforced. Back then, the "decency of God" trumped the "wickedness of

man" every time … but not anymore. Once you legalize pornography, it permeates **all** of society. And *today*, every form of *human dignity* and *God-honoring decency* must fall to the all-encompassing mantra of: *"America is a free Country!"* But as Tony Evans wisely observes, *"America is a free Country – but you aren't free to run a red light."* We Christians *must* stand with **God** and hold up **His Word** (the **Bible**) as the *Red Light* that will bring **"decency"** back to America. If it meets **God's Moral Standards**, we're free to do it; if it doesn't, that means **satan** is behind it and *we must reject it*. Without *Absolute Moral Laws*, "Christian America" will only exist in the memory of ole folks such as I.

I was one of the hold-outs who said she would *never* own a computer (while typing in this book, half my time was spent just trying to make my computer happy; I guess it's never read *The McCoy Manual of Stylish Writin'*). I only bought one when I realized I would have to submit my manuscript to a publisher in digital form. Therefore, all thirty-five chapters of *Dare To Be Jesus* were originally written out on paper. Pages and pages of hand-written "notes" had to be organized into a (hopefully) readable book. At the top of some of the pages, I would write a "title" for the subject matter. The title I gave to the following section was: "Girls Gone Wild!" I know, I know … boys have gone wild too. But let's face it, Folks, boys have always been wild. When it comes to a young man's nature concerning young women, he wants to hug, kiss, fondle and have sex *(dat's jest de way mens is)*. So, we can't lay the blame for the radical change in America's morals at *their* feet. The difference in our Country today is that satan has slithered into "The Garden" once again and "gotten through" to *our* daughters the same way he did to God's first daughter. Why did satan go after Eve in the Garden of Eden? Answer: That sly snake-in-the-grass knows that a woman's behavior determines a man's behavior. And so it was; Eve's sin led Adam into sin also. Things are no different in our modern world. Why is sexual promiscuity *sooooo* rampant in America today and abortion *sooooo* in-demand? Answer: Because our *satan-liberated* girls no longer hold up a "moral standard" to those hormone-driven guys and demand their respect, restraint and honorable treatment. Without **God** in her life, our modern-day Eve is "free" to take bite after bite of the forbidden fruit … and so she does. That Super Bowl halftime show was just one of *many* examples of *how far from God* girls are these days.

In the ole days, wise Christian Parents and Leaders **protected** us young folks from ole slewfoot so that he couldn't "get through" to us. We were taught **Christian Morality** and certain unwritten-laws that a "decent girl" *just knew* she had to live by. A girl *never* smoked cigarettes or drank whiskey. A girl *never* called a guy. A girl *never* "made moves" on a guy, no matter how cute he was or how much she liked him, lest she get the reputation of being "loose." A girl *never* ignored her parents' curfew. A girl *never* went out in public looking like she forgot to put her clothes on over her underwear. Today, Victoria's secret is that she no longer has any. *Mercy Me!* Elisabeth Elliot said that her mother drilled it into *her* to "let the boys do the chasing and always keep them at arms' length." *My, how things have changed!* And there is our answer: Parents no longer *teach* their daughters to *demand* that boys treat them as "ladies." Since young men have a problem controlling their sexual desires, it's up to young women to do it for them. That's just the way it has always been … until now. Today, the *Daughters of the American Sexual Revolution* have succumbed to that same ole devil God's first daughter succumbed to. They have turned themselves over to that sleazy, slimy serpent, and he has turned *them* into "Girls Gone Wild!" Unless our young men turn *themselves* over to **God** and become "men of honor" who love God more than they love themselves, abortion will continue to plague our Land.

The reason that so many of our young folks have gone wild these days is because "Girls Gone Wild!" and "Boys Gone Wild!" have grown up, had children and become "Parents Gone Wild!" Let's face it, Folks, parents who are *sexually immoral* themselves haven't the integrity to teach their sons and daughters the virtues of remaining pure – from pornography, sex, drugs, etc. I hear tell that it's fashionable these days for "Parents Gone Wild" to rent a hotel room for their child when they graduate from High School to party in all night long with no adult supervision. And other "Parents Gone Wild" let *their* children go with their "blessing." No one has to worry about getting pregnant. That's what abortion is for.

Our **Great God** didn't make us for such, and I guarantee you that the next day (even though she would never admit it to anyone) the girl who allowed her boyfriend to "use her" feels deeply dirty in the depths of her soul … because something *very precious* has been destroyed and lost. *God created sex* to be *"sacred"* between a **husband** and his **wife** (representing the

"Sacred Relationship" between **Christ** and His Bride, the **Church**). When you engage in *sexual immorality*, you defile yourself and sin against the God Who commands you to keep sex "sacred." You also do great harm to the *other person* because it leaves ugly scars on both of your souls. You will look back one day and wish *so badly* that you had never done such *sinful things* ... because they will *still* be hanging around in your **soul.** You will wish *so badly* that you could go back in time and change those ungodly choices you made. *But you will never be able to.*

Parents, you *must* once again drill it into your children that **God** expects **sexual purity** from them – and it's up to *them* to control their passions. Teach your sons and daughters that their virginity is a "precious treasure" which they must protect and keep – for **God** and for their future spouse. *"Give not that which is Holy unto the dogs; neither cast ye your Pearls before swine" Signed: Jesus* (Matthew 7:6). Then, you must use common sense to do all you can to help them. If you send your young folks to liberal colleges with co-ed dorms, you're in league with satan and his demons – who are waiting there for your precious children. When your daughter comes home and tells you she's pregnant ... well ... the sin is yours as much as hers. And don't think that an abortion will wipe it all out – it only doubles it.

Ray Comfort tells of being in a tempting situation with his girlfriend when he was young, *but fortunately* she looked at him and said, *"God is watching us."* The time has come, Christian Parents, for you to "be Jesus" to your sons and daughters by teaching them God's Truth: God is watching them *all the time. "Every day is Holy. Every place is Sacred"* (Adrian Rogers). Sin is *still* **sin** no matter *what* **satan** is saying to them through their teachers, friends, music, movies, TV and especially their boyfriend (or girlfriend-gone-wild). Our **Great God** sees it *all*, and they answer to **Him** – *always* (even in the dark when they're all alone with their boyfriend or girlfriend-gone-wild). Life is God's test, and the Teacher is always watching to see if you're cheating. *Don't fail Him. "Right is right even if nobody is doing it, and wrong is wrong even if everybody is doing it"* (Jeff Schreve).

"Girls Gone Wild" will never be tamed ... *until* ... they meet the Saviour. Only **He** has the *Power* to tame them – spiritually and morally. You won't be able to truly transform your daughter's behavior ... *until* ... the **Lord Jesus** has first *truly* transformed her heart. The way your

sons and daughters live out their lives doesn't depend on *what they're told* or *what they know* … but **Who they love** – *the most.* Fortunately for Ray Comfort, *his* girlfriend loved the **Lord Jesus** more than she loved Ray. He said that her words "sobered him up" and kept him from doing something he would have regretted *for the rest of his life.*

So it's elementary, my dear Watson, the answer to abortion isn't shutting down the abortion mills. Nope, it's going back to teaching our young folks **God's Agenda** for their lives: **SEXUAL PURITY!!** **God** commands us to remain *sexually pure* before marriage; then *sexually faithful* to our spouse after marriage. Now, I know what you're thinking, *"That won't work."* It won't work in a society that exposes our young folks to sex, sexual sin and sexual perversion in School, on TV, on their phones, on their computers, in movies, at the Super Bowl and everywhere else they turn. It won't work in a Country controlled by satan, his demons and his slaves. But it *will* work in *your home* – when you kick satan out and teach your children that **Jesus Christ is Lord and His Word is Absolute Truth!**

Trust me, Folks, we have no way out of this mess … **but God!!** It's going to take **Someone** greater than "religion" to **Save** America. At this point in time, America is in bed with *satan himself,* and she is foolishly allowing him to corrupt her by exposing *everyone* here to his explicit, sinful, sexual "entertainment." If America is serious about getting rid of abortion, she is going to have to get *serious* about getting rid of *pornography* (every form of it) by passing laws *against it* once again and holding up **God's Laws** to wicked people who scream, *"Censoring pornography is unconstitutional!!"* We will either be "One Nation under **God**" or "One Nation under satan" – and American Citizens must decide (not a few ungodly politicians and judges). I'm praying that important moral issues will be put on the ballot for **"We The People!"** to vote on. *Godly decency must prevail!!* All it takes these days is for a few of satan's slaves to go to Court and demand the "right" to do some indecent, ungodly "something," and thanks to ungodly leaders, the devil has his **ungodly judges** right in place to do his bidding. Then … *Wa La* … the demands of satan's *few* are "legally" forced on *everyone* (sound familiar?).

Let me take a few minutes and shock the young folks who may be reading this book. Like most of you, I always attended a Public School. But, unlike most of you, I never heard filthy language coming out of the

mouths of any of my classmates in all my years of going to School. I didn't know of anyone who drank or smoked (except for a couple of "bad boys" in High School), and drugs were something the doctor gave you when you got sick. No one ever showed me a pornographic magazine – they were non-existent because they were *illegal*, videos didn't exist and a telephone was a small black box (connected to a wall in your home) in which an "Operator" lived who said, *"Number, please"* when you picked up the receiver. We didn't have sex-ed classes (provided by Planned Parenthood and the homosexuals) teaching us how to have sex *and* perverted sex. Our Christian Teachers didn't teach us that a monkey was our Uncle. No decent person would *ever* get a tattoo or attach metal to their body through piercings (that was looked upon as being **satanic**). I didn't see fights or students spanked by teachers. Our School's bus drivers kept their buses orderly and under control. Boys always carried a pocket-knife in their pocket … and nobody cared. None of my classmates ever committed a crime and had to go to juvenile jail. In High School some of the boys drove ole trucks to School with their guns in racks behind their heads – and yet, School shootings were unheard of. Needless to say, I never saw a Policeman at our School.

So, what has gone **so** wrong? I'll tell you. Our Glorious God of the Bible has been rejected, voted out, evicted, banned and even criminalized over and over again in America. Our Government is perpetrating mass murder, so is it any wonder that many of our Citizens are doing the same? *Life* is no longer "sacred;" *sex* is no longer "sacred" and the *Bible* is no longer "sacred" … to those who regard **God** as no longer **"Sacred."** Today, *satan* is alive and evil and on the move in our used-to-be Christian Nation. More and more people are embracing satan's wicked occult world and becoming more and more like their evil leader – they openly sin and are proud of it. The devil now has so many people here with "satan in them" that he has no trouble a'tall finding well-groomed slaves who are eager to take up guns and take out as many innocent people as their demonic leader dictates – and I believe he uses "illegal drugs" to groom them. In the ole days, we didn't have "mass-shootings," nor did we have people "doing drugs." You would think that the people running our Government would wake up, pull their heads up out of the sand, see "The Light" and say, *"Hey! Now we see it!* **Satan** *is 'the evil-one' behind all of this! We need to find a way to bring* **God** *back*

*into our Country. Quick!! Only **His Power** can save us from that devil."* But they never do. Instead, they acquiesce to satan by passing laws that do away with capital punishment – even for mass-murderers. It makes one wonder, doesn't it? Could it be that many of *them* are satan's well-groomed slaves as well? *Mercy Me! "If you don't surrender to Christ, you surrender to chaos"* (E. Stanley Jones).

God commands us not to defile our bodies (which *He* created) by making any cuts or marks upon our flesh (Leviticus 19:28). And right on schedule, along comes the original hell's angel convincing everyone that tattoos and piercings are the "in" thing to do. Anything satan can do to get people in rebellion against God and in league with him suits him just fine. But he doesn't *tell* people they're in league with him. Nope, ole slick just runs his ole end-around-play and gets them totally obsessed with the vilest of video games full of killing and violence. Sure it's a *serious crime* to kill people ... *unless* ... you do it in "a game." Instead of wising up and *outlawing* the worst of them, this free-for-all-society just keeps on producing more and more – while more and more people are *becoming* outlaws, picking up *real* guns and killing *real* people!

The True and Living God is the "God of Love." Therefore, any Nation that *rejects God* ends up with a Country full of people "devoid of love." Expose those godless, spiritually dead folks to a steady diet of satan-inspired hate and bloody violence, and you've got the perfect recipe for a mass-murder scene acted out by a raging-angry, violent soul – the product of satan himself. Deadly crimes are committed by souls full of *demonic hate*. Satan hates God *and* the Crown of God's Creation; therefore, he uses every deception to devalue human life. The devil knows that if he can get a man to kill another man, it will hurt the God Who created and loves that man. That's why satan never warns the killer, *"Oh, and by the way, **God Created** that person you're about to kill."*

When people hear about horrific mass-shootings (and other terrible crimes), they ask, *"How could anyone **do** such a horrible thing?!"* Jesus tells us how: *"Ye are of your father the devil, and the lusts of your father ye will do; he was a murderer from the beginning"* (John 8:44). Their slave-master (satan) whispers in their ear, *"Hey, Big Man, there's no God; you're just the top-of-the-evolutionary-chain. And when you die, you're gone and it's over. There's certainly no God to ever give an account to. **You're** the master of your fate; the captain of your soul.*

*So, whatever **you** want to do – **just do it**. Yeah, it doesn't matter … because you'll never see it again anyway."* That ole serpent with the velvet tongue tells them exactly what they want to hear. They swallow his poisonous *lie* and do "it" … thinking they will never see "it" again. They just blow "it" off by saying, *"What will 'it' matter a hundred years from now?"*

Well, a hundred years from now … they're going to find out. "It" will matter a whole bunch to **The One** they actually did "it" to – **God Himself**. Therefore, we Christians must boldly let **"Jesus in us"** tell those deceived slaves of satan that they *will indeed* see "it" again – in the Presence of **Holy God** before His **Throne of Judgment**. On *that* Day, every poisonous **sin** they *ever* committed will be regurgitated out of their **sinful soul** before the Holy Throne of **Almighty God** – and they will have no way to clean up the **mess**. *Surprise!! Surprise!!* **"On that Day, vices will have voices as they testify against you before Judge Jesus!"** (Adrian Rogers).

Another reason America was a different Country back in the ole days is because we kids were **disciplined at home** by loving, wise parents who put "the fear of God" in us. My Daddy had a "Parent's Card" which read: *Have belt – will spank*. (I now realize that God gave me the Daddy that I had to discipline me like he did so that I would have the stick-to-itiveness I would need for God to use me like he does – *to write this book!* The longer I walk with my Lord, the more I see His hand in *everything!*) I truly believe that one the greatest gifts a parent can give their child is the gift of "discipline." Today, we're told that it's a **sin** to spank children, but our Godly Parents of yesteryear knew that it's a sin *not* to spank children. They put "the fear of God" in us because *they* feared God themselves. They taught us to honor and obey *them* because our Father in Heaven is always taking notes, and He expects us to honor and obey *Him* most of all. We *knew* to respect *all* adults – even the ladies in the lunchroom who served us our lunch. We had it drilled into us to *always* **obey the Law** and **respect Police Officers** … because if we ever broke the Law, got arrested and were sent to jail, we would get a **"Police record!!"** And if *that* ever happened … well … that was **it** for us – our lives were **over**.

Now contrast that with an interview I recently heard of a young woman who engages in protests against the Police. She was asked if she condemns the crimes and violent attacks on Police Officers committed

by the rioters, and here is her amazing answer: *"No. People can do anything they want to do!"* Has she ever heard of **"Laws"**?!! America has them, but she doesn't think anyone needs to bother with obeying them; she wants to live in a totally lawless, uncivilized Country. She was obviously raised in a home in which "she could do anything she wanted to do." She was probably never taught to obey **God's Laws** either. Sadly, **that** is our main problem in America today – a large number of our Citizens don't think they have to obey **America's Laws (or God's Laws)!** Our Country is "out of control" because so many of our **Citizens** are "out of control." They commit **crimes**; then *resist arrest* when our Police *try* to arrest them. They think *their crimes* are just fine because "they want to do them," *but* they condemn and violently attack *all* Policemen for the crimes of a few in the line of duty. *The natural man receiveth not the things of the Spirit of God.*

An entire political party is training black folks to convince their children to believe the **lie** that all of us white folks are evil racists who hate them; therefore, they need to hate *us* in return. This party's fake-president has gone on National TV with his **fake-news** that America is **"an evil Country of systemic racism!!"** The ones pushing this false race-war-narrative are feeding off all the chaos they are causing by relentlessly tearing our Country apart. What we see happening in America today is exactly what those corrupt politicians **want** to be happening in America today. They are blind followers of the "false-god." **They need Jesus!!**

Now contrast *them* with Gov. Ron DeSantis who made this statement when he passed a law prohibiting the "critical race theory" being taught in Florida, *"Teaching our children to hate their Country and hate each other is not worth one red cent of taxpayer money!!"* May his Tribe increase!

Many of the people I have witnessed to over the years have been black folks who turned out to be Born-Again Christians. *Praise the Lord!* So, they are my Brothers and Sisters in Christ. The great **"Joy!"** we share during those few *"Hallelujah moments"* is beyond the understanding of an unsaved person. We love each other now, and we will spend *Eternity* loving each other in Heaven ... because *we both love* **Jesus!** The real enemy in America today is *satan* – not a person with a different skin color. If those out rioting, looting, destroying and even killing could ever "see" that *satan* is their real enemy (and started fighting against

him), *then* we would have a very different America indeed. Instead of anti-Police riots, we need to have a whole bunch of **anti-satan** protests from people who have *seen The Light*. All of the turmoil, violence and chaos we are witnessing in America today is just the manifestation of **satan's** rule in the souls of *many* in our Country. **America needs Jesus!! America needs "Jesus in you!!" "For he whom God hath sent speaketh the Words of God"** (John 3:34).

Before *you* get taken-in by those wicked people trying to destroy our Beloved Country ... let me give you some sage advice: Don't let *anyone* convince you that living a life of **hate** is the best way to live. God created you, and He loves you; He wants you to live a life of **love** – for Him, His Son Jesus and others. When you live your life close to the Lord Jesus, you are able to bring everyone around you close to Him as well. **You** can help make America a **God-Blessed Nation** ... instead of a godless nation. Turn your eyes upon **Jesus** (The Chain-Breaker), and don't live your life chained to the sins of the past – this Country's past *or* your past. Instead, let *me* convince you there's a better way. No matter *what* has happened to you **don't** let it destroy the rest of your life, *for pity's sake!* It doesn't have to, you know. I know. I have been through things that could have (and should have) totally destroyed me ... **BUT GOD!!**

> *"I will never let another man ruin my life*
> *by making me hate him"*
> (George Washington Carver).

Let me tell you even *more* reasons why the world I grew up in was so different from today. Each morning, our School-day began with us sitting *quietly* and *reverently* at our desks while our Teacher read some Scriptures from the King James Bible (the *discipline* we received at home became a part of our very DNA). We respected our God and our Teacher as she read from His Word. Back then, it was remembered that the Bible was the first text book used in our Schools, which is why our **Founding Fathers** quoted it so much (tell *that* to the freedom-from-religion groups). Next, we stood, bowed our heads (and our hearts) and all prayed the Lord's Prayer together (no one *ever* said, *"I'm an atheist!"* and refused to pray). Then, we turned to our American Flag

(representing our Country which thousands upon thousands of brave Americans have given their lives to protect), placed our hands over our hearts and pledged Allegiance to our Country: One Nation under God (no one *ever* said, *"I hate America!"* and "took a knee" in protest against her). We were all united in our Prayer to our God as well as in our Allegiance to our Country, and we felt something stir deep within our hearts in gratitude to God for allowing us to be born in such a Great Nation. We loved being Americans.

I don't know how to explain it, but there was "something" in us that made us **want** to excel academically and achieve success; that made us **want** to obey our Parents and make them proud of us; that made us **want** to obey the law and be righteous, up-standing citizens; that made us **want** to live honorable lives of dignity and virtue as we did a "Great Work" for God and Country. It was more than what we were taught ... it was *who we* **were.** The blood of our Ancestors, those Great American Patriots, was still coursing through our veins! Today, many young Americans don't *want* to do *any* of the above. So, they don't – and all the King's horses and all the King's men can't make them. What *they want* is to rebel against their parents, the Police and anyone else who isn't a part of *their group.* They want to be able to do drugs, commit crimes, vandalize, destroy stuff, steal the rest ... *and get away with it!* To them, *that* is a really "cool" thing to do (trouble is, it sends you to a really "hot" place). *"Come unto Me, and I will give you rest unto your soul."*

In the America I grew up in, a young man was expected to be "an honorable gentleman" who treated a girl with the respect a lady deserves. A young girl was expected to actually *act like a lady*, and "modesty" was one of the highest virtues. Sex or sexual body parts weren't discussed at School; that just wasn't "proper" (somehow, the human race continued without "sex" being taught in Public Schools). Girls wore dresses or skirts (with crinolines) to School, and there was an unwritten law that they *had* to be below the knee. The night of the Senior Prom, every girl showed up in a "ball-gown" much like the ones worn by Scarlett O'Hara in *Gone With The Wind.* (I know you're thinking, *"That's not politically correct,"* but before you condemn Scarlett {and us}, take a look at the sleazy dresses girls half-wear today.) Life was fun! We felt like "Queen For A Night" ... instead of a "lady of the evening." Our clothes didn't send a message to the

boys: *"Don't you think I'm sooooo sexy? Of course, you do. And I am sooooo available to have sex with **you**."*

(Side-note: Speaking of *Gone With The Wind*, that classic ole movie has been banned because of its sinful content. *However*, if we Christians ever managed to ban pornography, there would be a **deafening outcry** from "the world" screaming, *"You can't censor pornography!! We have freedom of speech in America!!"{Hmmm}*. *Gone With The Wind* is too sinful to be viewed, but **PORNOGRAPHY** is just fine and wholly accepted. *Go figure*.)

We lived in the *real world* back then. We chased butterflies, fed animals, gathered eggs, milked cows (goats), went fishin', built tree-forts, drove tractors (before we were "of age"), rode horses (or whatever would let us ride 'em), chopped fire-wood, caught fireflies in a mason-jar, swam in the lake, went on hay-rides, drank sweet ice-tea, ate grits, swung on tire-swings, learned to sew our own clothes at our Mother's knee, went huntin' with our dog (then cooked for supper whatever we shot), were experts at using a fly-swatter, turned the crank on an ice cream churn to make ice cream fit for a King (then licked the dasher so as not to waste a drop), had huge "family reunions" with enough food to feed an army and picked apples, blackberries, sweet corn and wild flowers. We lived close to nature and in a world that was very *real*. Folks today live close to their "devices" which take them into the "cyber-world" where life is lived in the mind – and it all began way back when they introduced a new-fangled-box they called "television." *My, oh my!* In the evening, the few families who could afford one saw only "family entertainment" … because there actually *were* "censors" in those days who kept profanity, filth, obscenity, nudity, sex and bloody violence out of TV, movies, music, books and magazines. Back then, America was considered to be a **Christian Nation**, and **God** was still feared and highly revered. Therefore, Christians were also greatly respected.

Now, I know what you young folks are thinking, *"You're kidding, right?"* Nope, and if your Great Grandparents are still alive, ask *them* what America was like when they were your age. Then, we can all have a vote on which "world" we would rather live in. *You* think that all the violence, sexual perversion, drug use, obscenity and explicit sex you see every day is perfectly normal and acceptable. Yep, it *is* all normal … in *satan's* world … *but not in* **God's**. The reason you think that satan's evil,

corrupted, sin-saturated, sex-crazed, perverted world is perfectly normal is because it's the only world you've ever known. Trust me, the "good ole days" were a whole lot better than the "demonic new days" satan has *you* living in. Now, I'm not saying that *we* were all Angels while you kids today are all a bunch of demons in short bodies. Not at all; we were just like you … *except* for the fact that all the wickedness satan has you *drowning in* wasn't available to us (or even known about by us) back then. *Praise God!* We had wise Christian Parents and Leaders who **protected us** – and that's what **you** need *today*.

I'm sure that satan must really hate me for daring to still be alive *and* for daring to tell you young folks what America was like before *he* took it over. Satan hates me so much for doing all I do to bring him down that he would kill me in a heartbeat … if he could. The fact that I am still alive today on Planet Earth is *proof-positive* that there **is** a God on His Throne in Heaven controlling all things – including that rascal satan. **Almighty God** has *you* here for a *very important reason* also, and He has sent me to give you a *very important message* from **Him**: *"My Precious Child, I AM 'calling' you to be My Special Witness to a world in the grip of satan – the evil-one behind all the wicked things people do when they don't know My Son Jesus. Since you know Jesus as your Lord and Saviour, you are a member of the "Chosen Generation," and I AM sending you to defeat satan in America. You will be like those brave first-responders and fire-fighters who rushed into the Twin Towers on 911 to rescue people, and you will rush out into America to rescue people with the Gospel of Jesus Christ – satan's kryptonite! I AM giving you the faith, courage and resolve it takes to rush up the stairs when everyone else is rushing down!" "Run into the battle! That's the kind of courage that makes a man"* (Eugenia Bigham).

Another thing that has gone wrong in modern America is the rejection of **God** as our **Great Creator** and the total acceptance of satan's evil, made-up **lie** of "evolution" as scientific fact. Young folks are taught from kindergarten up that they are just evolved-animals. So, is it any wonder they live like it in every area of their life? Evolution totally *eliminates* God from our existence. If our Country still exalted our *Creator God,* people would still *know* that there **is** a God and He is **The God of the Bible**. They would *know* that He is *All Powerful* – worthy of our reverence; worthy of our praise. People would also know that after

death we are accountable to our **Creator** before His Judgment Throne. The Cowboys in the ole-timey Westerns knew it; one would draw his gun on another and yell, *"Get ready to meet your Maker!"* But sadly, America no longer acknowledges her Maker: **The True and Living God.** Our Nation has steadily rejected Him, and evil satan has been more than happy to steadily step in and take God's place. *Yes indeed! Now* the devil is *finally* getting what he desperately wanted in Eternity past – *to be "god." But* in the ole days, it was a very different story; satan may have been "the god of this world," but he sure *wasn't* "the god of **America.**" *No indeed! Not on our Godly Ancestors watch!!* They *knew* Who the *True God* was, and they steadfastly stood strong for the God they loved. Even out in the "Wild West" there was always a *Good Sheriff* around somewhere to enforce *Godly Laws.* Today, *satan* wants to do away with our Police and turn the criminals loose. **"Katie, bar the door!!"**

People are always saying: *You can't legislate morality.* But I say: *They are wrong ... because our Godly Ancestors sure did.* Those *Christian Super Stars* did *not* tolerate bloody violence, nudity, sex, perverted sex, profanity or obscenity in movies, magazines or TV shows. There were laws on the books *against* murder, sodomy and pornography because when **God** called something an *abominable* **sin**, that settled it for *them.* *Yes indeed!!* I can still remember the day when America didn't have **any** abortion mills, "adult" book stores, x-rated movies, homosexual parades, homosexual "marriage" or mass-shootings. Life was simpler back then because we *devoutly* lived under the **Laws** of **The God of the Bible.** In those days, people remembered that America was indeed birthed: One Nation under **God**! And I'm here to testify that our Godly Ancestors *did* legislate morality because America was a much more "Moral Society" back when they did. They knew that people **aren't** moral; they have to be **made** to be moral. But since their day, one Christian after another in America has just shut up, sat down and handed our Country over to satan's cronies – who are very close to totally taking over our used-to-be-Christian Nation. Now here's the situation; while Christians are wringing their hands and saying, *"You can't legislate morality,"* the *ungodly* are as busy as bees legislating **immorality** day after day after day. As I look around America today, I can clearly see that Christians are just dropping like flies. **"A Righteous man falling down before the wicked is as a troubled fountain, and a corrupt spring"** (Proverbs 25:26).

Where have all the Strong Christians gone? Seems to me, they have gone to graveyards everyone ... *long time ago.* When will we ever learn that if we don't stand strong for our God and give all we've got for His **Truth**, satan will *take* all we've got with his **lies!** *Satan* is the evil-one who has robbed our children of the wonderful privilege of growing up in a *Christian Nation.* Ungodly people have ripped *America's **Christian** Heritage* from their text books so that they can't even read about it, for pity's sake! Chalk another one up for wicked satan and *his* crowd as he wins another victory for *his* kingdom over Jesus' disciples and *His* Kingdom.

America's "public enemy number-one" is trying very hard to infect *all of us* with a good case of *insanity. Really!* Satan has taken over in America, and just like an evil dictator, he has sent most American Citizens to "Re-education Camps." With invisible demonic-chains around their souls, parents in satan's Camps are "convinced" that they *must* ask their young children which sex they want to be (the sex *God created* them to be is irrelevant ... because **God** is irrelevant). And until the child decides, the parents must not refer to them with gender names or pronouns. Satan's "new rules" don't allow parents to treat their child as a boy or a girl because *the child* is the one who must choose "its" own sex and name. *No wonder we have so many children in adult bodies in Washington trying to run our Country.*

In satan's "Re-education Camps," Americans are forcibly "inoculated" with the belief that engaging in homosexual sex *or* altering your birth-sex is so wonderful that it's actually the best way to go. *Yes!* What your evil slave-master *doesn't* tell you is that it's the best way to go deeper and deeper into his tangled wicked web that sucks you in and entraps you in **sins** you can't free yourself from. As satan's trapped victim, you are helpless to protect yourself from all the **poisonous sins** he injects into your **soul** – which he ultimately destroys. *Mercy Me!*

Prisoners in satan's "Re-education Camps" are also taught that "drag queens" are the perfect role-models for your young children – you know, the same ones you're brainwashing into believing that *they* must choose which sex they want to be *and* which sex they want to "marry." The homosexual indoctrination our children get in School these days is evil enough, but *now*, satan has the American Library Association on board for his "Drag Queen Story Hour" in Public Libraries *(can you believe*

it?!!). The first time I ever heard about drag queens, I was told that they are homosexual men who dress up like women and walk the streets at night looking for other homosexuals to pick them up and pay them for a night of perverted sex (now that's dragging the bottom of the barrel). Well, they are no longer just walking the streets at night. Nope, they are *now* being used by satan himself in Public Libraries and Schools across our Land to wickedly corrupt the next generation of Americans by teaching them the evil *lie* that sinful, perverted lifestyles are to be embraced and even celebrated. And only someone who has graduated from satan's "Re-education Camps" with honors would ever allow their children to be exposed to such. Where are the **Christians** outraged over this demonic activity?! I have a friend who says, *"My husband makes me crazy!!"* When you are "married" to *satan*, he does the same thing to **you**. *There's a hole in our soul where God once was – somebody's making us "Crazy"!! (his initials are: **s.a.t.a.n.**!!)*

(*Breaking News*: The US Supreme Court has just forced on *the entire Country* the abominable decision that homosexuality and transgenderism are now "Protected Civil Rights." The Justices who voted for it gave us a legally irresponsible, morally corrupt, reason-defying, ungodly decision. And satan *loved* it; *now* more homosexuals and transgenders than ever are going to be winning their cases against **Christians** in court. It seems that all it takes to get *"special treatment, protection and privileges"* in this Country these days is to just live a **sinful lifestyle**!! But let's look at the facts, Folks; then make our *own* judgment. Our skin color and sex are **God-given** – we don't choose either. Therefore, *their* protection *is* a civil right. *However*, homosexuality and transgenderism are **not** "God-given" (regardless of *what* they try to tell us). Nope, they are *sinful lifestyles* **chosen** by sinful people. Therefore, any "common-sense person" *knows* that they **do not** merit "special protection." The confused Justices who voted for this said that we can't discriminate against people because of their sex – and I totally agree. However, I totally **disagree** with those Justices' "definition" of our sex. Your sex is determined by the sex organs you are born with (male or female) – **not** by what you *choose to do* with your sex organs after you are born *(where is common-sense-intelligence when you need it?)*. Therefore, homosexuality is **not** your "sex" – it is the sinful lifestyle you are *choosing* to live. **The Lord Jesus** tells us in His **Holy Word** that only a **male** and a **female** can marry and become

"one flesh" (a child) (Mark 10:5-9). The Lord calls homosexuality an *abomination* (Leviticus 18:22). *God* clearly gives the same punishment for *homosexuality* as He does for *murder* (Leviticus 20:13). *And yet*, sinful man has legalized and protected *homosexuality!! Hmmm – just wait 'til the murderers get wind of this.* Yes sir, now that homosexuals have been granted "Special Rights," murderers are going to say that *they* were born that way too (yep, they've just got a "murder-gene"); therefore, *they* deserve special rights as well – and the Supreme Court will *have to* grant it to them. As ridiculous as that sounds, it is *absolutely true* ... because *God* makes no difference between those two *sins*. Since they are equal in *God's* eyes, they must be equal in man's eyes. If our Government is going to *legalize* and *protect one*, it has to *legalize* and *protect* them *both*. Otherwise, murderers will be marching down our streets and leading riots in our prisons demanding "Social Justice!" I truly wish our *Christian Founding Fathers* could come back. They had *Godly Wisdom* as well as *common sense*, and they *knew* who was "morally and mentally unfit for the bench." Godly, sensible *Christians* can *see* the *truth:* It was *God* Who was on trial in that Courtroom that day, and those ungodly judges voted *against God* and *for satan!! Lord, have Mercy!! But God* is still *God*, and *He* is the *Chief Justice* of the *True Supreme Court. He* is going to "Judge" *them* one day – and whatever His *Final Decision* is, there will be no other court to which they can appeal. *This issue will get everyone off the fence – either God and His Word are True, or ... God and His Word are false.*)

Sadly, satan has lots of "honor students" in our Country today. One campaigned to be President and vowed to take away the tax-exempt status of all Churches and religious organizations that refused to *totally embrace* the homosexual *and* transgender lifestyles. He was actually demanding that Christians reject *their very God* (the God of the Bible) and embrace *his god* (satan). *What is this world coming to?* I'll tell you. *Right now*, it's coming to satan and bowing down before *him*. *But Jesus* is the *True King* of this Universe, and the day *is* coming when time shall be no more. *Then*, every soul *will come* to *King Jesus* and bow down very low before His Majestic Throne of Judgment as they confess: *"Jesus Christ is LORD!" Worthy is the Lamb upon His Throne!!*

All of satan's prisoners are put on a starvation diet of absolutely *no* Bread of Life (Biblical Teachings of Jesus) or Heavenly Manna (God's Word). Spiritually malnourished children and young folks are also sent

to "Re-education Camps," aka Public Schools and Colleges. There, the supreme evil dictator of "the world" forces his homosexual, transgender, fornication, false religion, atheist, Communist, humanist, anti-God indoctrination on them. The devil's plan is to control the young folks, resulting in him eventually controlling the entire Country. Satan does this by sending many of his best "honor graduates" into our Schools and Colleges as teachers and professors who tell their students that they have been "indoctrinated" by their parents for years, *but now* they will be "educated." (Hitler would be so proud of them.) These satan-followers teach our children that their sex organs **do not** determine their sex. How insane is **that?!!** Now, Folks, either they're crazy, or we're crazy. The way I see it, satan is turning our Country into one big insane asylum with the inmates running the asylum – and if you're going along with it, *you're as crazy as they are!! May God have Mercy on America!!*

What is so amazing to me is *how many people* in our "One Nation under God" are actually going right along with satan's insanity and unbelievable sinful behavior. It's almost like America's "public enemy number-one" has put something in our drinking water, for pity's sake. *"There is a madness in the air!!"* (Mark Steyn). *But,* in your wildest imagination, could you *ever* see our Godly Ancestors bowing down to satan and accepting such craziness and wickedness? Me neither. If they could come back today, they would surely declare that they had landed on the wrong Planet. *Our* only hope is to do what they did – keep looking unto **Jesus,** Who gives us sanity in the midst of all the insanity swirling around us. *"It takes a special kind of stupid to be compliant with all the leftist craziness going on these days. But if you disagree with any of their nuttiness and refuse to acquiesce to it, you're condemned as 'an enemy of the State'."* (Rush Limbaugh).

Our Christian Ancestors strictly enforced *their* Laws against "public indecency" and ungodly **sins.** Back when *they* were in charge, a marching band performed during halftime at football games. You say, *"That's too dull and boring."* Well, unless your kid was in the band, you could make a pit-stop and get something to eat and drink without missing any of the game. But the best part was that we didn't leave there in a frenzy to go out and commit *sexual immorality.* Nor did we have to carry around ungodly mental videos in our brains for the rest of our lives. Pornographic images burn themselves into *your very* **soul** – and you

know it's true. If *you* are watching pornography and saying, *"It's OK; it's a victimless crime,"* let me warn you: *You* are falling for satan's *big lie.* Here's the truth: Even though you just *love* having your own personal "sex slaves" who are willing to do such sinful, immoral, degrading, wicked things for you, these people (created by God in His Image) must strip themselves of any human dignity, common decency or moral character in order to please you. But that's OK with you because you *love* joining them in their wickedness – which strips **you** of any human dignity, common decency or moral character. You are defiantly **sinning** against God … and you know it. After spending some *private time* with your sex-slaves and getting "down and dirty" with them, you **feel** down, dirty, defiled and *guilty* – and there's not a fig leaf in the world large enough to cover your **sin** before **Holy God.** Pornography isn't victimless. **You are the victim!!** *America* is also the victim because she's a Nation full of people just like you – addicted to corrupting themselves with demonic filth. Satanic pornography is one of the devil's favorite ways of using "the lust of your flesh" to destroy your **soul!** When you open your soul up to such wickedness, you open it up to demons … that flood into every corner and wreck your life from the inside out. Open your soul up to the **Lord Jesus** instead, and **He** will flood into every corner, giving you "New Life" from the inside out.

Sometimes (when Jesus isn't looking), I allow "Molly" to take me over (like an alien space-monster), and I think things like: *If America continues to allow all of this to keep on happening unhindered, unbridled and unopposed … well … she deserves what she gets.* **But Jesus** quickly glances over at me to see if I'm behaving myself … and I know I'm in *big trouble.* So, I fight off **Alien-Space-Monster-Molly** and become Jesus' Little Lamb once again. That's when He hands me my "Jesus Glasses." I put them on, and … *Wa La* … I can *see* once again! I see that *I* am part of the problem – which means that I can also be part of the solution. *Yes!!* So here's the situation; America's morals will remain on the "alley-cat" level until *I (and you)* start bringing her people back to the **God** Who created them and loves them. God loves them so much that He sent His own Dear Son to die for them in order to free them from their bondage to **satan.** *Praise to the Perfect Lamb of God!!* So here's the strategy; our Lord is looking to **us Christians** to bring those poor deluded victims of satan into **Jesus' Re-education Camp,** aka **The Church,** where they will get

Jesus' Living Water! When *that* happens, America will be "One Nation under God" once again. So, we Christians with "Jesus in us" are *God's Supernatural Solution* for a wayward Nation full of people with "satan in them." Now, I know what you're thinking, *"It's impossible to ever turn this ungodly culture around!"* But I'm thinking, *"**Christians** can turn America around ... if every one of us will become a Sold-Out-to-Jesus Evangelist who takes the task upon ourselves to 'be Jesus' to as many lost folks as we possibly can. With God all things are possible!"*

America's Founding Fathers answered *their* "Call" from God and pledged their lives, their fortunes and their sacred honor in order to give *us* the freedom to live "free under God." *But satan* (the ultimate con-artist) has conned America into abandoning her **God** in favor of *his* "candy." Instead of being "free in Christ," Americans are increasingly choosing to be "free from Christ." That translates into "being able to publicly commit almost any sin you want to" because, after all, America is a "free Country." Yep, she's free alright – free from **God** and in bondage to **satan**. Once you eat of the devil's evil "candy," you *must* keep coming back and coming back and coming back again and again and again for another "fix." America is having an "integrity crisis," and if she doesn't wholeheartedly return to **God**, she will soon be having an "end-of-life crisis." *"America is great because she is good. If America ever ceases to be good, she will cease to be great"* (Alexis de Tocqueville).

Our brave, committed **Founding Fathers** suffered, sacrificed and even died to make America "One Nation under **God**!" *But today*, ungodly governing officials all over our Land and in Washington, DC are in league with the **devil** to make America "One Nation under satan." And just how did all those ungodly politicians get in control? Sad answer: They were voted into office by America's own Citizens – who *love* being "free from God." After every election, I shudder to see how many ungodly people there are in our used-to-be-Christian Nation who voted for ungodly candidates. I just don't get it; they hate the candidates who love America and love the ones who hate America. How could so many American Citizens be so clueless as to actually vote to destroy their own Country? Who would vote for such demonic people? *"Americans get the kind of leadership they deserve"* (Adrian Rogers).

Now, I know what you're thinking, *"How dare you use such harsh words to describe such nice people!"* Well, those "nice people" are

DARE to be JESUS

against everything our **Holy God** is *for*, and they are *for* everything our **Holy God** is *against*. They are *against* our **Constitution** and the *"America"* our **Founding Fathers** gave us. They are *for* removing **God** (and **Christians**) from our Government and the entire Nation if possible. They cheer laws that legalize ungodly sins of *every* kind! They are *for* putting billions and billions of **our** tax-payer dollars into the pockets of people, organizations, companies and foreign Countries who are on-board with their evil agenda (and will funnel plenty of it back to *them*). Their goal is to totally bankrupt our Government so that they can achieve their *ultimate goal* of turning America into a godless Communist Country – which they are doing right in front of our very eyes, for pity's sake! Just like the evil-one they belong to, those "nice people" **lie** and hide the truth from the people of America in order to keep them under their demonic control (with the "fake-news networks" all-in on the scam).

No doubt about it, believing in God and His Son has fallen on hard times of late, and if you're like me, your heart is crying out, *"Lord, why is all this happening?!"* Perhaps, it's Habakkuk all over again, and God is using ungodly people to thrash *His* people … for our own good. Just as David used Goliath's own sword to defeat him, we Christians can pray that our Lord will use their own wickedness to defeat *them*. We can also pray that Jesus' Church won't wait until it's too late to "Wake Up" and realize that one of the largest "Mission Fields" in the world is right here in the Good Ole USA … because no Nation can reject the **True God** and endure. My Friend, **you** can intervene in America's demise by bringing the **Living God** she is rejecting back into her midst. America will be at peace when her people are at peace, and they will only find *True Peace* in the Presence of **Jesus**. *Proclaiming **Jesus** is the Victory that overcomes satan's evil world!!*

In 1865, President Lincoln abolished slavery in America, right? Wrong. Slavery is still thriving here because millions of people are *still* in bondage … to **satan**. *Mercy Me!* Spiritually dead slaves of that demon follow him because they don't realize they are actually following *satan*. *Spiritually Alive* followers of Christ must let "Jesus in us" open the *Spiritual Eyes* of those lost folks to the *reality* of the "Spiritual Realm" – where *only two* "Spiritual Kingdoms" exist: God's Righteous Eternal Kingdom and satan's evil kingdom of sin and death (which God presently *allows* to exist). Those are their **only**

two options. *So* ... they are either in God's Kingdom following **King Jesus**, *or* ... they are in satan's evil kingdom following the dead-end loser. Two kingdoms – two *very* different leaders. We Born-Again Christians have a different God from unbelievers. Our God loves them and wants them in *His* Kingdom. Their "god" hates Jesus so much he tried to get rid of Him at Calvary. **But Jesus** has shown up again in us Christians, and *now*, satan is leveling everything in his arsenal at *us* to get rid of *us*. We are the *only ones* standing in the way of his *total* take-over of America. Folks, we're not in a "culture war" ... we're in a **"Kingdom war!"** The winner of that war will be the "Supreme Lawgiver" in America – either God or satan. And shifty satan is getting closer and closer to total victory because he has convinced everyone (except Born-Again Christians) that morality should be decided by "the consensus of society" ... *not* by our **Creator God.** You can legally do "whatever" you want to in America these days just by getting enough people to go along with you. *"We now have morality-by-majority in America."* (Adrian Rogers).

They took a survey and discovered that most Americans don't want **God** telling them what to do anymore. *So*, God and His Word (the Bible) are no longer sought out, consulted or even considered. God is just an ole-fashioned, out-of-date, out-of-vogue idea. *Man* is now "god" and perfectly able to decide *on his own* what is best for him ... **to the destruction of his soul** (satan's ultimate goal for all mankind). *"Satan offers to fix you up with his 'medicine,' aka the sinful things of this world, but he hides the 'warning' on the label: If you take this 'medicine' ... it can kill you!"* (Tony Evans).

You have probably heard a little child quote John 3:16 by saying, *"For God so loved the world, that He gave His only forgotten Son ..."* We smile at the innocence of a little child, but, sad to say, America lost *her* innocence years ago. It was around the same time she forgot about God's Son Jesus. Alexander Solzhenitsyn spoke at Harvard in 1978 and said, *"The Russian Revolution killed 60 million Russians for one reason: We had forgotten GOD!! The same thing is happening here in America. You have lost your courage to confront evil. You have forgotten GOD!!"* His words were met with *rage* as he was *"booed"* off the stage! Those young followers-of-satan were *"booing"* *anyone* who would dare to confront them (and their

godlessness) with God's Truth. After all, this is America; they had the "right" to choose. And their children are still around today … still choosing *godlessness* … and still "*booing*" us Christians off the stage!

Wake Up, America!! Satan's throne isn't in hell. Nope, it's in Hollywood. It's in every Public School and College in America. It's in the corporate world and the media world where his cronies *love* pushing his evil agenda. Satan has even been known to wear a black robe and "vote in" his ungodly laws; then bring down his demon-empowered gavel to enforce them. And in case you're wondering who enthroned satan in America, I'll tell you. It was Christians. Yep, Christians – who failed to tell satan's slaves about **"The Saviour"** Who has the *Power* to *Save* them and free them from satan's grasp. Over the years, millions of immigrants have poured into America … without the Lord Jesus. They *think* their religion is all they need to make it into Heaven; they don't realize that the evil-one they belong to has them deceived. Sadly, Christians have failed to introduce them to the **Lord Jesus** by giving them **God's Gospel Truth.** Christians have even failed to evangelize *their own children*, for pity's sake. But starting today, you Christian Parents can help dethrone satan in America by dethroning satan in *your own home*. For instance, have you listened to the *words* of the "music" your kids are listening to? Satan knows the powerful, controlling impact music has over a person, and he loves it when they listen to *his*. He uses it to enter deep within a person's **soul** with his evil agenda. In fact, satan is holding an entire generation captive with his "music."

(Side-note: When I go to *The Symphony*, I look around at mostly older folks and wonder what is going to happen to music in America when *we* all die. So, I have a plan. Since you Parents punish your kids these days by putting them in "time-out" by themselves, why not *really* punish them by forcing them to listen to **Classical Music** while in solitary confinement? That would greatly cut down on their "crimes" while building up their character by exposing them to the **Greatest Music In The World** – the music of the **Grand Masters.** *Yes!* And as you play **Classical Music** in the background, play the **Bible** on CD over it! *Hide the Word in their hearts!!* The Lord would absolutely love it! **You** can be a "Rebel with a Cause" and *escape* from satan's "Re-education Camp!" And don't let your children be held captive

there either. Sneak them past that evil warden and bring them with you into **"Jesus' World!"** Then, put something into them satan can't take away. You may even live to hear them thank you for it. In fact, you may even enjoy it yourself. *Miracles happen every day!* {Do you suppose this idea would work in our prisons as well, or would the prisoners just sue the Government for "cruel and unusual punishment"?})

A studied look at the lives of people you know clearly reveals the fact that a person's "character" is the sum total of the choices they make. That is true of a person *or* a nation. America has made so many *ungodly choices* that she has little integrity or decency left. America is the loser; *satan* is the winner. And that ole devil gleefully does his wicked victory dance on top of a grave with a tombstone which reads:

"United States of America: One Nation under God.

Born: Eighteenth Century – Died: Twentieth Century."

Then, satan arrogantly takes his seat upon the throne of: *"United States of America: One Nation under the god of this world."* I don't know about you, my Friend, but I don't feel at home in this world anymore. Even worse, I feel like the disciples felt the day Jesus was crucified: *"It's all over! We're done! ALL is lost! We haven't got a chance!"* **But God** calms my anxious heart and reminds me that **He** is *still* **God**, *still* on His Throne and *forever more Powerful* than satan *(Hmmm)*. So ... what is our All-Powerful God **doing** on His Throne? Well, I'll tell you one thing He has done. In His Great Love, Mercy and Grace, God has *Gloriously Saved me* and has come to "live" in *me* in the Person of His Son's Spirit. *Hallelujah!!* Now, the Lord is able to speak His Anointed Gospel to folks He brings across *my* path. God didn't lose the battle to satan in *me!* God is *Victorious* over the devil in *me!* The Lord has at least *one* in-road into satan's evil kingdom of darkness ... in *me.* That devil *thinks* he has this whole world exactly where he wants it. *Surprise! Surprise! He doesn't have **me**!* *"For the prince of this world cometh, and he hath nothing in Me!"* Signed: Jehovah Jesus (John 14:30).

Now granted, I'm only one person, and I seem quite small and weak compared to all those high-powered *really important people* out in this world. But even though I'm only one, *I AM ONE.* And although I can't do everything, *I CAN DO SOMETHING.* And since I can do *something*, by the Grace of God and with His help, *I WILL DO THAT SOMETHING* I can do (and *ought* to do). How 'bout you? You wanna make it two? *We* could be the "two small fishes" Jesus uses to feed a lot of hungry people. *"There is a lad here who hath five barley loaves and two small fishes, but what are they among so many?"* (John 6:9).

Years ago, I heard Reinhard Bonnke speak, and he said something like this: *"When my Lord first 'called' me, I was just a zero. But I soon found out that **Jesus** is 'Number-One!' And when this zero stands beside The Perfect Number-One, you get a 'Perfect 10!' Now, if I can get another zero to join me, and you put The Perfect Number-One in front of us two zeros, you get a 'Perfect 100!' If we can get a third person to join us, then we're up to 1,000! If we get a fourth, we're up to 10,000! A fifth would be 100,000! A sixth would be 1,000,000, and so forth."* Isn't that a fantastic way to look at the *Supernatural Power* we Christians have when we join our hands, our hearts and our "Anointed Lives" together for our Lord Jesus? Imagine for a minute what a bunch of us Christians with the *Living Christ* "Alive in us" could do if we ever caught *Holy Spirit Fire* together!! *But* if we ever forget that it is *Jesus* Who is in front of all us zeroes, *then* what have we got? Answer: 000000. Jesus said, *"Without **Me** you can do 0!"* The difference between a zero and a hero is *Jesus*! *"One of the greatest joys in life is the feeling you get when you realize you're a part of something larger than your own life and personal experiences"* (Nick Vujicic).

Together, we Christians can catch the vision of a "New America" – with *God* upon her throne. However, there are "giants" in the Land; led by the giant of all demons, satan himself. Our adversary has an army of organized, determined slaves who are hell-bent on overcoming and getting rid of us "out-of-touch Christians." Now is the time for all of us "in-touch-with-Jesus Christians" to touch each other in faith, love and determination in order to *stand with* our Lord Jesus as we *stand against* satan and his slaves. Like those brave American Patriots in the Alamo, you and I are Jesus' last stand in America today. *"Yet I have left*

Me seven thousand in Israel, all the knees which have not bowed unto Baal, and every mouth which hath not kissed him" Signed: *Jehovah Jesus* (I Kings 19:18).

Jehovah Jesus is "calling" every Christian to *join* this fierce battle going on in the "Spiritual Realm" over the *Soul* of America. Folks, the battle lines have been drawn, and *we* are the only people here who are *not* under satan's control. America's only hope is *"Jesus in us."* This war will never be won if Christians just go to Church on Sunday but do nothing more during the week to try and reach those poor souls being held firmly in satan's grip. Let's start by entering into a "Spiritual Covenant" with each other and our *King Jesus*: We hereby agree that with the *Power of Christ* working through *us*, evil satan will *not* take America! *No!* We are going to *"Pray!"* and give the Gospel of Jesus Christ to those He brings across our path. We are going to find ways (many ways) to reach the *young folks* of our Country so that America will *not* be a totally demonic caliphate before our grandchildren die. Now, I know how you feel, *"Lord, two hundred penny worth of bread would not be sufficient to feed all these lost, hungry people!"* But **Jesus** is here to remind you of *Who* He is … and *where* He is. This hungry world needs **Jesus** – Who is "living" in *you*. **Jesus Lives!** And He speaks to us deep in our heart, *"My Dear Child, just one bite of **Me**, the Bread of Life (the Heavenly Manna sent down from the Father above) is all the hungry soul needs to be Saved from a life of famine in the wilderness of sin. Just give them **Jesus**!"*

"Be of good courage, and He shall strengthen your heart, all ye that hope in The Lord!" (Psalm 31:24). Christian Friend, pray for *courage*; then let "Jesus in you" take His *Saving Gospel* to those needy souls everywhere you look. *Together*, we will trust God that America's *greatest years* are yet ahead of her; He didn't bring her this far just to let her "fall" to His enemy now. Two thousand years ago in Israel, our Lord Jesus cast the demons out of demonized people who were brought to Him. Now is the time for us Christians to bring our needy Country to the feet of our Lord and pray, *"Lord, we bring our demonized Country to You and ask You to please have Mercy on America. Forgive us our sins and cast out satan's demonic power over America. We promise we'll help You, Lord … we'll have to … we're Your only Body and Soul on this Earth! Thank You, Lord, for*

*Your Faithfulness to America; for all You have done, all You are doing and all You are going to do. Lord, Bless our Great Country. Make America **Godly** Again! In the Mighty Name of Jesus, Amen."* **"And I will give them a heart to know Me, that I AM The LORD: And they shall be My People, and I Will be their God: For they shall return unto Me with their whole heart!" Signed: Jehovah Jesus** (Jeremiah 24:7).

In the previous chapter, I stated that the devil is "less than brilliant," but there *is* one thing he's good at. Satan is an expert at giving people more than enough of everything they need to self-destruct. America is his poster-child for that strategy. If America had started out in the Garden of Eden, satan would have run out of "forbidden apples" to dangle in her face so quickly that he would have gotten totally disgusted with all the apple cores on the ground ... and probably up left himself. I know, I know ... satan wouldn't have really left; he would have just danced with glee – the same way he's doing in the Good Ole USA today. Our Nation has managed to acquire all the desires of her heart, but tragically, her rejection of her **God** has brought leanness into her **Soul.** Only Christians can revive America with "The Bread of Life" (the Lord Jesus) Who speaks forth "Words of Spiritual Life." My Christian Friend, let **"Jesus in you"** speak to lost souls every day – *through you.* I realize that I'm just the voice of one crying in the wilderness, but I'm speaking to anyone who has ears to hear. Dare to "be Saint Telemachus" to this satan-following, sin-loving, God-hating society and cry out, **"In the Name of CHRIST – Forebear!!"**

Someone *must* step out into "The Arena" of *this* Land and stand against satan's wicked take-over of our dearly beloved used-to-be-Christian Country! **Someone** *must* bring her back to the God Who birthed her *and* still loves her. Our Nation's history is very clear: **America was founded a Christian Nation.** The vast majority of Colonists were **Christians,** and God greatly blessed America. This Nation is unique and exceptional because she was founded by **God** to always be a force for **"Christian Good"** in our world. *Blessed is the Nation whose God is The Lord!* Today, Christians must *humbly, sincerely* and *fervently* call on the True and Living God (the God of the Bible) the same way the Colonists did. Americans can sing "God Bless America" all they want, *but* until this Nation born in 1776 is

"Born Again" by repenting, returning to God and forsaking all of her *legalized sin*, she won't be *truly blessed* by God. **"Compared with ancient civilizations, America was born yesterday. But, and here is the rub – she is dying today, and she will be dead tomorrow unless there is a Spiritual Awakening!!" (Leonard Ravenhill).**

We Christians are fighting "Spiritual Battles," and we win with "Spiritual Weapons." We win by *believing, obeying* and *standing (and standing)* on God's Truth, the **Bible**. We win by *loving, praising, trusting* and *obeying* our **Wonderful Saviour** as we allow Him to send us into this lost world *equipped* with the *Gospel of Christ* and *empowered* by the *Anointing of God* to do a "Great Work" for Him and His Eternal Kingdom. We Little Lambs win by *praying* to our **Good Shepherd** Who carries us in His Strong Arms and lifts us up high above those evil wolves nipping at us from below. Ah, but some of those evil wolves are actually future Little Lambs. **"Jesus in us"** will draw them to His Cross through the *Power* of His **Holy Spirit** and the **"Word of our Testimony"** freely given to all.

Do you see any people around *you* who need Jesus? From where *I* stand, I wonder if *America* is Ezekiel's valley of dead, dry bones. If she is, only Born-Again Christians can speak *God's Glorious Good News* of "New Life in Christ" into her ... one soul at a time. **You** can start with that one lost person who will be right there in front of you *today* (or tomorrow, if you're reading this in bed ... unless that lost person is lying beside you). I'm sure you remember well the very moment *you* "heard" the *Voice of Jesus* as He spoke "New Life!" into your soul and raised *you* from the dead. *Now*, His Voice will raise *others* from the dead – and it will sound just like **yours**. *The hour is come that the Son of Man should be Glorified!!*

"No man can come to Me except The Father Who hath sent Me draw him" Signed: Jesus (John 6:44). God the Father bids people and draws them to Jesus by means of His Servant, the Holy Spirit. However, the Spirit of Christ is ... *a Spirit*. He needs a *physical body* to walk around in so that He can draw people to Jesus. Do you suppose He could use yours? He *will* use yours – if you will just *let Him*. When you allow *Christ's Spirit* to speak forth the Supernatural, Anointed Words of the Gospel of Jesus Christ through **you**, you are on very Holy Ground. Witnessing is such a Holy Work of God we should go out witnessing

barefoot. At the burning bush, God spoke *to* Moses. When God's Words were *received, believed* and *acted on* by Moses, God was able to speak *through* Moses. If you are a Born-Again Christian, God speaks to *you* – through His Holy Spirit, the Bible, prayer and other people. After receiving and believing God's Words, you are ready to take your Rod of God ("Jesus in you") and go find a lost person so that **Jesus** can speak to them – through *you*. As you go out witnessing, keep in mind that it isn't what you say *to* a lost person that gets them *Saved* but what the **Lord Jesus** says *in* them that has an impact on their life. When your Lord brings a "Called-Out One" across your path, He not only speaks *to* their soul, He also speaks *in* their soul with the *Voice of His Spirit* (Who is using *your* spirit, soul and mouth). Therefore, the folks who get *Saved* have "heard" the *Spirit of Christ* speaking to them in *their spirit*. Allow "Jesus in you" to be the "Fisher of men" *through* you as you treat *everyone* you witness to as a "Called-Out One" … and souls will be brought into the Kingdom of God! *"Only Jesus can impact a person with soul-bending Faith"* (Mark Dever).

"The Words that I speak unto you, they are Spirit, and they are Life" Signed: Jesus (John 6:63). Now, I know what you're thinking, *"Even though I'm a Christian, my words could never be powerful like* **Jesus'** *Words" (Hmmm).* Well, let me tell you about my friend Sam. He witnesses to people in a very powerful way. Sam engages them in a conversation and eventually gets around to asking, *"Are you in any pain today?"* If they answer, *"Yes,"* Sam asks, *"May I pray for you?"* They usually say *"Yes,"* and Sam discreetly places his hand on or over their pain as he prays to the Lord Jesus to heal them. Then, Sam asks, *"How's your pain now?"* They usually reply, *"Better (or, It's gone!). How'd you do that?"* Sam tells them it was the **Lord Jesus** working through him Who healed their pain. Then, he gets the chance to tell them about the Saviour. I asked Sam one time how he acquired such a wonderful *Gift.* I have never forgotten what he told me, *"Years ago, I was in deep prayer when the Lord suddenly spoke to me very clearly and said, 'Sam! If you will put your life completely in My Hands, your hands will be My Hands!'"* And the rest, as they say, is history (His Story). Listen closely, my Christian Friend, your Lord Jesus is still clearly speaking,

"My Precious Child,
if you will sincerely put your life completely in My Hands,
your hands will be My Hands; your mind will be My Mind;
your heart will be My Heart; your body will be My Body;
your life will be My Life, and your words ... My Words!"

When Jesus walked this Earth, His words had the *Power* to give "Spiritual Life" to those who had "Spiritual Ears" to hear them. *"My sheep hear My Voice, and I know them, and they follow Me!"* Signed: Jesus (John 10:27). When Jesus brings one of His "Called-Out Ones" across *your* path, the words of "Jesus in you" have the same *Power!* *"He that heareth you, heareth Me!"* (Luke 10:16). Jesus' promise is to *anyone* who will listen for His Voice and truly follow Him by **letting** *His Love, His Life* and *His Words* flow out of *them.* Our Lord's eyes are even now sweeping across our Land, looking for **someone** who will **trust Him** enough to step up, step out and dare to **"be Jesus"** to America. *"For the eyes of The LORD run to and fro throughout the whole Earth, to show Himself strong in the behalf of them whose heart is perfect toward Him"* (II Chronicles 16:9). Would **you** dare to be that person? **If not you – who? If not now – when? If not here – where? If not The Kingdom of God – what?**

Jesus is standing still; time is standing still ... as Jesus' eyes are riveted on **you.** So, be of good comfort. *Arise!* Cast aside your fear and doubt ... and come to **JESUS.** He is calling for **you!**

"My Dear Child, please. For My sake, Please, be that person.
I have already chosen you. Now, I AM asking of you,
Please, choose ME!!
You're drawing your water from the wrong wells –
the wells of this world.
Come!! Let Me give you Living Water from the
Eternal Well in My World,
and you will never again thirst for the fleeting,
vain things of Earth.

201

Yield yourself to Me; let Me use you to build My Eternal Kingdom.
I AM going to do many Mighty Works through you because
I AM in you always!!" Signed: Jesus

Years ago, an atheist got *Saved* while listening to a Pastor preach a long series of sermons on the radio. When the man got in touch with the Pastor to tell him about it, the Pastor asked, *"Since you were an atheist who didn't believe in God, why did you spend all that time listening to me preach about Him?"* The man answered, *"Well, Pastor, it's true that I didn't believe in God, and I didn't believe a word you were saying; but listening to you preach, I could tell,* **you sure did!"** Christian, that lost person you're witnessing to will instinctively *know* if you really believe what you say you believe. So, make sure you absolutely *know* that **"Jesus in you"** is **The One** speaking His **Gospel Truth** to that lost person *through you* ... as His **Holy Spirit** convinces them it is **Absolute Truth!** The Power of the Spirit of Christ Jesus "living in **you**" works the Miracle of Salvation in a lost soul. *Surrender* to His Will and *let Him* speak through **you**. The more you allow your Lord to be *Victorious* in *you*, the more your Lord is *Victorious* in *this world!* **Jesus** overcame satan, and He has given us Christians the *Power* to overcome him as well. Every time we let **Jesus** tell a lost soul about Himself through **us**, we're overcoming satan. **"And they overcame (satan) by the Blood of The Lamb, and by the word of their testimony!"** (Revelation 12:11).

I sometimes hear Christians say that our world is so bad and so wicked that we need to cry out to God to send Jesus back soon. When are those people ever going to realize: **Jesus is already here!** He is here "living" on the inside of millions of Christians – who don't think they matter. They don't think they have *any Power* to do *anything* for God. They think that if they ever tried to do something for the Lord, it would *never* count for *anything* in Jesus' Eternal Kingdom. Simply stated, they are suffering from the paralysis of analysis. Is that you? Well, let me help you analyze the situation. Back in the Garden of Eden, the only weapon satan had to use against sweet Eve was ... *lies.* Today, he figures that if it worked on Eve, it will *surely* work on *you.* So, he lies to you. Then, it's up to you. You must choose to believe the devil's

lies *or* … believe **God's Truth**. The deceiver (satan) yells at you, *"Hey Loser, you're just a **nobody** who knows absolutely **nothing** about 'Spiritual things.' Therefore, **nobody** would **ever** listen to **anything** you ever tried to say about **Jesus**!"* (*Now* you know where those thoughts are coming from.) **But Jesus** lovingly whispers the Truth to your heart: *"My Precious Child, you may be a nobody to this world, but you are loved with an **Everlasting Love** by the **King of Heaven**! So, you are definitely **'Somebody'** to **Me**! In My Great Love, I Redeemed you with My Blood and have taken up residence within your inner spirit-man. And today, **I've** got plenty to say … using **your** mouth!"*

Christian Friend, the Spirit of **"Christ in you"** is just chomping at the bit to get in front of a lost person so that **He** can tell them: *"Listen up! Jesus loves you! You can be 'Somebody' to **Jesus**! Let me tell you how."* "Jesus in you" will silence those stones – *but you have to **let Him**.* So now that satan's lies have run into your Lord's Truth, you have a choice to make. You can choose to let **Jesus' Truth** demolish satan's lies, *or* … you can choose to let satan keep you believing that you will *never* be anything but a "Spiritual whimp."

"A man went into a pet shop one day
where a talking parrot was sitting on a perch.
When it saw the man, it yelled out,
'Hey, Mister! You ain't nothin' but a punk!'
The man was shocked but ignored the ill-mannered bird.
A few days later, the man went back to the pet shop.
The same parrot saw him and yelled,
'Hey, Mister! You ain't nothin' but a punk!'
Once again, the man just ignored the bird. A week later,
the man returned yet again. The parrot saw him and yelled,
'Hey, Mister! You ain't nothin' but a punk!'
That did it! The man found the owner of the shop and said,
'Every time I come into your shop, that
parrot insults and offends me.

You'd better do something about the way he treats your customers!'
So, the owner 'laid down the law' to the rude bird.
The next time the man entered the shop,
the parrot saw him and yelled,
'Hey, Mister! You know.'"
(Tony Evans).

So, are you going to keep listening to that demon ... you know, the one that keeps yelling at you, *"You ain't nothing but a Spiritual punk!"* While you're making up your mind, listen to a very different message sent *special delivery* to you from the very heart of your **Heavenly Father:**

"My Dear Child, in My Love, Mercy and Grace,
I sent you My Precious Son Jesus. The time has come
for you to let 'Christ in you' do what I sent Him into you to do.
Jesus does all things well. 'Jesus in you' can do anything ... but fail.
He will take your cup of cool water and turn it into a flowing
River of Life!
My Son loves pouring Eternal Life into the souls of lost folks ...
through YOU!!"

My Christian Friend, there's no time like the present to start. *Today* is the "Day of Salvation" for the lost and a "New Day of Resolve" for *you*. Never again will you let that liar satan tell you who you are. **No!** After you get through telling him who *he* is, you're going to tell him who *you* are ... in Christ Jesus. **You** are the Disciple whom **Jesus** *loves*, *Saved*, *indwells* and *empowers* to be a **Mighty Witness** for **Him!** *Yes indeed*, my Friend, you may not know everything, but you know just enough to be dangerous – to *satan!* If you will obediently go out into this needy world letting **"Jesus in you"** tell people about Himself, they will be amazed. It will absolutely *amaze* people that someone is out loose in this world actually speaking the Name of **Jesus** – and even bragging on Him boldly. What a phenomenon! I dare you to try it. **"Now therefore**

go, and I Will be with thy mouth and teach thee what thou shalt say" Signed: Jehovah Jesus (Exodus 4:12).

All things were created *by* the Lord and *for* Him (Colossians 1:16). God created **you** for Himself. Have you ever wondered why? Do you see yourself as being infinitely valuable and important to your Lord Jesus? You are, you know ... and more than you know. You are a Member of the Royal Family; **you** are a Child of **The King** of the Universe. The King Himself sealed you there when He purchased you with His own *Supernatural Royal Blood* – which is flowing through your *Spiritually Alive* spirit-man. You are now "in Christ," and Christ is now "living in you" ... and He's got some things on His Mind. Wouldn't you like to know what they are? Jesus is right there, and He's listening – *ask Him.* "Jesus in you" is waiting for you to *want* to do those things He's in you to do ... and *He's just sitting on ready!* What are *you* sitting on – the fence? *Mercy Me!*

People look at me all the time like I must be from another planet. And the truth is ... I am. I'm from *Another World*, and I'm going back there when my Lord is done with me here. Jesus sent me to Planet Earth to help Him do some "Eternal Work," and when He has used me up, He will take me up. In the meantime, I look at it like this: *Somebody* has got to do this job ... and it may as well be *me*. It may as well be *me* allowing "Jesus in me" to use *my (His)* mouth to tell lost folks about Himself. It may as well be *me* letting my Lord Jesus use *my (His)* body to finish "The Work" our Heavenly Father gave us to do. *What a privilege!* Now, what about you? Does your Lord have anything He wants to say or do using *your (His)* body? Have you asked Him lately? Jesus would love to hear from you. He would also love to put more *true meaning* and *pure joy* into your life than you ever thought possible. *The Lord is my Shepherd; He's all I want ... my cup runneth over!!*

In the Providence of God, I once met someone who had *true meaning* and *pure joy* in *his* life. It was that faithful Servant of the Lord who first witnessed to me. He was such a bold witness for Christ that he dared to just walk up to me in a public place and start telling me about **"Jesus!!"** Some folks probably told him, *"That doesn't do any good,"* **but God** knew better – and here I am *all these years later* as living proof that his bold witness for Jesus *did a lot of good!* Here's the way witnessing

works. God our Father has given His Son Jesus a "Matching Grant," and every time you tell someone about *Jesus (and He "Saves" them)*, God not only *doubles* your witness but He keeps on *multiplying* it until the end of time. *Really!* Ever heard of Edward Kimball? He was the Sunday School Teacher who led Dwight L. Moody to Christ. Wilbur Chapman received confirmation of his Salvation from Moody. Billy Sunday was mentored by Evangelist Chapman. Mordecai Ham was sent by Billy Sunday's Evangelical Group to Charlotte, N.C. in 1934 for a Crusade – during which Billy Graham was gloriously *Saved!* All of those Evangelists brought millions of people to "Salvation in Christ Jesus." Today, the descendants of those Evangelists and the millions they led to Christ are *still* bringing millions of people to Christ. God alone knows how many souls will be in Heaven because of one man (Edward Kimball) leading just one man (D.L. Moody) to our Lord and Saviour Jesus Christ! *God moves in mysterious ways His Wonders to perform!!*

If you don't think that *you* could ever be an "Edward Kimball," don't worry about it. Just spend your life (time, *same thing*) loving your Lord and pouring all of your energy into letting "Jesus in you" "be Jesus" to the folks all around you every day. Wherever you are right now is exactly where your Lord Jesus wants to use you right now. So, become a Servant of the Most High God. Then, *every deed* you do is like a stone you throw into a placid lake – the ripples of which continue out until they reach the shores of *Eternity!* It's true, my Friend, we are all going to be in Heaven in a heartbeat, and I feel so sorry for you if *no one* comes up to you and says, *"THERE YOU ARE!! YOU are the one Jesus used to get me here! Oh, thank you!! THANK YOU!!"*

I'm looking forward to saying those words to a man by the name of Earl in Heaven. I haven't seen him since he boldly told me about *"Jesus!"* and His *So Great Salvation* those many years ago. Therefore, I have asked my Lord to have Earl at the "Beautiful Gate" welcoming me Home to Heaven. Wouldn't it be wonderfully *Divine* if you spent the first part of *your* "Heavenly Life" at the Gate Beautiful welcoming Home those souls who are there because you allowed *"Jesus in you"* to tell them about Himself through *you*?! You may even be greeting folks you've never seen before who are thanking you for telling someone who told someone who told someone who told *them* about *Jesus!* And Jesus

will also be there – somewhere close by with a great big smile on His face. *"I'm so old I've forgotten where I've been … but I do know where I'm going!"* (Ken Davis).

"I have left orders to be awakened at any time during a national emergency – even if I'm in a Cabinet Meeting" (Ronald Reagan). Is your life just one long, boring "cabinet meeting" … and you've got nothing more to look forward to? Well, my Christian Friend, it's time for you to **"WAKE UP!"** and realize that America is in the middle of a **"NATIONAL EMERGENCY!!"** Each new generation in America has fewer and fewer **Christians** because the previous generation of Christians failed to pass along their *Faith in Christ.* How could so many Christians have dropped the ball (the Baton of the Gospel of Jesus Christ), and today we're wondering: *Where did the Good Ole USA go?* You know, the one that was "One Nation under God." Well, it's time for at least one person in *this* generation *(you)* to wake up and smell the fragrance of Christ Jesus; then open your eyes and *see* that God has blessed *you* so that you can *be a Blessing.* When God *Saved* you, He didn't just *Save* you for yourself. No siree, once God is *Victorious* in *you*, He has *Big Plans* to be *Victorious* in other people as well – **and YOU are His Plan!!** *Mercy Me!* *"For we preach not ourselves, but Christ Jesus the Lord; and ourselves your servants for Jesus' sake. Signed: Every Born-Again Christian* (II Corinthians 4:5).

Christian, your Lord needs three *Victories* in you in order for His Plan to work. The first *Victory* (after your Salvation) occurs the day you put your "Jesus Glasses" on and **see** that God truly *does have* a "Big Plan" for you: You are to faithfully allow "Jesus in you" to speak His Gospel *through you* to people who need Him and His Salvation. The second *Victory* occurs when you *look beyond yourself* and actually **see** those spiritually dead people, aka "lost folks," all around you who *need you* in a very important *Eternal* way. So, do you? When you look around at people, do you really *see* them? Do you see them … a hundred years from now? Do you care where they will be? When you look in the mirror, do you see a Christian looking back at you who is happy to spend the rest of their life doing anything and everything *except* that *one thing* called "witnessing"? Could it be you don't realize that God loves those lost folks as much as He loves you? His next *Victory* in you will remedy that.

The third *Victory* occurs when you sincerely "purpose in your heart" to pursue a closer, more intimate, dynamic relationship with **Jesus** – and then actually *do it* with your **whole heart.** Once you truly *love* the Lord your God with *all* your heart, soul, mind and strength, He will then turn your heart toward all those *other folks* He loves just as much as He loves you. So, open your heart up to God's Powerful Love and let it pour into (and through) your soul. When you do, your heart will grow bigger than the Grinch's heart did in Whoville that Christmas Day. And instead of giving out toys to kids, you'll be daring to let your Resident Saviour give His Glorious Gospel to lost folks all around you ... because **Jesus Himself** is the Best Gift of all. So, draw up close enough to Jesus to feel His heart beating, and you will feel it beating for and breaking over all those lost souls everywhere you look. Then, you will love Jesus enough to let Him love them through *you.*

God's Victory in you is now complete, and you are well on your way to being a Mighty Witness for your Lord. With your "Jesus Glasses" on, you are able to *see* folks all around you that Jesus wants to *"Love"* ... through you. You suddenly *see* bunches of folks you've never even noticed before that Jesus wants to *"Save"* ... through you. You can also see that *your* job is to just get out of Jesus' way and "let Him." When you do, "Jesus in you" will be an *Unstoppable Force* in God's Eternal Kingdom. **"We will have all Eternity to celebrate the Victories, but only a few hours before sunset to win them!"** (Amy Carmichael).

After writing the first half of this chapter, I felt like praying, *"Lord, would you just please wake me up when all of this is over!"* But I didn't; I already knew what He would say: *"Fret not thyself, My Child; rest in Me and wait patiently for Me. On the day of My choosing, I will wake you up from 'The Twilight Zone,' and you will be in Heaven with Me – forever!"* Until that day, I must stay at my post, serving at the pleasure of my King as His faithful Soldier, doing what He has "called" me to do – and so must you. *"The worth of a soldier is never known in times of peace"* (Thomas Manton).

"I have cerebral palsy, but thank God,
cerebral palsy doesn't have me!
I don't have a disability; I have a platform

from which to tell my story.

I don't have a burden to bear – I have a Blessing to share!

Jesus is worth living for; He thought I was worth dying for.

The Eleventh Commandment is: Thou shalt not bellyache!

It's time to get the 'lead' out and put The Lord in!

Cerebral palsy isn't a handicap … it's a Blessing!

I've got cerebral palsy – now what's your problem?"

(David Ring, *A Victorious Christian!*).

You've probably noticed by now that this book isn't full of "secrets to success." It doesn't need to be … "Success" is already *living* right on the inside of you. So, the secret to true success is *surrendering* to "Jesus in you" and His Will for you. *Pray* to Him as you *listen* for His voice; then *surrender* to Him as you *do* what He tells you to do – and you will be a "success" to **Jesus!** However, *your* success doesn't mean that every person you encounter will surrender to Jesus as well. The *Victory* here is that Jesus has been successful in making *you* a "fisher of men." Your only failure now is failing to *let* the Master Fisherman "fish for men" through you. **"Come ye after Me, and I will make you to become fishers of men" Signed: Jesus (Mark 1:17).**

Now, I know what you're thinking, *"Yes! I've made my decision. I'm going to be Jesus' faithful Disciple, and starting today, I'm going to let Him 'fish for men' through me!"* That's a very good plan. But satan's not worried; he's got a good plan too. Yep, that devil is going to make sure that the first dozen people you try witnessing to are some of his most rude, insulting, vile, full-of-hate, foul-mouthed, all-round-vicious slaves he can come up with. Then, you will have another decision to make: *Do I keep on trying … or just give up?* Instead of giving up, look up … into the eyes of your Saviour. Then, keep on loving Jesus, trusting Jesus and faithfully doing what He "calls" you to do (with the strength He gives you), and you will be a *success* "in God's eyes" … every time … *no matter the outcome.* Your Lord is just giving your "Spiritual Muscles of Faith" a work-out. Yes siree, your spirit-man is getting *Spiritually Stronger* every day! So, when those foul-mouthed slaves of satan call you a *"Loser,"* just smile … knowing that **Jesus** calls you a **"Winner!"** The *Victory* here

is your *faithful obedience* to the Lord you love – and trust me, your love for your Lord is what is being tested. ***"No man is a failure who loves God"*** **(Paul McCusker)**.

Satan may knock you down, my Friend, but don't you ever let him knock you out. Your Lord Jesus is right there with you to take your out-stretched hand of Faith with His strong hand of Love, Mercy and Grace. Jesus will lift His fallen Soldier up off the ground and plant your feet solidly on The Rock of Ages – *Himself!* Standing safe and secure on The Rock, you can see the world a whole lot better. *Ah, yes! Now* you can see the enemy (aka shifty satan) down there … slithering around from rock to rock … just waiting for the perfect moment to use the lust of your flesh to get you back down there in the mud with him again. Little does he know that *this time* God's Victory in *you* is as complete as **Jesus'** *Victory* was over *him!* *This time*, you are going to join young David in proclaiming, ***"The battle is the Lord's!"*** You're also going to remember that David slew Goliath with *Goliath's own sword!* So, when your "Goliath" comes against *you*, you'll know that no weapon formed against you shall prosper but will be an opportunity for your Lord Jesus to be *Victorious* over His enemy once again. *"The Greatest Winner of all time is living inside of you!"* (Jeff Wickwire). Never forget that the Victory is the Lord's – and so is the Glory. Give all the Glory to your Lord Jesus! *We are unprofitable servants; we have done that which was our duty to do.*

One hundred years ago was the beginning of the "Roaring Twenties" in America. Looking back, we can now see that it was the beginning of the end of "Godly America." Little by little, a roaring lion named "satan" started fulfilling his dream of reigning "as god" in our Country. And today, that vicious lion has America firmly in his sharp teeth … *quickly devouring her.* **BUT GOD!!** God still loves His Beloved America which was originally founded by **Christians** as a "Church-plant." They were answering the "Call of God" to take the Gospel of Jesus Christ to the shores of a foreign Land (check out: **The National Monument of the Forefathers**). I truly believe that our Country still has enough **Christians** here today who will answer God's "Call" to make the 2020's the "Roaring Twenties" all over again – America roaring *back* to the God Who loves her!

Listen closely, my Christian Friend, and you will also hear the *Roar* of The Lion of the Tribe of Judah – **Jesus Christ**. Our Majestic Leader "lives" within us, and when **Jesus** roars (or speaks) folks listen. **"Jesus**

in you" will help make "America first" – first in showing this dark, lost world what God can do with a Nation full of **Christians** totally sold-out to His Son **Jesus**. So, come join me in this "Jesus-Inspired Spiritual Revolution" against God's evil enemy satan who is taking over our beloved America in a blitz. We'll declare our own "war on poverty" and go out making people "rich in Jesus!" *He is our Treasure! "Lift up your eyes and look on the fields; for they are white (ripe) already to harvest!!"*

God's strategy to defeat the walled-city of Jericho was for Israel's army to march and march around it until God gave the command through Joshua to *Shout!* So, Israel obediently marched … *until* … the God-ordained moment arrived; Gen. Joshua gave the command; they all shouted and *Victory* was theirs! I truly believe that the God-ordained moment has arrived. Christians have marched around in circles long enough. **King Jesus** has given the Command for His "Soldiers of the Cross" to *Speak Forth* our Victory Message of **"Salvation in Christ Jesus"** into lost souls all around us. When we obediently do our part, God faithfully does **His** … and demonic strongholds will fall.

Even though it may *look* as spiritually dark as midnight in America right now, I believe that we are going to live to see our Lord Jesus, "The Light of the World," bring *Revival* to America! Remember that it was **midnight** when God's earthquake shook the prison holding Paul and Silas – and their chains fell off and the doors flew open! It all happened *while* they were praying, singing and praising our **Great God**! With millions of Born-Again Christians doing the same, America *still* has the chance to be a **Christian Nation** once again. **Let's roll!! Jesus** is a *prison–shaking* **Saviour!!** His earthquake will shake up *everything* … but **us**. So brace for the Good Ole **USA** to have a jail-house rock and "go over the wall at **midnight!!"**

> *"Christianity has a God*
> *Who knows His way out of the grave!"*
> (G. K. Chesterton).

As I was driving to the store to get some grub the other day, I passed a business that was opening up again after the lock-down for the

coronavirus, and this was on their marquee sign: *The War is over – and WE WON!!* That is the *Victory Cry* of every **Christian** in America! We have a Strong Saviour Who gives us the *undefeatable spirit* of those who know their God and do exploits. Instead of this world hearing the death-rattle from Jesus' Church, let's make sure it hears our shout of *"Victory in Jesus!"* *"But thanks be to God Who giveth us the Victory through our Lord Jesus Christ!"* (I Corinthians 15:57).

King Jehovah Jesus is on His Throne!!

"WELCOME TO MY WORLD!"

WORLD ABLAZE

"I am come to send fire on the Earth,
and what will I, if it be already kindled?"
Signed: Jehovah Jesus (Luke 12:49).

Charlie and I were attending a "dinner on the ground" at our Church one time (you don't really eat on the ground), and we were sitting at a table with some other couples. One of the husbands (a retired fireman) was reminiscing about some of his heroics back in the good ole days, *"I was on duty the day the ole First Baptist Church caught fire. I went and fought that **big blaze** at the ole First Baptist Church!"* He looked around to see if anyone was impressed when his wife turned to him and said (as only a wife can do), *"Well, you didn't do a very good job, did you – **it burned down!**"* What could he say?

Sunrise, sunset; swiftly flow the days … as we go about our everyday life in our own little Christian bubble, and *all the while*, God's number-one enemy, satan, is burning **America** down all around us! What can *we* say? I know what we *do* say: *"I can't help it." "I can't keep it from burning down." "It's not my fault it's burning down." "I can't make a difference."* Well … can you make a difference in the life of that person standing (and standing) next to you in the checkout-line at the store? Can you make a difference in the life of that neighbor you're always talking to over the back fence? Can you make a difference in the life of that young man loading your groceries into your car? Can you make a difference in the life of that faithful mechanic who always fixes up your ole car every time it breaks down? Can you make a difference in the life of that young girl who babysits your children? Can you make

a difference in the life of that person who _____? (*You* fill in the blank.)

The truth is: **You can.** The question is: **Will you?** Will **you** allow the Lord Jesus (Who is "living" in you) to make an **Eternal** difference in **someone's** life? I remember well that night so long ago when a "Faithful Servant" of our Lord Jesus took the time and made the effort to overcome all of my resistance in order to make a *gloriously* **Eternal** difference in *my* life. I can't wait to get to Heaven and thank him and thank him and thank him! (Do you think I am *oh so* glad he did?) I pray that I will have the great joy of seeing that *faithful Christian* at the Beautiful Gate of Heaven, welcoming me into my Eternal Home. So, will **you** do what that man did? Will you just *yield* yourself to **"Jesus in you"**? Never forget: There is an incredible **Supernatural Person** dwelling within you Who is *so worth living for!*

As I look around modern America, it is quite evident that the ole First Baptist Church isn't the only Church that has been destroyed. The ole First Baptist Church's problem was *too much fire*; the problem with many Christian Churches today is *too little fire* – **Holy Spirit Fire!** The young folks aren't finding **Jesus** in many of *His own Churches,* for pity's sake (as if they were looking for Him in the first place). Well **you,** my Christian Friend, must go looking for **them!** And when you do, take the best "demon fire extinguisher" known unto man – **the Gospel of Jesus Christ!** All the **fiery** missiles satan and his demons fire at it can never destroy it or even lessen its Power. *They all bomb out!*

As I write about our young folks, my mind goes back to a very physically alive, spiritually dead, empty, clueless, lost-in-sin young Molly and that "Faithful Servant" who first witnessed to *me* (when I was such a lost worldling only God Himself could have ever found me). That total stranger (who was very well-known to God) kept saying to me, *"You need **The Lord** in your life."* Right. Truth is, I didn't have a clue what he was talking about *(I told you I was clueless)* because I hadn't been spending any of my life (time, *same thing*) "seeking **The Lord.**" But, *Praise God, He* had been seeking *me! And **God** is still seeking young folks today – *through* **us Christians.** Yes sir, God has chosen *you* to go tell those lost young folks (who are in no way seeking God) that **The Lord** is seeking **them** and has shown up in their life (in you) to prove to

them that He is indeed **Alive!** **"Jesus in you"** wants to tell those clueless free-spirits that He has tracked them down in order to bring them the "Best News" they've never heard! So, let "Jesus" tell those "rich young rulers" (of their own kingdom) that they are being confronted by the **True Ruler** of this Universe. **He** is offering to give them *"Eternal Salvation"* – *but* they must choose **Jesus** over every other "god" in their life. Jesus can't be their Saviour as long as they have plenty of other "saviours." But when they get rid of all their earthly rulers, **Jesus** can become their *Heavenly Ruler*. Then, He will use them to defeat His enemy (satan) like He did in I Kings 20:13-20 – *and there were only 232 of them!*

"Joshua (and all his generation) died ... and there arose another generation after them which knew not the Lord, nor yet the Works which He had done" (Judges 2:8,10). *What?!!* How could this be?!! How could people who had crossed the Red Sea and the Jordan River on dry ground by a **"Miracle of God" not** have passed along their "Faith in God" to their children, for pity's sake?!! *(Hmmm).* Have **you** ever *crossed the Red Sea* (been **Saved** by a **Miracle of God**)? Are **you** letting anyone know about *your* **"Miracle of the God of Heaven and Earth"**? Is it because you're still doing laps around the wilderness? And every time you *think* you see help on the horizon ... it turns out to be a mirage. If so, I'm here to lead you to *Living Water*. It's elementary, my dear Watson; the help you need is so close to you that you just can't see it (yet). *"We constantly ask God for what we already have"* (John MacArthur).

Intriguing, exciting mystery novels have always been very popular, and you have probably read a few. On every page and at every turn are new clues of "whodonnit." Well, you may not realize it, my Christian Friend, but every day of your life, you aren't *reading* a mystery novel ... you're *living* one! Yes siree, you get up every morning wondering what's going to happen – then you go to bed at night wondering what happened. Well, on *this* morning, a different **Son** has risen upon you, and He has sent His Servant to help His Favorite Child figure it all out. Now here's the situation; the greatest Mystery in the entire Universe is *God Himself*, so He knows a thing or two about mysteries. In fact, He has designed *your life* to be like a mystery novel that you are being sent clues to every day. Little by little and day by day, God

is giving you *new thoughts* and *new ideas* you have never had before. He is giving you *new opportunities* you could never have imagined. Your Lord is even bringing *new people* into your life you never saw coming – like *me*. Yep, here I am … with God's new clues to your mysterious life.

I have always called a hand-held magnifying glass an "Inspector." And you, my Friend, are going to need a "Spiritual Inspector" (plus a pair of "Jesus Glasses") to unravel the mystery of your life. You need these to find "Spiritual Clues" to what God is doing in your problem-ridden, mystery-novel life. I hope you won't mind me spoiling the ending, but if you look real close, you will *see* your first New Clue: **God is The One Who is doing it all!!** *Aha, now* you know "Whodonnit" – and continues to do it. This bedrock truth is the "Key" that unlocks those *Secret Doors* through which you discover a deeper understanding of all the mysteries of life.

Now, look even closer and you will see your Clue Number-Two: **Jesus**, your Good Shepherd, is taking you *through* that dark valley you're in to a "Brand New Day" where you will be able to *see* "The Light" of **why** you are here on Planet Earth. As you walk in the Light with **Jesus**, He illuminates your life with Heavenly Light – much of which shines through His Truth (the Bible) as His Spirit uses it to help you solve the mystery of your Christian Life *one day at a time, one step at a time*. Looking at life through your "Jesus Glasses" and "Spiritual Inspector" brings your life into focus. Things become so clear that you no longer have to cry out, **"Lord! Why is all this happening to me?!!"** Nope, you unflinchingly *know* that it's all part of God's Perfect Plan for you. Even when a big storm hits your boat – **"Whoaaaaaa!!!"** – and it *looks like* you're going under, you will know beyond a doubt that **Jesus** is in your boat **with you.** *So* … you can just mosey on over, lie down beside Jesus and join Him in some peaceful sleep. *However*, if you choose *not* to follow your Good Shepherd into His **Perfect Plan** for you (but keep following your *own* clues to finding true *Joy* and *Purpose*), you're just on a treasure hunt with no "treasure" at the end of "the hunt." And Clue Number-Three will be that you're lost in the weeds of this world on the wrong path of life. *Mercy Me!*

Precious Christian Friend, don't let ole slewfoot lure you onto the best path *he* has to offer you. **No!** All *he* has engineered for your life is a train wreck. Run after satan, and you always run amuck. **You** have a "Calling" from **God. He** will "call" you to a **passion** that will become a **fire** in your bones! It will literally *burn* to fulfill God's Plan for you. "Jesus in me" longs to inspire in you a *burning desire* to live up to your **Divine Potential** God had in mind when He sent you to Planet Earth. *Yes!!* It starts when you answer your "Divine Call" from the **Eternal Son of God** and continues through every trial and hardship until He "calls" you Home to Heaven. And that brings us to Clue Number-Four: God is going to override every problem in your life in order to use **you** mightily as His Building Partner. Your Lord is laying the foundation for His Plan to build His **Eternal Kingdom** using *you* in a way you have never even considered before. Jesus is giving you the great opportunity of making an **Eternal** *difference* in the lives of people you haven't even met yet (and some you've known for years).

With that in mind, you're ready for Clue Number-Five: When you allow "Jesus in you" to speak forth His *Gospel Message of Salvation* through **you** to a lost soul walking around in bondage to satan, you are bringing the *Power* of God in Heaven to Earth. If you are spending (wasting) your life (time, *same thing*) playing video games because they make you *feel* like a powerful warrior, go to war against satan (and his evil kingdom) and *you really will* **be one!** Do **something** with your life that won't end when you take your last breath. Don't let death end *your* "life" on Planet Earth. Leave "Jesus' Life" behind in lots of folks who will let "Jesus in them" tell many more people about **Jesus!** God has given you the *Spiritual Power* to do so through His Gifts: Christ's Spirit, God's Word (the Bible), God's Love, God's Gospel of Salvation, God's Armour, Prayer, Faith, Spiritual Gifts, God's Anointing and the Prayers of your Lord Jesus – Who took on the devil … *and WON!!*

"Hallelujah!!
For the Lord God Omnipotent Reigneth!"
Signed: Every Born-Again Christian

Satan wants everyone thinking *he* is reigning. (When I typed in that last word, my computer flagged it because it thinks I meant to say "resigning" {the machines are taking over!}. I laughed out loud and said, *"Ha! Satan isn't about to resign!"* But don't despair, my Friend, because neither is our **Lord Jesus** – no matter how hard satan and his evil cronies try to impeach Him.) God didn't let satan "be God" in Heaven, so he's making another run at it here on Earth. Yep, the father of lies deceived Eve; then rode that lie all the way to the Throne of Planet Earth! And *today*, that demon-rat thinks he's really the "big cheese" because he's finally getting what God denied him in Heaven in Eternity past – he's getting to "be god" (over some worldling slaves). *Whoopee!!*

Truth is, satan can only reign over people who *give* him the power to do so by rejecting **Jesus** as their **Lord and Saviour**. Much to our former master's great dismay, we *Christians* have gone down to the Cross of Jesus; we've gone through the Blood of Christ and come out the other side in **Jesus' Kingdom** – where every knee bows to **King Jesus!** The time has come for each of us to *embrace* our **"Almighty Christ"** *(Who embraces **us** so intimately close to His heart)* and start living our God-given life on purpose – **God's Purpose! Our God Reigns!**

Christian, your Lord Jesus is ready to show you that *He* is the *Mighty God* – as soon as *you* are ready to *let Him*. There is a **"Jesus Dimension"** to your life that your Lord is just waiting for you to shut the world out of ... and quietly step into. *So*, when you are ready to draw up close enough to Jesus to feel His *Spirit's Breath* upon your soul, you're ready for Clue Number-Six: God the Son will show His Power and His Glory to *anyone* who sincerely wants to see it bad enough to actually **do** what He tells them to do. Jesus longs for **you** to *love* Him enough and *trust* Him enough to **be** that "someone." Without a doubt, your Lord is by your side and on your side to help you turn the tide! Jesus says the same thing to you He said to Thomas, **"Be not faithless, but believing!"** So, **believe** that your **Lord Jesus** is powerfully **"Alive"** *in you* for the purpose of telling everyone *around you* about **God** and His love for them. Then, *show* your Lord you believe it by letting "Jesus in you" speak *through you* "as you are going" about your everyday life. You are one of Jesus' "Called-Out Ones," and folks are going to *see* that there is "something

different" about *you*. That opens the door for you to say, *"The difference about me is 'Jesus in me!' And* **you** *can have 'Jesus in* **you**!' *Let me tell you how."*

Now you're ready for Clue Number-Seven: Jesus called you *out* of this doomed world, my Christian Friend, in order to send you back *into* it – **Spiritually Alive!** This world may be burning down with **sin,** but **you** are **ablaze** with the **Presence** of **Jesus Christ** "living" within you. If you will let the **Living Christ** set you **on-fire** for Himself ... this world will come just to watch you **burn!** **"Set me on-fire for You, Lord! I seek not a long life but a full life like You, Lord Jesus."** (Jim Elliot). Jesus has a **burning desire** for *you*, Christian, that is as *deep* and as *strong* today as it was the day He willingly went to the Cross to die for you. Now let Jesus ignite such a **Holy Fire** in you for "Witnessing for Him" that nothing or no one can ever put it out – neither the Angels in Heaven above nor the demons down under the sea! *"But His Word was in mine heart as a burning* **fire** *shut up in my bones!"* (Jeremiah 20:9).

I have a dear Sister-in-Jesus who is a vivacious, fun-loving, full-of-life person. Even old-age can't dampen Marjorie's zest for life. I love to see people loving Jesus and loving life (may their Tribe increase). A few years back, her husband needed to go into a health care facility for a while; so Marjorie, her daughter, her son (who was visiting from another State) and I decided to drive around town and check out a few. Before we left, she read off the names of the ones she was considering – one of which was on Fleming Island. We went to a different one first but didn't like it, so we left there to go to another. As we pondered where to go next, Marjorie's son (who was sitting by me in the back) asked, *"What about the one on Flaming Island?"* I laughed, turned to him and said, *"It's Fleming Island – not Flaming Island."* **In a flash,** Marjorie popped her head around and excitedly exclaimed, *"It* **will be when WE get there!!"**

I laugh every time I think about that because those words sum up my friend's life so well. No matter what she's doing or where she is, she turns it into a *"Flaming Island!"* This dear soul lives her life in the **"Charge!"** mode. That's the way we Christians should be living for **Jesus** – even while living in a world **ablaze** with every **fiery sin** satan can fill it with. *So*, here is God's Clue Number-Eight: Now that your Lord has

made you *Spiritually Alive* and put a *Holy Fire* in your soul, He wants you to go out into this *World Ablaze* (wearing the Armour of Christ) and turn it into *"God's Flaming Island"* full of *on-fire-for-Jesus Born-Again Christians* who are compelled by their *burning love* for their Lord to speak forth the *Glorious Gospel of Jesus Christ* to lost folks who are *ablaze* with *sin* and headed for a *fiery hell*. *Mercy Me!*

While you're strapping on your Armour, I'll let you in on your Lord's Clue Number-Nine: God never intended for your life on this Earth to be a long, dull, boring ordeal … or a prison sentence to be served and endured without parole for the crime of being born. *No!* Your life is a "Gift" from the God of this Universe Who loves you with an *Everlasting Love;* He intends for you to receive His Gift with great Joy and live it out to His Glory. Your life is to be a "glorious adventure" with the God of Glory, *Jesus Christ Himself!* When you leave your faithful Traveling Companion out of your life, out go the "Glory" and the adventure.

The reason the Apostle Paul was such a dynamic Christian was because he had met the Living Lord Jesus *personally*. If you, my Friend, have met Jesus *personally*, then we have another Apostle Paul on our hands! No one can shut you up from telling this clueless world: *"Jesus is Alive! Jesus is Lord! Jesus has the Power to Save!"* As you share this profound *Truth* with a lost person, you are opening their "Spiritual Eyes" to the fact that they must deal with a *Living Saviour*. Now, you let them know "why" they need a Living Saviour: *"Everyone is born into this world with no 'spiritual life' in their spirit due to our inherited sinful condition. Jesus is 'Alive!' – but you won't be 'Spiritually Alive' until Jesus is 'Alive' in you. Jesus is 'Alive' in me because I have received Him as my personal Lord and Saviour, and it was by far the best thing I ever did. Now, let me tell you how Jesus can be 'Alive' in you!"*

Even though *everyone* won't accept our Lord Jesus as their Saviour, we can still strive to reach the people who *will* and give *them* the opportunity to do so on *our watch*. I can't reach everyone alone; you can't reach everyone alone – *but God* can, with His Clue Number-Ten: *All of us together* can turn this world upside-down, inside-out and right-side-up! It's time we took our Christianity on the road – *"The Romans Road"* that leads folks to Heaven! With the *Power* of

Christ's Spirit working *through us*, a bunch of us dedicated *Sparks-for-Jesus* will make one *big bonfire*, all to the Glory of God. *Many of the people I witness to claim to be Born-Again Christians.* If that be true, then *"We The Church of Jesus Christ"* are truly a *sleeping Giant* in this Country today. When we *all* decide to stand up, stand for and stand with our Saviour in this Epic Battle, God's Kingdom will spread like *wildfire* on this Earth. His Kingdom is here in me. Is it here in you? Good, now don't just sit there; go tell those lost folks all about your *Saviour.* Show them *God's Mighty Power* to *Save* a person (you!) and work through a person (you again!) in order to *Save* another person (them!). Faithfully do *that* and I can guarantee you: *Your living will not be in vain.* *"Now therefore go, and I Will be with thy mouth, and shalt teach thee what thou shalt say!" Signed: Jehovah Jesus* (Exodus 4:12).

In America's National Anthem, "The Star Spangled Banner," Francis Scott Key was wondering if tattered and torn Ole Glory was still flying over America. Today, do you ever wonder if "Jesus' Blood-Stained Banner" is still flying over America? I talk with enough people to know that it is still flying over many Christian homes in our Great Nation. Satan's rockets' red glare and bombs bursting in air haven't defeated Jesus' Kingdom yet – *and never will!* However, we *all* need to hear our Lord's Clue Number-Eleven: God's Kingdom would be a lot stronger in America if *Jesus' Church* would be "the Land of the free and the Home of the brave." We Christians, who have been set *"free"* by our Lord Jesus, must be *"brave"* enough to take our Saviour's Saving Gospel to lost folks who need Him to be *their* Saviour and set *them free. The Shout of a King is among us!* Do you hear the shout of *King Jesus*? *I do!* Rally to the Banner of His Cross! *Bravely* take the Gospel of Christ to those who need to be *set free.* And trust me, you won't have any trouble finding them – you pass them every day. *"If you live gladly to make others glad in God, your life will be hard, your risks will be high and your Joy will be full"* (John Piper).

Born-Again Christians should live out their Christian Faith in every area of life – especially when they go to the polls to vote. We Christians know that wherever man rules, our Most High God over-rules. A good example of that was the 2016 election of President

Donald Trump. It was a *Miracle* of God Himself! Our gracious Lord gave America a "Divine Reprieve." We were on the path to destruction from within our **own** Government – **BUT GOD!!** Well Folks, *today* there's a **Bigger Movement** than the Donald Trump Movement going on here, you know. Do you sense it? God's Clue Number-Twelve is: Open your "Spiritual Eyes" and **JOIN IT,** *for **Jesus'** sake!* This could be the beginning of **God's Revival** in America – we just need **one more!** *"It's not an issue of 'the Right' or 'the Left.' It's an issue of 'what is right' and 'what is wrong'!"* (Adrian Rogers).

"Vote for Donald for President. He knows how to shake things up!" Melania Trump made that statement about her husband during the 2016 Presidential Campaign. When I heard it, I immediately thought about my Lord Jesus. Folks, the "Trumpet Call" is going forth! The time has come for **Christians** everywhere to rally to our **Anointed King Jesus** ... because **He** knows how to shake things up! And the first thing **King Jesus** is going to have to shake up is ... **you,** my Christian Friend. Then, He's got to *"Wake Up!"* His **Church** by shaking her down, around and ever which way but loose! The Lord's Plan is for *every Christian* to **"be Jesus"** to this lost-in-space world. **"Until we win ... or until we die!"** (King Leonidas).

As I encourage you to be a **"Strong Soul-Winner"** for your Lord, you may think I'm being a bit hard on you, but trust me, when you get to Heaven, you'll thank me. You will hear your Lord saying to you, **"Well done, thou good and faithful Servant!"** And you will be *so thankful* for every person you ever talked to about **Jesus** and shared His Gospel with ... because many of them will be there thanking **you.** **You** won't be empty-handed! You will be so glad that I clued-you-in to "The True Meaning of Your Christian Life." *"A coach is someone who tells you what you don't want to hear; who has you see what you don't want to see, so that you can be who you have always known you could be"* (Tom Landry).

Do you ever think about Heaven and what it's going to be like when you get there? Well, your final Clue is that Jesus is preparing it right now – *with His eye on you.* Heaven will be **"ablaze!"** with the **Love** and **Joy** of Jesus. The Glory of **Jesus' Presence** will make Heaven the ultimate **Flaming Island!** So Christian, get crackin' and fan the **flame** burning within *your* **soul!** Dare to **"be Jesus"** to this world. You will

be *Eternally* glad you did. You will break the tape a "Winner!" And your Lord Jesus will be there with your reward. Actually, *Jesus is* your "Reward!" He will hold out His nail-pierced hand to you, lovingly call your name and say,

"WELCOME TO MY WORLD!"

THE POWER OF GOD

"All Power is given unto Me in Heaven and in Earth.
Go ye therefore!" Signed: Jehovah Jesus
(Matthew 28:18-19).

People of Faith look through their "Jesus Glasses" at our amazing life-filled, life-sustaining Planet (floating around in a vast Universe) and *"see"* the Infinite, Eternal Power of God revealed in *everything*. Without a doubt, it would take an *infinite* number of books to cover all the aspects of God's Infinite Power. However, in this chapter, I would like to focus in on God's Power in (what else?) witnessing – and I will humbly leave all the rest to the Bible Scholars.

"Ye do err, not knowing the Scriptures nor the Power of God" Signed: Jesus (Matthew 22:29). According to Jesus, the "Key" to God's Power in witnessing is found in the Word of God, the Omnipotence of God and the heart of the one holding this book. Reading God's Word; knowing God's Word; believing God's Word; acting on God's Word *in Faith* while trusting the God of the Word to faithfully *do* what He has promised to do results in the manifestation of the Power of God on this Earth. We Christians know that … we just don't always do it. But the more we obediently *do* the things our Lord tells us to do, the more we are amazed at *His Faithfulness*. Jesus absolutely *loves* to amaze us. Therefore, He is always looking for people who *love* to be amazed – by their *Amazing Saviour*. This book is Jesus' challenge to *you* to listen closely for His still small Voice, *"My Dear Child, just believe Me, try Me, trust Me … and **see!**"*

"I will build My Church, and the gates of hell shall not prevail against it!" Signed: Jesus (Matthew 16:18). Now, I'm no theologian, but every time I read that verse, a picture comes into my mind. I can see satan's stronghold like a

big ole medieval castle, standing on a high, craggy mountain shrouded in dark clouds. The enemy's castle has towering walls of stone and a tall, thick gate of iron – and on the inside are many prisoners *in chains*. Those poor wretched souls are being held captive by their cruel slave-master … **satan**. *Mercy Me!*

I talk to people all the time who are in bondage to satan. They are being held fast in chains of **sin** by the enemy of their soul, the devil. Yep, ole slewfoot makes them *think* they are "free" – when all along they are actually *his slave*. Satan fools them into thinking they are so **"alive!"** when they are actually in his death-grip – being squeezed to death by *him*. They are spiritually dead, spiritually blind, spiritually deceived – and they don't even realize it. Those poor souls are prisoners of a devil they can't free themselves from because satan is stronger than they are. Their friends can't free them because satan is stronger than their friends. I can't free them either because satan is stronger than me. Let's face it, my Friend, the devil is stronger than all of us – including *you*. *Mercy Me!*

So, what's the answer? Jesus tells us, *"When a strong man armed keepeth his palace, his goods are in peace. But when a stronger than he shall come upon him and overcome him, he taketh from him all his armour wherein he trusted, and divideth his spoils"* (Luke 11:21-22). The strong man in this verse is satan himself, and Jesus admits that he **is** strong. Notice also that Jesus tells us he is armed. Well, whoever armed *that* rascal?! Answer: Adam did. When he bowed down and obeyed satan, Adam turned himself, his God-given "Authority," the dominion of the Earth, all the kingdoms of the world and all of mankind over to that devil. Satan is also armed with devilish **lies** which keep his powerless slaves under his control. Therefore, satan's "goods" are all his prisoners (thanks, Adam), but trust me, they are *not* at peace. They may put up a good front and look like it on the outside, *but on the inside* they are full of turmoil … because there is no peace to the wicked, saith my God. When Jesus says that the strong man's prisoners are "in peace," He actually means *they can't escape*. That's because there is no one strong enough to free them from him … *until … The Stronger Man* **(The Lord Jesus)**. *YES!!* Our Lord *overcomes* "weaker satan," takes his captives from him and *sets us free. Thank You, Lord! However*, satan has many more prisoners in his castle of horrors, and our Strong Saviour is just sitting on ready to

set *them* free as well. But how can He? Answer: By using – **Ta Da – us Born-Again Christians.** *Mercy Me!*

So, we start obediently marching toward satan's big castle-stronghold with high stone walls and a tall, thick iron-gate. As we approach it, we stop, look up and freeze. We remember Jesus' Words, *"The gates of hell shall not prevail against My Church,"* and we think, *"Is Jesus serious? How in the world am I **ever** going to get in **there**?!"* Well, let's search the Scriptures once again. *Ah yes,* our good friend Paul says, **"For I am not ashamed of the Gospel of Jesus Christ: for it is the Power of God unto Salvation to everyone who believeth!"** (Romans 1:16). I think we have a clue. The word Paul uses for *Power* is the Greek word "dunamis" from which we get our English word "dynamite." When I think of dynamite, I remember the ole Westerns I loved going to see at our country town's Movie Theater when I was a little girl. The cowboys always had a box of dynamite handy in case they ever wanted to blow something up. They could put it in a wagon and drive it around for miles … and it would just sit there, bumping along in the back of that wagon. They could pick up a stick of it and carry (or even throw) it around – and nothing would happen. So, where's the power? *Ah yes,* it was when somebody struck a match and lit the end of the fuse; *that's* when everybody ran for cover … because they *knew* they were getting ready to see some **POWER**!!

That is a good illustration of the Gospel. You can carry it around with you all day and all night, and you won't see any dynamite power … *unless* … you light the fuse. So, how do you light the fuse? *Ah yes,* it is only when you *speak forth* the God-Anointed Words of the **Gospel of Jesus Christ** that you light the fuse of that "Dynamite Power" you've been carrying around with you all this time. The Power of God has a Name. His Name is **Jesus.** According to the Apostle Paul, the **Christ** we *preach* is the **Power of God**! If you are a Born-Again Christian, **Jesus Christ** is "Alive!" in *you*, and He wants to be unleashed *through you* so that *God's Power* can *ignite* those dead souls you pass every day. When you let **Jesus** speak forth His Gospel Message *(using your mouth, of course)*, you're going to see some **POWER**!! **You, Christian,** are America's only hope … *when* you let **Jesus** come **"Alive!"** in **you.** *Mercy Me!*

Now, let's go back to satan's big castle-stronghold sitting on top of Ole Smokey Mountain. The stone walls are still high, the iron-gate is still

DARE to be JESUS

thick, and you still can't get through. *But Jesus (the Strongest One in the Universe)* is approaching it *this time* (in *you*) with the Dynamite Power of His Gospel! *Yes siree*, Jesus and you take your stick of Dynamite Gospel (which you lit *on fire* when you *spoke forth* the Message of *"Salvation in Christ Jesus"*) and run as hard, as fast and as straight as you possibly can … right up to that impenetrable fortress. When you reach those high stone walls … you stop. *Then*, with all the strength of a Mighty Witnessing Warrior for Jesus, you fling **Jesus'** stick of **Dynamite Gospel** over those towering walls … right-smack-dab into the middle of satan's castle-stronghold. *Mercy Me!*

Then … you wait. You wait to hear the sound of a loud explosion coming from the other side of that stone wall. **Woo Hoo!! Now** we're talking **Power!!** Do you know what that explosion does? *Ah yes*, the *Power* of God's Holy Spirit (unleashed into a lost person's inner-being by *your* spoken words) applies the Precious Blood of Jesus Christ to their spirit and soul. The *Power* of Christ's Sacrificial Blood breaks and destroys the chains and shackles off the wrists and ankles of satan's slave being held captive within the walls of the devil's evil stronghold – and sets him **FREE!** *Hallelujah!* **"For by Thee I have run through a troop, and by my God have I leaped over a wall!"** (Psalm 18:29).

Do you remember the day when *your* chains fell off and Jesus set **you** free? I do. *Thank You, Lord Jesus!* So, let me ask you a question: Are you willing to let God use **you** to break the chains off of someone else and set *them* free as well? He *will* use you to do that – *if* you will just present yourself to Him and pray with all your heart, **"Lord, here am I. I'm Yours! Use me. I'm willing and ready. In the Mighty Name of Jesus, Amen."** Now, maybe you're willing, but you just aren't ready. You're saying, *"I have so many other important things to do first"* (Hmmm). I agree they're important, but are you sure they are *more* important than the **Destiny** of another person's **Eternal soul**? I realize that our most famous mountain in America is called "RushMore," but can you slow down long enough to hear what your Lord is saying to you? Jesus is telling you that if you will just seek **FIRST** *His Kingdom* and *His Righteousness*, **He** will take care of **all** the rest – and give *you* rest. Why not just **trust Him** enough to *do* what He says … and see what happens? *Jesus' Love … limitless! Jesus' Grace … measureless! Jesus' Power … boundless! Jesus' Care … endless!*

228

Meanwhile, back at the ranch (castle), let's check the latest News Report to see what's happening with our new "Brother in Christ" who has just been set free inside satan's castle-stronghold. *"Houston, we have a problem!"* Even though our Brother has been unshackled, that big iron-gate is *still* bolted tight; satan has plenty of his slaves guarding it, and there is no other way of escape. *Mercy Me! But wait!!* Didn't Jesus give us Christians some Keys? Yep, *His Presence* in us gives **us** *His Authority* to do *His Work* on this Earth. **"Jesus in us"** is "The Key." **The Spirit of Christ** is "The One" Who entered into the *spirit* of our new Brother, opened his heart, washed him clean with Jesus' Precious Blood, cast out satan's dominion over him, broke the devil's chains of bondage on him and set him free from that demon's rule. *Now*, **Christ's Spirit** dwells within his inner spirit-man. *Praise the Lord!* A *new* **King** "Reigns" on the throne of his heart – **King Jesus** – Who says to that big iron-gate, *"Open, says* **Me***!!"* The stones of that castle cry out, **"Jesus is Lord!"** That big iron-gate swings open wide! And satan's ex-slave walks joyfully past those petrified guards … right out of the devil's demonic domain into God's Glorious SonShine – *a free man "in Christ."* Hallelujah! **"Jesus breaks the power of cancelled sin and sets the prisoner free!"** (John Wesley).

In times past, I always enjoyed going to the post office to pick up my tracts. I would order over a thousand at a time, so the box was pretty heavy. The person who handed it to me would usually say something like, *"Oh man, that's heavy! Whatcha got in there?"* So, I would tell them, *"Oh, something very important and very powerful. It's very powerful indeed. Would you believe that in this box – IN THIS VERY BOX – is one of the most Powerful Things in the entire Universe?!!"* I loved how big their eyes would get. *NOW*, they *really* wanted to know what was in that box. So, I would open it up and show them – *the Gospel of Jesus Christ!* They were always *so* disappointed. But they shouldn't have been. Did I tell them the truth, or not? I told them the truth; their problem was: They didn't believe it. Now, what about you? Do *you* believe it? Do you believe that the **Gospel of Jesus Christ** is one of the most *Powerful Things* in the entire Universe? Do you believe that the **Gospel** is the "Power of God" unto *Salvation* to all who *believe*? If so, what are you doing with it? Anything? Ever? *Just asking.*

It is undeniably true that when Billy Graham preached from the Crusade Pulpit, he had God's Anointing upon him in a powerful way. You, my Friend, may never preach before thousands of people from a pulpit, but you *can* experience the same *Anointing of God* as you stand before that *one lost person* and tell them about your Lord Jesus and His *So Great Salvation*. That lost person needs to hear the *Voice* of the Son of God in order to be *Saved* (John 5:25). God's *Divine Plan* for that to happen is … **YOU! You** are God's Plan! He has anointed **"Jesus in you"** to speak to that person *through you* so that they can hear the Voice of His Son Jesus and be *Saved*. Christian, you are breathing and your heart is beating so that Jesus can use *your mouth* to speak His "Good News" to the people He created, loves and died for. Those folks don't just need to know that there really *is* a Heaven – they need to know "The Way" to get there. "Jesus in you" is *The Way*. *Praise to the God of our Salvation!!*

The secret to letting "Jesus in you" live through you isn't rocket science. It's fairly simple – just stay connected to Him. As you go through your day, converse with **Jesus** about everything that comes up along the way. The more you talk with your Lord, the more you are acknowledging: **"I am living my life in the very Presence of God Himself!"** Living in your Lord's Presence (and your Lord's Presence living in *you*) empowers you to tell others, **"Jesus is Alive!"** Your heart and soul will overflow with **The Spirit of Christ Jesus** "living within you," and your God-Anointed mouth will let **Jesus** give the *Wings of His Spirit* to your words – *His Words!* *"This is the Word of the Lord unto Zerubbabel saying, Not by might, nor by power, but by My Spirit, saith the Lord of Hosts!"* (Zechariah 4:6).

"(Abraham) staggered not at the promise of God through unbelief, but was strong in Faith, giving Glory to God: And being fully persuaded that what He had promised, He was able also to perform" (Romans 4:20-21). Has God promised to bring "Revival" to America? Not exactly, **but God** *has promised* that everyone who comes to the foot of His Son's Cross (in *Faith* and *Repentance*) and lets **Jesus** die for them (to pay the penalty for their **sins**) will be gloriously **Saved!** *Now* is the time for **you**, Christian, to start leading some folks to the foot of Jesus' Cross – **so that God can keep His Promise.** Giving the Gospel of Christ to lost folks is **urgent!** *"Maybe I will … or maybe I won't"* isn't an option. **No!** It is of

the utmost importance that you render this service to your Lord here on Planet Earth – **now!** It is a matter of life or death! Here's why: **You** are Jesus' "Doctor-on-duty" in an Urgent Care Clinic (this world). It is full of people who are dying (an *Eternal death*) all around you. **But "Jesus in you"** can give them the *One Thing* they need to survive – **Eternal Life!** Pray for your Lord to give you a compassionate "Doctor's heart" for the lost – *like His.* Karl Wallenda (Patriarch of The Flying Wallendas Trapeze Artists) once said, *"Life is on the wire … all else is just waiting."* My prayer is for my Lord to so work in *my* heart that I can truthfully say, *"Life is being on-fire for **Jesus** and telling others about Him … all else is just waiting."*

A while back, the movie "Star Wars: The Force Awakens" opened at theaters everywhere. I didn't go see it, but the title intrigued me. Stretch you "Spiritual Muscles" for a minute and imagine with me that our **King Jesus** is sending us Christians a *Divine Code Message*:

"Behold, Ye Soldiers of The Cross!
Strap on your Mighty Spiritual Swords!
I AM 'calling' My Powerfully Supernatural Church to
AWAKEN! And storm the gates of hell, one soul at a time!
I AM showing 'Darth Vader of the dark spiritual realm' that
I AM The Supreme King and Sovereign Ruler of MY Universe!
My Spirit in My 'Called-Out Ones' is the Powerful Force that
overcomes the enemy's evil empire – for lo, his doom is sure.
My Majestic, Mighty Kingdom is striking back! Follow Me!!
Be of good cheer, I AM here! I have overcome the world!!"

The word "Stars" is used in the Bible to refer to God's Angels – one third of which were cast out of Heaven along with satan their evil leader. So, to say that today we are engaged in "The War of the Stars" would not be so far-fetched. The battle is real, and it is raging. Are you engaged in it (on God's side along with *His* Angels), or … are you just sitting on the sidelines oblivious to it all? You pass people every day that you will never see again … *unless* … you see them in **Heaven** because **you** gave them the

Gospel of Jesus Christ! Go for it! *"While the Church is waiting for Jesus to come down, Jesus is waiting for His Church to stand up!"* (Sammy Rodriquez).

"I'm not going to shut up. I'm going to stand up!" (Jeff Schreve). The "Living Word of God" (Jesus) is "living" His Life *again* in *you*, Christian, and He has brought with Him God's Love, Wisdom and Courage. *Jehovah Jesus* knows how to wield "The Sword of The Spirit" as He prays and witnesses – *through you*. Your Lord is awakening you to that *Truth* so that you will live your life in the moment by moment *reality* of it. In this war against satan's wicked kingdom, we Christians are Jehovah Jesus' Soldiers who have been dropped behind enemy lines by our *High King* of Heaven. *Rally to His Blood-Stained Banner!* Don't be MIA or AWOL. *No!* You have your King's Spiritually Supernatural Weapons. *Onward Christian Soldiers!* The *Power* of your *God* goes with you! *"And he wrote in the King's Name, and sealed it with the King's Ring, and sent letters by posts on horseback. So the posts that rode went out, being hastened and pressed on by the King's Commandment!"* (Esther 8:10,14).

Spiritual Warfare is a reality you may as well get familiar with … you will be engaging in it every day. The same devil that is God's adversary is now *your* adversary because *The Spirit* of God's Son is living in you – and satan *hates Jesus.* So, you can be sure that when you start messin' with satan's evil kingdom, *evil satan* will start messin' with *you*. Trust me when I tell you that in the battleground of *your soul* the devil will try to confuse, frustrate and intimidate you at every turn … in order to "take you out." There will be times when what you see in front of you and what you hear your Lord saying to you will be two entirely different things – and it will take every fiber of your being and every ounce of your soul to *trust* your Lord and *believe* that what He is saying to you is *true.* That is when the *Power of Prayer* is so important in the Christians' battle with demonic forces. Your strongest spiritual weapon against satan and his evil kingdom is your *constant communication* with your *King!* The satanic world may be strong but just remember: *Jesus Christ is LORD* and on His Throne … and nobody else is. *He* is stronger than satan – *always!* Unwavering *Faith* in your *Lord* (Who is on the throne of *your heart*) is the *Victory* that overcomes evil satan. *"Gird Thy Sword upon Thy thigh, O Most Mighty, with Thy Glory and Thy Majesty!"* (Psalm 45:3).

232

When Jesus walked this Earth with His disciples, they had the amazing privilege of witnessing *The Power of God Incarnate!* They took great comfort in that ... *until* ... the day they were sailing with Jesus across the Sea of Galilee, a great storm arose *and, alas* ... Jesus was asleep! *"And they came to Him and awoke Him, saying, 'Master, Master, we perish!' Then, He arose, rebuked the wind and the raging of the water, and they ceased, and there was a calm"* (Luke 8:24). Let me ask you a question: Are you going through this stormy life, day in and day out, just sailing through life ... with **Jesus** asleep in your boat? Don't you think it's time you woke Jesus up so that He can **ARISE** in **you?** To do that, you are going to have to give **Jesus** (not your fancy-phone) your serious, undivided attention. It's called: *Prayer*. It's called: *Bible Study*. It's called: *Devotion*. It's called: *Obedient Service*. It's called: **Your Life!!** Love is spelled: T-i-m-e. You must call Him, **"Master!"** You must actually let Him *be* your *Master*. You will either be the slave of your smarty-pants phone, your computer, your TV, (or perhaps: your drugs, your pornography, the race track, the casinos, the bottle) ... *or* **Jesus Christ**. You alone must make the choice. When you choose **Jesus,** He will *ARISE* in you and do some *Miraculous Works!* The first *Miracle* He will do is start freeing you from all of the above ... because He knows that you won't find **God** at the bottom of that bottle, at the end of that needle or at the end of that sex-show. So, just come to **Jesus** and show Him your "little Faith," and He will show *you* what He wants you to do with it – for His Eternal Kingdom. The things you're living for *right now* have **no Eternal Value** ... *but* "Mustard-Seed Faith" plus "Living Water" yield much Fruit! **"Is the world crucified to you ... or does it fascinate you? How can you pull down strongholds of satan if you don't even have the strength to turn off your TV?"** (Leonard Ravenhill).

"God's Word tells us to trust in the Lord. Do you trust the Lord today? If you don't trust the Lord Jesus, it's because you don't love Him. If you don't love Jesus, it's because you don't know Him. And you don't know Jesus because you aren't spending time with Him" (Adrian Rogers). Yeah, I know your struggle. There are *so many things* in this life that compete to be your "master." So, how do you make **Jesus** your Master? Jesus will only be your Master when **His Love** has first mastered *you*. Living the Christian life is always a matter of the heart. You go after that which your *heart* is set on. So, ask yourself some hard questions:

"What is my heart *really* set on today? What do I love *most* in life? Who do I love *most* in life?" At your life's end, will you be able to look back and say, *"Lord Jesus, I lived my life the best I could for You ... because I love You so much!"* Or will you have to face Jesus knowing that *He knows* all those things in your life that you loved more than you loved *Him*?

Think for a minute of all those things that are so important and so valuable to you on this Earth. Think about what matters the most to you right now. When you stand before your **Lord Jesus** in Heaven, you will suddenly know what *should* have been most important. In the Light of *Jesus' Presence*, you will see what *should* have been most valuable – what *should* have mattered more than anything else. Don't wait until your dying day to start giving some attention to the next world ... because when you take your last breath on this Earth, the only thing that will matter *then* is how many people will be in Heaven because of *you*. And now you know.

My Friend, when you became a Born-Again Christian, you didn't just "believe in a religion" ... you "received a **Person!**" And not just *any* person – you received the Spirit of **The King** of this Universe into *your* spirit! Have you even talked with Him lately? You may never meet with the President, but you *can* meet with **The King** every day! Do you know what He's thinking about you right now? *Ask Him!* If you will sincerely listen for His Voice, He will sincerely let you know. Then, let your **King** know what *you* are sincerely thinking about *Him*,

"King Jesus! Reporting for duty, Sir! I'm at
your service today, Sir!
You and I have Something Wonderful to give to this lost,
sad world, Sir!
God our Father hath Anointed us to bring Good News
to the afflicted, Sir!
So, go ahead, Lord Jesus, and use my earthly body and
Eternal Soul for
the Glory of Your Kingdom and the Honor of Your Name!!
Amen."

Our Mighty King has already won the war for us. *Now*, we just have to show up for the battle, stand on His Word and speak forth His Truth. The reason we Christians are losing the war against satan is because ... *we aren't even showing up!* We are just too timid to let "Jesus in us" take the *Gospel of Christ* and the *Sword of The Spirit* and wield them ... *for* **Heaven's** *sake.* When the disciples woke Jesus up in the storm, the first question He asked them was, *"Where is your Faith?"* I hate to admit it, but there are times when Jesus has to ask *me* the same question. And I have to confess that the only faith I have is *His* Faith – so He will have to give me some more of *His*. That's when Jesus reminds me that Faith comes by hearing "His Word." So, as I prayerfully read my Bible and listen to Bible-believing, Jesus-lifting-up Preachers, Jesus speaks to me in my soul through His Spirit's still small Voice ... and *He* grows my Faith. The Living Word "living in me" draws me into the *Divine Presence* of **Jesus** Himself!

Our Lord doesn't want the Churches in America full ... of empty people (complacent pew-sitting-Christians). *No!* He wants an Army of *totally sold-out, all-in* Mighty Witnesses for **God!** As Oswald Chambers encourages us, **"Abandon yourself to God!"** So, if *you* decide to jump into "Jesus' Supernatural World of Witnessing," go ahead – *Jesus will catch you!* Then, He will fling you out into *this* world in a mighty way for the **KING** of kings and **LORD** of lords! Revelation 17:14 calls us God's "called, chosen and faithful." I am so thankful to my Lord for choosing me and calling me. *Now*, I want to be a *faithful Soldier* of **The One** Who has always been *faithful* to me – especially when He hung on that Cross and died for me.

As you obediently walk through life in close fellowship with the "Spirit of Christ" within you, He will show you just how *Miraculous* your "New Life in Christ" really is. You quickly discover that "Jesus in you" **loves** people; therefore, He *never* meets a stranger. "Jesus in you" loves *talking* with all these folks, and you soon learn that Jesus' favorite topic is the *Best News* in the whole world – *His Glorious Gospel!* As you allow "Jesus in you" to *come forth* and tell someone about Himself, He floods your soul with His **Great Joy.** And after all the depressing things you've been through lately, *that* will be a *Miracle!*

In the Introduction to my book *Ole Slewfoot*, I stated that letting the Christ Who "lives in you" actually "live through you" is a radical

concept. *But* it is only radical to a *superficial Christian* who has never tasted what it's like to be a *Supernatural Christian.* It starts with "learning to love" and "learning to lean." Jesus will use you to the extent that you *love* Him ... and *let* Him. The more you get to know and fall in love with "Jesus in you" the more you will let Him flow *through you* to others. *Such Joy!!* The Joy of Jesus is your strength. Let Jesus' Joy infect the people all around you. *Be contagious!* Touch them with your heart of "Joy" and spread the "virus" of "loving Jesus with all your heart" to *everyone. Go viral! "These things have I spoken unto you, that My Joy might remain in you, and that your Joy might be full!"* Signed: Jesus (John 15:11).

The next Miracle your Lord has for you is: *Peace in your soul.* The Lord told you He was leaving it for you, and now you've found it. It's the Peace of *knowing* that you are doing *The Most Important Work on Earth*: **Letting your Lord Jesus work through you.** Many years ago, **True**tt Cathy (a **True** Christian and founder of Chick-Fil-A) was at a party talking with a man who didn't know who Truett was. The man asked him what he did for a living, and Truett's answer went something like this: *"Well, my Real Job is bringing people into the Kingdom of God by introducing them to my Lord and Saviour Jesus Christ. That's my Real Job ... and I sell a little chicken on the side."*

I love it! When your *Real Job* is bringing people into the Kingdom of God, you have the *Peace* of knowing that no matter what walls might fall down around you in your life, you have your Lord's assurance that "The Foundation" is solid and sure. Your life is now built upon *The Rock of Ages*, and *Jesus* will never be shaken. *Never!* Even if you ever do hit rock-bottom, you will just discover that **Jesus** is *The Rock* at the bottom! **Jesus** is *The Rock* in a weary land. You can rest assured that when troubles *do* come, it's because your Lord has allowed them – for a season and for a reason; they give you the opportunity to make **Him** known to this lost and dying world in the grip of satan. When people see you suffering, they will see you suffering with *Peace in your heart* (because **Jesus** is in your heart). As you rejoice in Jesus' Love and praise Him for His Glorious Presence, a quiet *Peace* settles over your soul. *The Peace of Christ* reigns within your heart ... and everyone will see "Jesus in you." *"Peace be unto you; as My Father hath sent Me, even so send I you."* Signed: Jesus (John 20:21).

Then, there's the Miracle of seeing a person who is far from the Lord *(but closer than he thinks)* being softened by the tender *Love of Jesus* right before your eyes! The *Love of "Jesus in you"* reaches out and draws that Precious Soul unto Himself – *through you!* You will be so amazed that you will say (to yourself), *"Wow! This is a Miracle!"* Yes it is, and you *know* Who did it. *Thank You, Lord Jesus; one more Lazarus raised from the dead!*

It will also be a Miracle that you are talking to a total stranger about **Jesus!** That may be the greatest Miracle of all. Get used to it. Your Lord Jesus wants to boldly reveal Himself to His world, and now that He has *you* willing to allow Him to do it through **you**, get ready for a wild ride! When the fullness of time came, Jesus was born into our world – and when the fullness of time came, Jesus was Born-Again in **you**. *Now*, the fullness of time has come for Jesus to live His Life *through* you. *In Faith*, go forth in the Fullness of Christ's Spirit, and He will show Himself *Faithful* and *Strong*. *The Lord Jesus will not be ignored; He will not be denied … He will not be defeated!!*

A challenge I encountered in the writing of this book was trying to figure out a way to take "the passion for witnessing for Jesus" that I have in *my* soul and put it into *yours*. I know that I can't – **but God** can (and only God can). It starts with "The Call." When the Lord Jesus "calls" you unto Himself, He makes sure you "hear" His Voice … in your spirit. *"God has never fired a shot and missed!"* (Charles Stanley). When you answer "The Call" of the **Eternal Son of God** and receive Him into your inner spirit-man, He brings with Him a "Passion" for lost souls. *So … one would think that we Christians would be the most passionate, courageous, driven, dedicated, focused, disciplined, energetic people on this Celestial Ball. But*, more often than not, it's *the worldlings* who have the burning passions to discipline and drive themselves to do whatever it takes to achieve awards, titles, prominence, position, wealth and "a place" in the history of *The Late Great Planet Earth*. **They want it!** Nothing matters – except the *desire of their soul*. However, it goes even deeper than that. More than physical; more than mental; more than emotional; most of all, it is … *Spiritual*. Even people who aren't Christians feel a stirring deep within their heart to accomplish something **"Grand."** It's as if they are mysteriously drawn into *another world* of just *them* and their "passion." Without a doubt, God hath set

Eternity in our hearts. *"When you set your mind on doing something Magnificent, you lose yourself in your Passion. Something that I could not resist – and didn't make any thought to resist – called me upon that cable"* (Philippe Petit).

My Christian Friend, are you ready to put your "Jesus Glasses" firmly on your *Spiritual Eyes* and focus your attention on your Lord Jesus – Who is "calling" **you** into the "Supernatural Work" of doing something *Magnificent* with *your* God-given life? You will become a "Passionate Christian" when you *personally* go to the *very passionate* "Jesus in you" and let Him give you *His Passion* for lost souls. The only question that remains is: *Do you want it?* When your Lord Jesus and His Eternal Kingdom are *more visible* and *more real* to you than this world is to the worldlings, then **you** will be *more passionate* for **God's Invisible Kingdom** than worldlings are for this visible world.

People are fearlessly doing all kinds of daring things these days just to get on TV or in the movies. But *you*, my Christian Friend, don't have to do what *they* do to get attention. Nope, just get out into this "politically correct" world and start talking to people about **Jesus** and *His Gospel*. You'll get plenty ... and Jesus will love it! He also loves **you**, and *Jesus' Love for you* will turn you into a brave, enthusiastic "Witnessing Warrior" with a *dream* and a *passion*. Jesus will give you the same "passion for lost souls" He has. Love takes risks, and *your love for Jesus* will compel you to take the riskiest risks of all.

My Friend, no matter what you may achieve on this Earth, there is one thing you will never be able to do ... stop your ole Timex from ticking (yep, those ole-timey Timex TV commercials were **true!**). As surely as the sun is coming up in the morning, the day *is* coming when you won't see it go down. When *your* time comes to die, you will be leaving here in a heartbeat. Will you be *leaving* your treasure ... or *going to* your treasure? Our Lord tells us, *"Lay up for yourselves treasures in Heaven"* (Matthew 6:20). If you're wondering how to get your $ into Heaven, it's time to put your "Jesus Glasses" on so that you can start looking at life from *His* perspective. Notice that Jesus says "treasures" not "treasure." So, what are Jesus' Treasures? Easy – the souls of people. *Every person* you see is a "living soul/spirit" who will spend all of **Eternity** ... *somewhere*. Every time you let "Jesus in you" tell a lost person about Himself and His

Plan of Salvation *(and He Saves them)*, Jesus and you have just laid up another **Treasure** in Heaven.

With every tick of the ole Timex, you get closer and closer to standing before your Lord and giving an account to Him for what you did (or didn't do) with the time (life, *same thing*) He gave you on this Earth. Don't stand there guilty of being a fraidy-cat. Don't stand there ashamed of being ashamed of **Jesus.** *No!* If the worldlings can be *passionate* and *courageous*, then we Christians with **"Jesus in us"** should be even more so. *Yes!* Rewards, titles, positions, wealth, power and prestige acquired by the worldlings will *all* pass away – *forever. But* he who wins souls is wise ... because *people's souls* are **Eternal!** *"Don't let fear silence the song of your soul."* (Philippe Petit).

Christian Friend, don't let fear silence the **Saviour** of your soul ... Who sweetly abides in your soul as the "Love Song" you will sing forever. We Christians can sing our Lord's Song in a strange land because Jesus *is* our Song! Deep within our heart lives a Melody ... by the Name of **Jesus,** singing His "Love Song of Salvation" to a lost world that desperately needs Him, His Love and His Salvation. Our loving Saviour's Sweet Presence within us overcomes our fear. Then, we can tell folks all about our Lord and His Plan of Salvation – and *that* is the loveliest *"Melody"* in His ears we could ever sing to Him. *Sing to your Lord a New Song!*

I often hear testimonies of young people revealing why they became drug addicts. They usually say that they just felt *so alone* and were desperately looking for *someone* who would accept them and love them. They pierce their tongue, dye their hair purple, cover their body with tattoos, give their body to anyone who wants it, drink anything, take anything, say anything, wear anything, agree with anything and do anything just to be loved and accepted. Our young folks are longing to "belong," *but* they are longing to belong to the *wrong people.* They join their "friends" in "doing drugs" trying to escape their problems ... only to run into their biggest problem of all! Even sadder is that they never find the love and acceptance they're looking for (and need) in their worldly, equally lost "friends." Many of those relationships that our young folks *think* are the answer to all of their troubles are actually the *cause* of all their troubles. They are searching everywhere for "peace" while running away from "The Prince of Peace" – and running right-

smack-dab into satan, "the evil prince of darkness and death." Satan's world is completely void of "True Love" and "Real Fellowship." Since when does the devil give our young folks anything to live for other than themselves, their own pleasure and his evil agenda? *Can you say, The Twelfth of Never!!*

We have an entire generation in love with their fancy-phones because they desperately need the attention and "love" they receive through them. That attention makes them feel *important* and *valued*. Girls send indecent photos of themselves on their phones because it makes them *feel desired*. How sad. You and I know that the "love" and "acceptance" folks *really need* can only be found in the Lord Jesus Christ – Who wants them to know how much **He** desires them. The heart-cry of our young folks today is: *"I don't know who I am. I'm trying to 'find myself.'"* Oh, Christian Friend, *you* know that they just need to find **Jesus** – Who will tell them who they are. Jesus is "living in you" – *you* need to arrange a meeting ... soon. Dare to be a Christian who goes out into the highways and byways of this world proclaiming to everyone along the way the Gospel Truth: *"Jesus Christ is Alive on this Earth today (in me), and He is Mighty to Save!"* Or better yet, let *Jesus* tell them Himself – *through you.* God loves to see "a surrendered Christian" who lets His Son Jesus *live again* on Planet Earth through *them*. When **you** dare to be that Christian, my Friend, "Jesus in you" will become *very visible* to everyone around you. They will see the "Joy" God gives a person who will surrender themselves to Him, sacrifice their life for His Son and dare to "be Jesus" to a world that desperately needs Him. *"There is one thing better than going to Heaven, and that is to encourage at least one other person to go with me!"* (Nick Vujicic).

The *Divine Light* of Eternal Life (God's Spirit) dwelling in *your spirit* gives you Light from the inside out, *but Jesus* doesn't want you to keep His Light all bottled-up inside of lil ole you. *No!* Let it shine *through you* into those lost, dark souls all around you. Let them *see* **"Jesus in you."** The more you make **Jesus** visible to this world He came to *Redeem*, the more He can use *you* to give *others* **Eternal Life.** Just as your reproductive organs have "seeds" within them to reproduce your physical life, your spirit-man has the "Seed" (the Spirit of Christ) within *him* to reproduce the "Spiritual Life of Christ" in the spirits of those into whom you "sow" Him. You do that by letting "Jesus in you" tell them about the *Man*

of Salvation and His *Plan of Salvation*. *"I died on the Cross for **you**!"* *Hallelujah to the Lamb!*

The Miracle of speaking in tongues experienced by the Disciples on Pentecost is something of a mystery to us ... but there was a time when it may have happened to *me*. I was walking through a mall when I passed two guys who looked like they were from a foreign Country. *For some reason*, I turned around and started walking beside them. I politely offered the one nearest me a tract. He smiled, took it and nodded without saying a word. As I walked, I talked to him about my **"Lord Jesus!"** ... but he just stared at me. So, I stopped and asked, *"Do you speak English?"* In a very broken accent, he replied, *"A leettel."* He was kind *(be kind, it costs nothing)* and still smiling, so that's all I needed ... I continued. I quickly and enthusiastically gave him the **Gospel of Jesus Christ!** The whole time, he just stared at me as if in a trance – his eyes as big as saucers. When I finally stopped to catch my breath, he turned to his buddy and in very broken English excitedly exclaimed, *"I can understand what she is saying! I know what she is telling me!"* It was only *then* that I remembered, *"Oh yeah, he told me he didn't really speak English."* My Lord had blocked that fact from me so that I would continue telling him about **Jesus** and His **So Great Salvation!** Acts 2:6 tells us that as the Christians spoke, "every man *heard* them speak in his own language." Could *that* have been what happened? All I know is that the big smile on his face told me he had definitely gotten "The Message." Therefore, I fully expect to see that guy again – *in Heaven! Start thinking like Jesus ... and you will start living like Jesus!!*

If you have started thinking that there is something special about me ... you are absolutely right. The *Something Special* about me is "Jesus in me!" And guess what, if you are a Born-Again Christian, my Friend, that's the very same thing that is so special about **you**. We Christians have the Lord Jesus "living" right on the inside of us with all of His **Power**. We *should* be storming the gates of hell every day! But, sad to say, we are too busy, too doubtful, too fearful, too distracted, too shy, too unmotivated, too broke, too sick, too old, too young, too disinterested, too stubborn, too uncommitted, too timid, too lazy, too "Biblically challenged" and too scared to ever tap into *His Power* and **trust Him** to do *Miraculous* things through **us** – and you know it's true. This world presses in on you with so many things you *must* do. I understand that.

But are you willing and ready to allow "Jesus in you" to speak to lost people *through you* "as you are going"? Just how long will it delay you to turn and politely offer a Gospel tract to that person standing *(and standing)* behind you in the check-out line at the grocery store as you graciously speak a few words about your Lord Jesus? How 'bout at the post office? At the filling station? Walking down the sidewalk? Playing with your kids at the park? I could go on, but you get the picture. Now, I know what you're thinking, *"But what do I say to that person?"* Wrong question. Right question: *What does **Jesus** want to say to that person?* (Matthew 10:20).

When Ian McCormack was a young man, he was a free-spirit atheist. **But Jesus** had plans for that young man. *So*, the Lord arranged for Ian to be stung by five extremely poisonous jelly fish and die – physically. *But* life isn't over when it's over … because Ian found himself still very much *Spiritually Alive!* During his "out-of-body" experience, Ian also found himself standing before **Jesus** – **The King** of the Universe. *Lord, have Mercy!* Jesus *did* have *Mercy* on Ian and filled him with His *Great Love.* Then, Jesus asked him if he wanted to go back. Ian said, *"No, why would I want to go back, Lord?"*

The Lord answered, *"Look behind you, Ian."* Ian turned and saw a great crowd of people down on Earth. He was puzzled and asked, *"Lord, why would I want to go back for them? I don't even know those people."* To which Jesus replied, *"Ian, I know those people."* When I heard those words, I got Jesus-bumps. Jesus was showing Ian all the folks He already knew He was going to *Save* through Ian's testimony. **Amazing!** "Jesus in me" intimately knows *every person* I pass every day. Of course, He knows them – Jesus is our *Great Creator God!* So, the answer to your question is: Jesus intimately knows and deeply loves that lost person standing in front of you; therefore, He also knows exactly what **He** wants to say to them. Your part in this is to just let *"Jesus in you"* *pour His Heart out* to this dear soul He came to seek and to *Save.* And never forget: "Jesus in you" is the *Flame of Fire*, lighting the fuse of the Dynamite Gospel – the **Power** of God unto Salvation to all who *believe!*

However, you've still got concerns, *"But what if I tell them about Jesus, and they _____ me?"* (Your vivid imagination is busy filling that blank in with all sorts of terrible things.) Well, let's think for a minute about all the terrible things they did to **Jesus** when they crucified

Him (your imagination can fill *that* blank in as well). Jesus suffered more than we could ever imagine in order to redeem our souls, and *now*, He says to *us*, *"Take up your cross and 'Follow Me' – all the way to Calvary, if necessary. They hate Me; therefore, they hate you. They persecuted Me, and they will continue to persecute Me by persecuting you. But just keep dodging their stones as you lift up My Cross and follow Me ... down the Via Dolorosa (The Way of Suffering)."* *"Jesus was a Master at shrinking the congregation"* (Tony Evans).

So, whadda you think? Do you want to take Jesus up on His offer? Are you willing? Are you ready? While you're thinking about your answer, let me offer you another thought. Instead of putting bad things in that blank about what people might do if you tell them about Jesus, put in *good things. Glorious Things!* Ask Jesus to give you some of *His* ideas. Remember: He knows these people, and He knows what He's going to do in their life. After all, look at **all** He has done in **yours!** So, instead of being afraid of what they might do to *you*, rejoice in the expectation of what **Jesus** is going to do with *them!*

Now, just in case you *do* have a bad experience, let me share one of mine with you. A person told me one time that he thought I was just demon-possessed. After we parted, I took it to my Lord in prayer as I walked along (**He** understands when nobody else does), *"Lord, did You hear what that person said to me?!! Of course, You did. You heard him accuse me of being demon-possessed. Can You believe it, Lord, he thinks that I just have an evil spirit!"* My Lord knew the anguish of my soul and how badly I needed an answer; so He gave me one, *"Cheer up, My Child, that's the same thing they said about Me, you know. So, you're in good Company, aren't you?"* And I will never forget what happened next. *I promise you,* I heard Him *laughing!* So, I took Jesus' advice, cheered up and laughed along with Him as we walked on together. I am convinced that our Faithful Saviour is more than able to deliver us from the worst things that ever happen to us in this life. *"Trust Me, My Child, I have everything under control!"*

Maybe you're still not convinced that your Lord could ever use you as His Witness. Your favorite prayer is, *"Lord, I'm just not able to do this!"* If you stick around long enough to hear Jesus' response, you will hear Him say, *"My Little Lamb, I know you aren't able, but don't worry about it ... because I AM! I AM Strongest in your weakness."*

So, proclaim the Glorious Gospel of our **Mighty God** and watch *Him* work! You will just stand back in awe and say, *"I can't believe Jesus is using someone like **me** to do this!"* Well, who else does He have to work with? Jesus uses us ordinary garden-variety Christians to do extraordinary *Supernatural* things. And when He does, always be very careful to remember that it's not you – it's **Him!** All Glory goes to **Jesus** (*you* are just the unprofitable servant).

Do you ever wish you were an undercover-cop? I do. I could make *soooo* many arrests – especially when I'm driving (I need a bumper-sticker that says, "I May Be Slow, But I'm Aheada YOU!"). I was thinking about that one day (as someone sped around me doing 90 miles-an-hour) when it dawned on me that *God* has a Divine Undercover Cop – the Holy Spirit. *He* doesn't miss a thing, and as my Aunt Margaret used to say, *"Payday someday!"* All those lost folks (out there recklessly breaking God's Laws) *aren't* going to pass "Go" but are going to pass into Eternity one day with an endless number of "offenses" on their record against *"The One"* Whom they will then be standing before in **Judgment.** What a day that will be when our **Jesus** they will see. They will look upon His face – *The One* Who offered them His Grace – but they rejected Him, for pity's sake! People who refuse to set foot inside of a Church on this Earth are going to **die** one day and face God – Who will refuse to let *them* set foot inside of *His* Holy Heaven. King Jesus won't be taking *them* by the hand. Sadly, the Angels of God will take those whose names are not found written in *The Lamb's Book of Life* and (like a maitre d' in a restaurant who checks to see if you have a reservation, or not) will escort *them* to the "smoking section." Jesus wants so badly to warn those lost law-breakers of their future "Day in Court," and He already has someone picked out to do it through ... **you.** *Mercy Me! "Be not simply good ... be good for something"* (Henry David Thoreau).

The Gospel of Jesus Christ is *Powerful* – but only if you speak it. *"For the preaching of the Cross is to them that perish foolishness; but unto us who are Saved it is the Power of God!"* (I Corinthians 1:18). Throughout history, great men of God have been *convinced* of the truth of that verse. In Colonial America, the early Preachers rode on horseback throughout our Land. They were called "Circuit Riders," and it's hard to believe how many miles they traveled and how many sermons

they preached, tirelessly proclaiming the "Good News of Jesus Christ." So, why would they willingly spend all of their time (life, *same thing*) enduring the unbelievable hardships of a totally unselfish sacrificial-servant? Because they *knew* that the *Presence of the Living Christ* dwells within every Christian, ready to unleash the *Power of God* through the *preaching* of His Gospel. They also knew that Jesus gives each one of us *The Great Commission* … not *The Great Suggestion*.

But, alas, they have all gone to their "Reward" and are no longer living and breathing on this Earth. Never again will they be able to speak for their Lord Jesus in person – *but they sure did while they were here!* Their lives were **God-given** – and they knew it. *God* had given them only one short span of history (His Story) to proclaim the Glorious Gospel of Jesus Christ, and they were *faithful* to their "Heavenly Calling." Today, they have Joy unspeakable and full of Glory, and they have passed the Baton of the Gospel on to **us**. Now it's *your* turn. What are **you** doing with the Gospel? All of life is "God's Test," and He is watching you to see what *your* grade is going to be. Are you going to take that loooong look into *Eternity* and do what **God** wants you to do, *or* … are you going to let satan keep you from receiving all that God has for you? Don't lead a life of quiet desperation and then go to your grave with your *Song* still in you. *Sing your Lord's Song of Salvation!!*

Your Lord is challenging you to use God's Dynamite Gospel to blow up a few of satan's strongholds! The day is far spent; the night is rapidly approaching, so don't waste any more of **Jesus'** precious life (time, *same thing*). *"Only one life, 'twill soon be past, only what's done for Christ will last"* (C. T. Studd). My Friend, the *Living Lord Jesus* has chosen *you* and called you to a "Life" that will *last forever! Now,* Jesus is choosing to use you to do some "Spiritual Work" on this Earth that will *last forever!* So, live this day for Christ Jesus – Who gives you God-given Power, God-given time and *plenty* of God-given opportunities to share your Faith with souls who will exist for *all Eternity!* The *Ball* is definitely in your court. Make some *Divine* racket as you serve the Gospel to a lost world – and do it in **Jesus' Love.**

"If Jesus Christ be God, and He died for me, then no sacrifice can be too great for me to make for Him" (C. T. Studd). God's Son was willing to pay "The Price" for your Salvation. Now are you willing to pay the price for *others* to be *Saved* – through you? The Lord Jesus has "Good

News" for this satan/sin-saturated world, but He can only proclaim it through *you*, my Christian Friend. Most Christians would never be honest enough to admit it, but when God dials their number and their *Spirit-phone* rings, they look at their Caller-ID and shriek, *"Oh no, it's God!! No way am I answering that 'Call.' He's probably just wanting me to go tell some lost folks about His Son Jesus – Who Saved me all those years ago (and I really am thankful), but right now I'm busy with other things ... you know, the things of the world that I need to make my life really great on this Earth. So, I just don't have any time at the moment to go make another person's life really great for all Eternity."* (*But* as soon as *they* get into some serious trouble, they've got God on speed-dial, expecting Him to answer right away ... eager to do what they're wanting Him to do. *Hmmm.*)

Christian Friend, promise your Lord Jesus that from this day forward you will no longer just *say* you belong to Him, but you will start actually *doing* some things *with Him. Don't make Jesus come get you.* Jesus once told a story of a rich man who had to wake up in hell to finally get a "missionary heart." Since you are a Born-Again Christian, you won't end up in hell, so start living your life with your "Eternal Celebration with Jesus" in view. Begin each day by asking yourself: *How much am I willing to do, and how far am I willing to go so that another soul can join the Eternal Celebration with Jesus in Heaven?* I would like to submit to you that how much you are willing to do for Jesus will depend on how much you love Him. Malcolm Muggeridge once described Mother Teresa as a person who was motivated purely by love alone. Those words moved me in my heart to pray, *"Oh, Lord Jesus, the passion of my soul is to be Your faithful servant who is motivated purely by love for You alone. Amen."*

I'm at that age when I have to alert the Fire Department before lighting the candles on my birthday cake. But looking on the bright side, I'm praying that my *life* will be like my birthday cake and shine ever brighter and brighter *for my Lord Jesus!* So, as long as I can stay clothed and in my right mind, I'm going to keep on telling lost folks (who are being held hostage by satan) about my Saviour and His So Great Salvation. I want them to know *Jesus* (in Whose Presence is fullness of "Joy!") and join His Family (who are traveling through life on "Jesus' Joy Train"). One of the best compliments I ever got was from

a couple I was witnessing to in the middle of a grocery store. After enthusiastically telling them about my Lord Jesus, the husband looked at me, smiled and said, *"You remind me of a little girl at her Birthday Party!"* Bingo! *"For he shall not much remember the days of his life, because God answereth him in the joy of his heart"* (Ecclesiastes 5:20).

As the years go "bye," I have more and more health problems. Some mornings when I first wake up, I feel like I'm a lot closer to going on into Jesus' World than I am to staying in this one. Now, I know what you're thinking, *"Well, if Jesus loves you so much, then why doesn't He just heal you?"* Answer: Jesus *is* healing me. My Lord is in the process of giving me the "Ultimate Healing;" He's just getting rid of this ole temporary body so that He can give me my *new Eternal body* (and I will gladly make the trade). The shadows lengthen as the sun sets on my life, and Jesus will soon deliver me from satan the *second* time. The first time, Jesus delivered my *soul* from satan. The second time, Jesus will deliver my *body* from satan; then that ole devil will never be able to cause me any more grief. *Hallelujah!* Our Lord Jesus always has the last Word with ole slewfoot; so there is no way to defeat a Born-Again Christian. Even when we "lose" … WE WIN!! *Like JESUS did.*

"WELCOME TO MY WORLD!"

HEAVEN EVERY DAY

"These things have I spoken unto you,
that My Joy might remain in you,
and your joy might be full!"
Signed: Jesus (John 15:11).

I f I injected you with "truth serum" right about now and asked you if your life is "Heaven Every Day," what would you say? Do you wish it *could* be? Well, you won't find the answer in this chapter of my book ... but in the **Living Lord Jesus** Who is with you as you read it. The *Living Presence* of "Jesus in you" is the only One Who can truly make your day a Heavenly Day. "Jesus in me" is always speaking to *my* heart and teaching me *Spiritual* lessons using just about anything. Years ago, I was walking through a Library when I spotted a book titled *Heaven Every Day*. On the front cover was the picture of a smiling man sitting on his motor cycle, and in the background were beautiful snow-capped mountains. I didn't pick it up, but the picture said it all – for *this* man, biking through beautiful places makes *his* life *Heaven Every Day*.

When I saw that book, I immediately thought of my own life. *My* life is also "Heaven Every Day" but for a completely different reason. It's not the scenery I'm looking at that makes it so; it's my **Heavenly Companion** Who goes with me every step of the way, giving me His **Divine Light** in a dark world. *"For I know Whom I have believed."* As I walk with my Lord in the Light of His Presence, what a Glory He sheds on my way. Every day, I walk and talk with my Best Friend Forever, *Jesus*. We have such a *gloriously good time* telling all these folks He knows here on Earth how much *He loves them*. We tell them He loves them so much

that He came to Earth and *died for them* on the Cross. And *now*, He's dying to meet them!

Yes siree, God *loves* to hear us speaking well of His Son. And when we do, He rewards us with a heart that is full to overflowing with *Jesus' Joy*. If you lack "Joy," you don't have to sing a silly song to get it – just go out witnessing, and Jesus will *give it to you*. There is nothing in all the world that can take away the "Joy" God gives us when we actually *do* what He sent us to Planet Earth to do. **Jesus** is our best example of that; He surrendered Himself to His Father and lived a life of *Self-sacrifice* – which produced in Him the *Great Joy* that comes when we *delight to do God's Will*. Surrender *yourself* to **Jesus** and delight to do *His Will*; then His Joy will be your Joy! You are in the Strong Hand of your Good Shepherd, and He is well able to hang onto His weak little Lamb. Up the hills and down the hills, through the sunshine and through the rain, you travel along, singin' a song, side by side. No matter what, Jesus will never leave you.

David Ring is a lot like our Lord. David is a real Blessing and one of our Lord's choice Arrows that He shoots around all over the place … even though he has cerebral palsy *("So, what's your problem?")*. David says that the Lord has given him a beautiful wife whom he deeply loves. He also loves telling her so, *"Honey, I sure do love you. I love you so much that I don't want you to leave me. Don't ever leave me. Don't ever even think about leaving me. Sweetheart, if you ever leave me … I'm going with you!"*

Well, I'm here to tell you that **Jesus**, your Heavenly Bridegroom, *loves* **you**. He loves you so much that if you ever try to leave *Him*, He's going with you! But who in their right mind would ever want to walk away from Jesus? In His great Love, Mercy and Grace, Jesus *Saved* me all those years ago, and when He did … I fell in love with Him. Only **Jesus** can give you a "Love" and a "Life" that just keeps getting sweeter and sweeter as the days go by. The more that you love and serve Jesus, the more of His Love and Joy He floods into your heart … making your life *Heaven Every Day!* The Christian Life is so simple; it's falling more and more in love with Jesus each day.

Since you're still under the influence of that "truth serum" I injected you with, you are probably confessing by now that all your problems and troubles are going to keep *you* from being happy any

time soon. *Newsflash!* Joy and happiness are two different things. Happiness depends on what's happening. But even on my worst day, I *still* have the "Joy of Jesus" because my problems and troubles don't stop me from sharing Jesus' Love and Gospel with lost folks who need Him – and *when I do*, my Gentle Shepherd turns my sorrow into **Joy!** *Try it.*

He that observeth the wind shall not sow, and he that regardeth the clouds shall not reap. Does that sound like you – just sitting in your lonely room watching all the dark clouds in your life blow by? Well, don't just sit there watching dark clouds and blustery winds. *No!* Put your jacket on, hitch your oxen up and go plant a field full of Gospel Seeds with **The One** Who says, *"Take My yoke upon you – My yoke is easy; My burden is light."* Even if you don't feel like your burden is light at the moment, just go tell *others* about "The Burden Bearer" ... and *He* will lighten yours. When you have a burden for lost folks, **Jesus** carries you *and* your burden. *"In the morning sow thy seed, and in the evening withhold not thine hand: for thou knowest not whether shall prosper, either this or that, or whether they both shall be alike good"* (Ecclesiastes 11:6). *Throw caution to the wind and sow Gospel Seeds into lost souls!!*

Now that Jesus and you have sown lots of *Seeds*, it's time to go *harvest* a field with Him. That's what **Jesus** loves to do. Listen closely and you will hear Him saying, *"Behold, lift up your eyes and look on the fields, for they are white (ripe) already to harvest. Just go down to your local mall and take a good look around, for pity's sake. Go to a park, go to the grocery store, go to work, go to school, go for a walk, go anywhere and lift up your Spiritual Eyes and look around you!"* **Jesus** sees lost folks *everywhere!* Do you? Jesus wants you to; He wants to harvest the field of "your world" *with you.* Do you want to harvest that field with *Him*? Does **Jesus** have the pre-eminence in your life? Is He the **President** of your spirit-man *or* ... just a Resident in your spirit-man? Is Jesus the **Driver** of your life *or* ... just a Passenger? Does *He* have the wheel, or do *you*? If you're not letting **Jesus** drive, maybe you should check the passenger seat to see if He is still there. Jesus won't settle for being your Co-Pilot, and if you don't let *Him* pilot your life, you just may find yourself flying solo (hope you've got a parachute handy). Totally *surrender* your life to **Jesus** – *and buckle your seat belt!!*

"There's one thing Jesus can't do – He can't be 'second' in your life" (Tony Evans).

You have probably heard Preachers say, *"Jesus could come back at any moment, so you had better be ready!"* I personally don't spend much time thinking about Jesus coming back. I spend *my* time thinking about the fact that Jesus is *already here – in me!* And *I'm ready* to be about my Father's Business. He has employed me, empowered me, appointed me and anointed me to let His Son **Jesus** live His Life *again* in me *and* through me – *right now!* Preachers will sometimes try to motivate Christians by saying, *"If you truly believed that Jesus could come back at any moment, it would impact your life."* It's true that Jesus could come rapture us Christians outta here at any moment, *but* when you truly believe that Jesus Christ *is already here* – in **you** – *that* will impact and transform your life like nothing else can. *"I AM in My Father, and ye in Me, and I in you!"*

Every morning when I wake up and realize that my heart is still beating, I know it's going to be a good day … **for JESUS!** My Christian Friend, Jesus is **The One** Who keeps *your* heart beating too … *for* **Him.** Your presence on Planet Earth and Jesus' Presence "in you" is proof-positive that your Lord has a very good reason for you to be here. Jesus wants to give you *good days* full of "Greater Works" that He has *purposed* for you to do … *with Him.* So, get in cahoots with "Jesus in you" – *today!* Enjoy the company of His Presence *in you* and *with you* every moment. Spend your life (time, *same thing*) loving Jesus and spend some of your $ on some good Gospel tracts to offer to people as you let "Jesus in you" tell them all about Himself and His Love for them – using *your* mouth. Withhold not thine hand! Sow those Gospel Seeds of "Salvation in Christ Jesus" into every person you possibly can. Like the verse says, you don't know which seeds will take root and grow … **but Jesus** sure does. *"I know My Sheep!!"*

Maybe you're a Christian who doesn't have the heart to tell *anyone* about **Jesus** … because you just feel dead and lifeless inside. Your life is such a mess that you've given up on yourself – and you're sure that everyone else has given up on you too … even **God.** Well, who hasn't been right where you are at one time or another? But before you throw in the towel and "take missing," let me tell you about my ole mailbox.

I was living in a sixty-year-old house with a mailbox out by the street that looked like it must have been the original one. The metal post was terribly corroded, and the ole mailbox clinging to the top was equally battered. I finally got around to replacing it with a new one, and on trash-pick-up-day, I leaned the old one against my trash bin out by the street. Well, would you believe that those trash-pick-up-guys emptied my trash bin but *rejected* that ole mailbox and threw it down on the ground? They did. *But* the recycle truck hadn't come by yet; so I leaned that ole mailbox against the recycle bin, hoping that the recycle-pick-up-guys would take pity on it and count it worthy of recycle status. However, as I watched for them out my window (ole folks do such things), I witnessed something very strange. When their truck was just a block away, an expensive, late-model SUV stopped in front of my house. A nicely dressed lady got out, opened the back hatch and shoved that ole mailbox into her nice SUV. Then, she got back in and drove off. **I couldn't believe it!!** What would an obviously well-to-do lady want with that beat-up and battered ole mailbox? Answer: The same thing **God** wants with beat-up and battered ole **you**. *Mercy Me!*

The God of this Universe has been watching you every minute of your life. He saw you rejected and thrown down on the ground by heartless people. Your Lord has been watching as those heartless people kick you around while you're down. But *now* (with satan breathing down your neck) **God** is going to have *Mercy* on you ... because **He** counts you worthy of recycle status. *Praise the Lord!!* **God** hasn't given up on you – not by a long shot. Aren't you glad God never comes to the end of His patience with you? Not only you, **but God** even *Saved me* in order to show forth *His perfect patience.* God can afford to be patient ... He's got time on His hands. He's also got "Big Plans" on His mind for His Children – but all in *His good time.* God's Big Plan right now is to pick you up outta that trash heap you're in, wash you up, sand you down (it'll hurt), tighten up all those loose screws about to fall out, repaint your life with pretty colors and display you to the watching world (including those heartless people who rejected you and threw you down) as a "Trophy of His Grace." *Yes!* From His "New Creation Mailbox" God is going to send out the "Gospel Message of His Son Jesus" to people all over the world. *Double Yes!!*

I know ... because *I* have been that ole mailbox on numerous occasions. I can tell you for certain that there is a Faithful Saviour standing close by Who is forevermore in the "Reclaim Business." ***"When you give up as a Christian and throw in the towel, Jesus just throws it back. He won't let you give up!!"*** (Jeff Schreve).

I know you. You're just like me. You got troubles. You had troubles yesterday, and you're spending your day today dreading all those troubles you're gonna have tomorrow. Opportunity only knocks once ... but trouble kicks your door down! Well, if you can take a break from all your troubles for a minute, I'll give you some sage advice: *Spend your day today safe and secure in the Everlasting Arms of God ... praising Jesus for taking such good care of you.*

Now, I know what you're thinking, *"Hey, that doesn't work. There have been plenty of days when the Lord didn't solve all of my problems."* *(Hmmm).* Your problem is that you can't see your *real problem* because you don't have your "Jesus Glasses" on – and ***that*** is your *real problem!* So, put your "Jesus Glasses" on, and you will clearly *see* that your Lord *has* solved all your problems ... that you really *needed* solving. You needed a *Glorious Saviour* Who would take you Home to Heaven when you die. *Check!* You needed a faithful *Good Shepherd* Who would walk with you (or carry you) every step of your journey through this life. *Check!* You needed a *Gracious Servant* who would show up in your life and tell you about your "Jesus Glasses" – through which you are able to *see* God's Wonderful Love and Grace toward you. *Check!*

Truth be told, *I've* had all the same troubles you've got. I have stood beside the caskets of the dearest on Earth to me. I've looked at an almost-empty bank account. I've lain on a sick bed that I didn't think I would ever get up from. I've been "done wrong" by those I loved and trusted. ***BUT GOD!! "Giving thanks unto The Father ... Who hath delivered us from the power of darkness, and hath translated us into the Kingdom of His Dear Son." Signed: Every Born-Again Christian*** (Colossians 1:12-13).

However, you've still got complaints, *"Yeah, I hear people saying that God is always faithful, but He isn't always faithful to **me**."* Ah, ***but God is*** always faithful to you ... because He is always *with you* ... and He is *for you.* Jehovah Jesus promises you that your battles are *His* battles. Your Lord loves you more than you could ever possibly imagine or comprehend, and He never leaves you to face your troubles *on your*

own. Jesus is a Saviour Who *ever* has "a Plan." Sometimes, His Plan takes time, and when it does, you will have to choose how you're going to wait: *"Will I choose to sincerely thank my Lord for what I'm going through, or ... will I just grumble in my tent?"* I have been through many a situation in which I had to wake up each morning, look into my Lord's loving eyes and say, **"Lord, I trust You!"**

"God sent a man before them, even Joseph, who was sold for a servant: Whose feet they hurt with fetters; he was laid in iron" (Psalm 105:17-18). My trusty (but not dusty) ole Bible gives another translation for the last part of that verse: *"Iron entered into Joseph's soul." Aha!* **You** think that God is surely trying to kill you, **but God** is just turning you into His "Iron Man!" Put your "Jesus Glasses" back on and you will *see* that you are just in God's Boot Camp – which is producing a *Faithful Servant* and *Mighty Witness* for **Jesus.** God knows that only the *Power* of "Jesus in you" can overcome the power of "satan in this world." So, yield to *God's Will* for you, and *you* will know what *He* knows: *"My Child, these hard times are necessary ... because I can't use a marshmallow to defeat a foe as vicious as My enemy satan!" Mercy Me!*

In case you're thinking that I don't know anything about you and *your* problems, let me tell you about one of mine. As you might guess, satan was not at all happy with the publication of my first book *Ole Slewfoot*; he hates stories that end with **Jesus winning** and him losing. That ole devil can't stand *anyone* on Jesus' Winning Team; so ole slewfoot set out to torpedo *Ole Slewfoot* (even though I named it after him). Soon after the book was printed and sent to the distributor, my Faithful Saviour revealed to me that a quote included in it was attributed to the *wrong person. Oh, no!* Yep, and that meant the mistake would have to be corrected and the book *totally reprinted (groan).* In my mind's eye, I could see flocks and flocks of dollar bills with wings – *all flying away. Mercy Me! "When God opens the windows of Heaven to Bless you, satan will open the doors of hell to blast you!"* (Adrian Rogers).

However, rather than turning into a basket-case, I decided to thank my Lord for the mistake instead, *"Lord, we're going to laugh about this in Heaven one day, aren't we? So, let's just go ahead and laugh about it now."* And that's what we did (the smile that comes through tears is the

smile Jesus treasures). But like most of you, I did wonder, *Why would my Lord let this happen?* Jesus heard me and decided it was time to let me in on "His Plan" – which is always way better than mine (of course).

First, Jesus brought to my attention the fact that those flying-away-dollar-bills weren't *my* dollar bills. Nope, they were *His* dollar bills, and He didn't mind spending them to reprint *Ole Slewfoot* one bit … because it was all part of "His Plan." Yep, *now* I would have *lots* of copies which I could correct with a pen and give to everyone and anyone who would take them off my hands. My Lord had some folks in mind who needed the Gospel … but would never have gotten it otherwise. *Jesus is so wise!* Only our Saviour can take our musty straw and spin it into "Gold" – *Eternal Gold!* I am convinced that people are going to come up to me in Heaven and say, "**There you are!!** *I'm here because you gave me one of those corrected-copies of Ole Slewfoot back on Earth.* **Thank you!**" (Be it unto me according to my Faith.) *"Jesus didn't come to get you out of trouble, Mister; He came to get into trouble with you"* (Adrian Rogers).

No one can bring good out of bad like the Lord, and He used the reprinting of *Ole Slewfoot* to consume some dross out of my life. I'm an ole widow lady living on Social Security and some savings. It's enough to live on for the rest of my life … provided I die within the next few years. So, like most ole-timers, I'm always "concerned" that I will out-live my savings (I couldn't say "worried" because the preachers tell us that worry is a sin). I had just come through a *very* financially draining situation when the mistake in *Ole Slewfoot* was discovered, and *that* was the Proverbial straw that broke the camel's back. Actually, it broke *me*. It brought me to my knees before my Lord, and I was finally ready to truly give everything (even my dwindling savings) over to Him. *He loves me, for pity's sake.* My Lord is my Heavenly Father, and I can trust Him – even in my deepest valley and on my darkest day *(when cotton is down to a quarter a pound and I'm busted)*. **Jesus** is our *Good Shepherd* – He watches over His Sheep every moment, and He will take care of His own. **"My Presence will go with you, and I will give you Rest" Signed: Jehovah Jesus** (Exodus 33:14).

"Lord, glorify Yourself in my life today … and do it at my expense" (Erwin Lutzer). True Christian maturity comes when we can honestly *embrace* "The Refiner's Fire" – no matter what it costs us. And *when we*

do, God's Supernatural Grace totally transforms us. Our Lord promises that He is working all things together for good – *Eternal Good*. Our job is to believe Him, trust Him and look for that good … with our "Jesus Glasses" on. *"The Lord is good, a Stronghold in the day of trouble; and He knoweth them who trust in Him"* (Nahum 1:7).

Now, I know what you're thinking, *"I thought you said the Lord helped you write your book. So, how could it have any errors in it?"* Easy. The parts that are good, encouraging and inspiring … the Lord wrote. The parts that are dull, boring, uninspiring and full of errors … I wrote. What can I say? Jesus never says, *"Oops!"* But I sure do. **The Lord** is perfect; we aren't. *"God is … we ain't"* (Tony Evans). God works through us weak, frail, "mentally challenged" cracked pots of clay because we're all He's got to work with. But take heart, Dear Heart, if the Lord can use me, He can use *anybody*. At times, I feel like such a complete idiot that I think I need a "brain transplant!" *Mercy Me!*

Some days, our walk with our Lord is like a tennis match. We ball up all of our problems, troubles, trials, needs, fears, etc. and whack the ball over the net onto Jesus' side of the court. And He just whacks it right back with Zephaniah 3:17 attached: **"The Lord thy God is with you; He is Mighty to Save!"** *Now* the ball is definitely in our court. So, what are we going to do with it? Are we going to believe Jesus and trust Him – or not? *Well* … to whom shall we go? Actually, we've got that all figured out. We know plenty of folks we can go to. Yep, and if we whack our ball into *their* court, we will definitely end up going out of bounds. The secret is to whack your ball back onto Jesus' side of the court with Mark 9:24 attached. Jesus whacks it back to you with Jeremiah 29:11 attached. Then, with renewed Faith, you whack it back to Jesus with Psalm 139:23-24 attached – and in love, He will. *Everybody wins! The Christian life is like a tennis match – you can't win unless you serve!*

Your Lord Jesus is always right there in your spirit-man wanting to listen, talk, fellowship, laugh, share or have any kind of contact with you that you're willing to have with **Him**. So, the "ball" is always in *your* court. Jesus is just waiting for you to serve it to Him and begin the dialogue. It's all in the game. The more prayers you serve over the net to your Lord, the more answers He returns to you with *His Blessings* attached.

If you aren't giving Jesus much of your time and attention, it's because you either don't really believe He's actually there (waiting for you and wanting to hear from you), *or* you know He's there … but you just don't care. *Mercy Me!*

Time to make amends; go to your Lord Jesus in the "secret place" of your soul and talk with Him. Then, listen for His still small Voice. You won't hear an audible Voice, but you will know beyond a doubt that **God** has spoken to you … in your spirit. God loves speaking to you through the Wisdom of His Word, the Bible. And who knows, He may even choose to speak to you in an audible voice … of another person.

I was witnessing to an atheist one time and asked him my favorite question to ask the lost, *"What is going to happen to you when you die?"* Without blinking an eye, he replied, *"Nothing. I'll just be dead. Gone. It's over." (Little does he know!)* So, I told him that I know exactly where *I'm* going – I'm going to Heaven to live with **Jesus** – *forever!* When he heard those words, he looked at me as if I were an escapee from the "funny farm" being sought by the Police. He said, *"You mean to tell me* (he couldn't believe I was serious) *that you actually know where you're going when you die?!"* I thought about it for a second; then replied, *"Well, truthfully, I don't really know where Heaven is; so I don't know exactly where I'm going. What I do know is "Who" I'm going to. I'm going to be with my Lord and Saviour Jesus Christ, and wherever Jesus is will be Heaven for me!"*

So, let's think about this, Folks. Jesus is already "living within us" *right now*. Therefore, *at this very moment*, we can have "Heaven on Earth" in our soul … because *that's* where **Jesus** is! Heaven isn't just a destination – Heaven is **"A Person"** – Who dwells within **us**. Today, *we* can be in Paradise with **Jesus!** As we bask in the warm Son-Light of our indwelling Lord, Jesus gives us an assignment, *"Take My Heavenly World to satan's hellish world! Satan's slaves walk around in darkness … while thinking they are so 'enlightened.' Go! Shine My Light into their dark souls!"* And "go" we *will* – because their darkness can never put out "The Light of the World" living in **us**. Never! Our feet are on Earth's terra firma; our eyes are on our **Heavenly Bridegroom**; our minds are full of **Jesus' Gospel Message**; our hearts overflow with **Jesus' Great Love**; our tracts are in our hands, and our lips are proclaiming that our **Living Christ** is **The Mighty God** Who has

returned to Planet Earth ... **and is living in us Christians!** Ole slewfoot won't know what hit him. An Army of "Jesus Followers" – *that's what!* This world may call us "Jesus Freaks," but we'll just take that as a compliment. **On Judgment Day You Will Wish You Had Been A FANATIC For JESUS CHRIST!!**

"If I have brought any message today, it is this:
Have the courage to have your wisdom regarded as stupidity.
Be fools for Christ. And have the courage
to suffer the contempt of the sophisticated world"
(Antonin Scalia).

I have a nine-foot-tall wooden Cross in my front yard, and when the sun goes down, I light it up with a spotlight in honor of JESUS – The Light of the World! I daily pray for God's Anointing on my Cross so that the people who see it will be deeply touched in their hearts by the deep Love of God – Who sent His Precious Son Jesus to die on a cruel Roman Cross ... for *them.* Much like Lewellyn Hudson, I try to use every available opportunity to lift up **"JESUS!"** If you are a Christian living your life in "Jesus' Secret Service," put a tall wooden Cross in *your* front yard, light it up every night ... and your neighbors will label you a *"Jesus Freak!"* But don't worry about *them,* because **The One** Who matters *most of all* will be smiling. **"Well done, thou Good and Faithful Servant!"**

(Side-note: Do you ever get weary of hearing about the atheists taking down all the Crosses all over our Country because they are on Government land? I do, and I have an idea. I got land; you got land; all God's Children's got land to live on – that *isn't* owned by the Government. *So* ... Christians who own property can start putting up impressive Crosses, Bible verses and Christian Christmas decorations in *very visible places* all over America ... and there won't be a thing satan (or his followers) can do about it *(hee-hee).* It's time to stand up for Jesus, Folks, and confess Him on this Earth to the Eternal Glory of God our Father! I can just see millions upon millions of Crosses lighting up the darkness all over our Land. It

may even spread to other Countries. Remember: America First –
for **JESUS!**

The reason atheists want all Crosses and Christian symbols removed
from our Country is because they just *hate* the fact that America was
founded as a Christian Nation and there are still Christians here today
who love and honor the God of the Bible. Cross-hating atheists belong
to *satan* – the evil-one giving them their marching orders. The devil
hates our Lord so much that he doesn't want *anyone* to be reminded
of Jesus in *any way*. Taking Crosses down isn't just the atheists trying
to take our Christian symbols down. Oh no, *satan* is trying to take
JESUS down! Yep, that devil thought he had *defeated Jesus* when he put
Him on the Cross, *but* much to satan's great dismay, he now knows that
it was **Jesus** Who defeated *him* ... *on the Cross*. So, every time satan
sees a Cross, a knife goes through his evil heart {like the spear that
pierced Jesus' side}, and *he* is the one who is reminded that *the Cross* is
where Jesus won the victory over *him* and set us all free from his evil
clutches. *Hallelujah! "Thine arrows are sharp in the heart of The
King's enemies!"* (Psalm 45:5).

Folks, this is *Spiritual Warfare* between us "Followers of Jesus" and the
followers of satan. We Christians fight on our knees through "Prayer!"
Then, we rise to our feet, stand on our Lord's Powerful Word and raise
up our Christian Crosses to the *Glory* of our Wonderful Saviour. We
will remind satan *everywhere he looks* that **"JESUS IS LORD!"** – and he's
just chopped liver.)

On the day of your Salvation, your Lord came into your inner spirit-
man and brought Heaven with Him. *Now*, Jesus wants you to live like
it! So, go ahead and trust Jesus, love people and rejoice in your soul as
if you're *already in Heaven*. Christian Friend, dare to live with the total
abandon of a joyous Child of your Heavenly Father. Perhaps one of the
reasons you can't live joyously in Jesus is because of that person you just
can't forgive for what they did to you. The reason you can't forgive them
is because you can't get rid of *you*; it's all about you. *"Pity parties are
the most tedious, unproductive and unrewarding events you could ever
attend"* (Nick Vujicic).

Well, I hate to have to be the one to ruin your pity party, but it is
not about *you*. It's first and foremost about **Jesus** and that other person.
You see, that person didn't do "that" to *you*. Nope, they actually did it

to *Jesus* – Who still suffered and died for them on the Cross – where you were crucified *with Him* … for that person. *Mercy Me!* You will only be a free soul when you realize that you have *already* forgiven that person from your position "in Christ" on the Cross. Since you are "in Christ," their sin hit *Christ,* not you; therefore, you no longer have to deal with them for their sin against you. They sinned against the Lord Jesus and must answer to *Him*. Your job is to just get out of the way so that *Jesus* can deal with them.

I'm just like you. There have been people in my life who once feigned love and affection for me – but are now cold and distant. I wish it could be different, but I can't change them. Let me share with you my secret of how I rise above that. I look beyond everything in this life on Planet Earth and focus my attention on how everything is going to be *in Heaven* – no more hurtful words, no more hateful deeds, no more hard feelings, no more sad thoughts, no more painful memories, no more pain of *any kind*. God's Love, Jesus' Joy and *Peace like a River* are awaiting us there, my Friend. In Heaven, we will finally love one another as Jesus loves *us – perfectly*. *Oh*, if we could only start living a "Heaven on Earth" life *now! "Count up everything you have that money can't buy and death can't take and you will find out how truly rich you are"* (Adrian Rogers). I got stuff; you got stuff; all God's Children got stuff on this Earth. *But* the most valuable thing we have (besides Jesus) is *each other*. You may not consider some of the folks you know as "gold" … *but Jesus* sure does! Just start looking at them with your "Jesus Glasses" on and He will do a work in your heart … because *He's living there.*

While reading recipes for Key Lime Pie the other day, I ran across one described as "Heaven on a plate." Well, may I describe to you what the life of a Born-Again Christian living close to Jesus tastes like: *"Heaven on a Planet!"* We have Heaven in our heart, Heaven in our spirit, Heaven in our sight, Heaven on our lips and Heaven on our mind. Now granted, we can never experience Heaven here on Earth like we will when we shed these Earthsuits and go there in person. Heaven is so unimaginably wonderful and so full of the "Glory of God" that we will need new *Supernatural bodies* just to experience it, take it all in and spend *forever* there praising our Lord.

In the meantime, I wrote this book for you, Christian Friend, in hopes of delivering you from a dull and boring life. You do disservice to

The One you belong to (The King of the Universe) and the *Position* you've been granted (Ambassador for Jesus Christ) when you spend your life in a laborious doing of "nothing." *DON'T DO IT!!* God has included **you** in *Jesus' Building Project*, and *you've* got an **Eternal Kingdom** to build! Get yourself some good Gospel tracts (or however you witness best) and get out there and *brag on* **Jesus!** Get yourself a *"Real Job!"* Get in on **God's Eternal Plan!** You won't be bored for long. Your Lord gave you a job to do. *DO IT!! Don't let death catch you empty-handed.*

You can either spend your life doing laps around the wilderness *or* … you can start taking baby steps of obedience toward your Heavenly Father. When your Father sees you coming Home to Him, He will be like the father of the prodigal son and come *running to you* with so much in His hands you won't know what to do first. For instance, I have spent many years telling folks about Jesus, but it *never once* crossed my mind to write a book (so writing this book was definitely not *my* idea). **But God** was watching me, and He started speaking to me deep in my spirit: *"Molly, what is that you have in your hand?"* I didn't have much, but I *did* have, *"A pen."* Little is much when **God** is in it because He uses small things to do big things. God can use something as small as a pen to bring down mighty demonic-strongholds. So, God responded, *"Ah, yes. I AM going to use you to bring Glory to Me … using that which you have in your hand. Through your pen, I can lead many out of their bondage to satan by bringing them to the Cross of My Son Jesus. Once there, they will go through His Precious Blood and come out the other side in Jesus' Little Flock. Then, I will lead them into the 'Promised Land' of living a Spirit-filled, faithful Christian life."*

Your Lord has been watching **you**, my Christian Friend, as **you** have been faithful to Him. *So,* what do you have in *your* hand that He can use to bring Glory to Himself? Now, I know what you're thinking, *"I don't have anything in my hand – except this book you didn't even want to write."* You're right. Not only did I have no interest in writing a book, I didn't even think I *could* write a book. You've heard the ole saying: If you want to hear God laugh, tell Him your plans. Well, when God told me *His* Plans, *I* laughed! I said, *"Lord, You mean You want me to just take this pen and some paper and start writing a book, for pity's sake?!!"* My Lord answered, *"Do you know of any other way?"*

So, not having any other means, I took my pen and some 3X5 cards (I didn't think I had much to say) and started scribbling down some thoughts. Well, that was all my Lord needed me to do … because once I did *that,* *He* started pouring so many ideas into my mind that when I stopped long enough to catch my breath, there were 35 chapters in the book. *Mercy Me!* Here's how it happened. I would write and write and finally reach the point that I would say, *"OK, Lord, that's it. That's got to be it. I've got nothing left to say. It's done."* The next morning (you know what I'm going to say), my Lord would wake me up early and say, *"Get up and write this down."*

"Lord! There's more?!! There couldn't possibly be any more."

"Pick up your pen; you'll see. Write this book along with Me; the best is yet to be."

"But Lord, it's *so* early. It's still dark outside!"

"My Child, it may be dark out there, but it is *Bright* in here. **I AM** 'The Light of the World!' Remember? Now, get up and let My Light shine through you. Surrender your pen and your life to *Me* so that I can use *you* to set My People free!"

Fellow Christian, allow me tell you on your Lord's behalf that when *you're* all done-in, **He** is just getting started! With **Jesus,** there is always more. *"But what about when I die?"* MORE! MORE! MORE! A Universe of MORE!! With **Jesus,** the BEST is *always* yet to be! So, even if you don't have anything "in your hand" *at the moment* that your Lord can use for His Glory, I would challenge you to pray and ask God to *show you* what He is just sitting on ready to *put* into your hand that He will then use to do His "Mighty Works." And don't say you're too old to do anything; if I didn't get a pass … neither will you. But cheer up, my Friend, and keep your eyes on "The Prize!" *"I press toward the mark for the Prize of the high calling of God in Christ Jesus"* Signed: *Every Born-Again Christian* (Philippians 3:14).

When you hear people talking about *"living by Faith,"* do you ever wonder what that really means? In my humble opinion, it means faithfully doing those things in this *visible world* which *prove* what you believe to be true about the *Invisible World.* That translates into being willing to sacrifice temporal, material, earthly things (including your time, energy and $) in order to build **God's Eternal Kingdom,** knowing that **Jesus** promises: *"Great will be your reward in Heaven!"* Your Lord

may suddenly surprise you with a "Big Idea" to do something that looks totally impossible – to *you*. Just keep plodding along, if necessary, as you ask Jesus to fill you with *His* energy, enthusiasm and wisdom. Then, watch what **Jehovah Jesus** will do *in* you and *through* you.

Let my story encourage you. As I confessed, *writing a book* had never crossed my mind, **but Jesus** has turned it into the *passion of my life* ... because my Lord (Who loves me and knows me so well) gave me the desires of *His* heart – and He will do the same for you. If you're a really brave soul, dare to pray and *ask* your Lord to give you a "Big Idea." Trust me, when you get to the end of your life, you are going to wish that you had taken *more risks*, attempted *greater things* and done much more that would *live on* long after you leave Planet Earth. The clock is still ticking, so you *still* have the chance to make a "*Big Difference*" for your Lord's Eternal Kingdom – *if you do it now!* **"Go out quickly into the streets and lanes of (America), and bring in hither the poor, and the maimed, and the halt and the blind." Signed: Jehovah Jesus** (Luke 14:21).

If you are an older Christian reading this book, have you ever wondered why we are too soon old and too late smart? It seems that just about the time we get life all figured out ... it's time to die. Well don't despair; there is a time for every purpose under Heaven. Remember, the leaf turns a beautiful brilliant color *just before* it dies and falls off the tree. I have heard that the reason the color changes is because the leaf returns all the nutrients in it back into the tree – then dies and falls off. I think that's pretty neat. We Christians need to be like that leaf. We should spend the last years of our life pouring everything that's *in us* into the people *all around us* – then die, drop off and fall into the waiting *Arms of* **Jesus!** I don't know about you, my Friend, but that's what *I'm* gonna do. *"After all, what are us older folks still doing here if not to help out these younger folks?"* (Jeanne Robertson).

Like that leaf, the sun gives us a gloriously beautiful sunset *just before* it goes down. So take heart, Dear Heart, our Lord is using me to get His Message out late in *my* life, so there is still time for Him to get His Message out through you in *yours*. It's always too soon to quit – and *never* too late to start. We older Folks just have to feel "the urgency of the moment" a little more, that's all. No doubt about it, we're all going to die one day, but make up your *Mind of Christ* that *you're* going out in a blaze of "Glory" – *for* **Jesus!** Sadly, as I look back over *my* life, I

see lots of wasted time and missed opportunities. Not so for Lewellyn Hudson. Nope, he's a man who is using the best opportunity he could think of to let His Lord speak His Message to this world through *him*. Lewellyn was born in 1797; let me tell you how I met him. *(Hmmm; he's how old?)*

It all happened quite a few summers ago in the quaint little town of Eatonton, Georgia. On this beautiful day, I was taking the time to do something I always enjoy doing. I was strolling through an old cemetery, reading what the ole-timers had engraved on their tombstones. Back then, they could be very creative. Just look at all the beautiful homes and buildings they built – especially the old Churches. I never miss the opportunity to attend one. I love the way their steeples point up to **The God** they were built to "Glorify." Some of those old Churches have the most exquisitely beautiful woodwork and stained-glass windows you will ever see. One of which is in Eatonton, by the way. Another one in Newberry, SC still has the bell in the belfry with a long rope for the children to pull and ring it – calling the people to "Worship." I love it! I can *feel* God smile. For me, a visit to one of these beautiful old Churches is a little trip to Heaven on Earth. As I sit there and look around, my mind goes back to the Godly Christians who built it and first worshipped there. They made great sacrifices in order to build the most beautiful Church they possibly could ... in honor of "The **King** of all Creation!" Then, they came to Church to present themselves before their **King**, dressed in their *Sunday Best*. Oh well, I think it's time we moseyed on back over to the old cemetery.

As I strolled from one tombstone to another, I was very disappointed. They were so old that the engravings had long since worn off most of them. That Georgia sun was high-noon hot, and I was ready to give up when ... *Oliver Sutton*, I came across a tombstone with the engravings still fairly visible! *Eureka!!* Excitedly, I came back to life and studied it for quite a long time, trying to decipher what it said. That broiling-hot Georgia sun was suddenly forgotten as I asked Jehovah Jireh to provide His help. After all, the elements of nature had been constantly wearing it away for almost two hundred years! I had to carefully trace many of the words with the tips of my fingers as if reading Braille. It posed quite a challenge, but here is what I was able to discern. The man buried there was Lewellyn Hudson (1797-1836). He never reached his 39th birthday

(*he* wasn't too soon old and too late smart; in fact, he didn't even live to be old) but read what he had engraved on his tombstone.

LEWELLYN HUDSON

1797-1836

READ IN THIS COLD AND SENSELESS MARBLE

THIS DARK AND NARROW HOUSE OF DEATH

SILENTLY BUT EMPHACTICALLY TELLS

THE UNSPEAKABLY IMPORTANT TRUTH

THAT THE ONLY RATIONAL,

THE ONLY VALUABLE USE OF LIFE

IS TO PREPARE FOR ETERNITY.

REMEMBER THAT BUT A MOMENT MORE

AND YOU TOO, AS SILENTLY AND IMPRESSIVELY,

WILL TEACH TO OTHERS THE SAME SOLEMN LESSON

YOU NOW LEARN FROM HIM.

As I slowly ran my fingers over those faint engravings, I knew that I was standing on Holy Ground. I could hear **God** speaking to my heart. Our Heavenly Father was sending a profound message to His world … because *truer words* were never spoken – or chiseled. I remembered Jesus saying, *"The stones will cry out"* and as I stood there reading those powerful words, that tombstone was crying out to *me!* In a strangely transcendent way, those words on Lewellyn's tombstone were more than mere words; they were the heart-cry of his God – Whom he deeply loved. The Lord deeply loved Lewellyn and gave him the *Grace* to know the mystery of life – which he revealed in the message on his tombstone: God sends us to Planet Earth to find our way to the foot of Jesus' Cross, where our sins are forgiven and we enter into a *Spiritual Relationship* with our Heavenly Father (our Infinite God becomes our Intimate Friend). This is the most worthy quest in life because God, His Word and our souls are the only things on this Earth that will last for

all Eternity. That is why I witness to lost folks and give them the Gospel. That is why I wrote this book – to prepare people for *Eternity!* *"And this is Life Eternal, that they might know Thee, the only True God, and Jesus Christ Whom Thou hast sent" Signed: Jesus, God The Son* (John 17:3).

As I stood there reading Lewellyn's tombstone, I felt like I was in a "time-machine" … because, in the depth of my being, I could actually *feel* the longing of Lewellyn's heart; he desperately wanted to get his Godly Message out to the world – *any way he could.* So, he had it engraved on his tombstone. It was his last chance to teach others the solemn lesson that life is short (quite short for Lewellyn); God is real (very real to Lewellyn); Eternity is forever (staring us in the face), and we must choose our own *Destiny!*

Christians and non-Christians look at death so very differently. An unbeliever looks at death as a sign that nothing matters. We live. We die. It's all over. Nothing matters. A Christian looks at death as a sign that *everything matters.* We live … because God gives us life. We die … because God takes us Home to Heaven to be with Him. Nothing is ever over … because everything we do on this Earth echoes into Eternity as we live on forever in Heaven praising our Great God! *EVERYTHING MATTERS!!*

I tried to research some facts on Lewellyn's life, but all I was able to discover was that he married Evelina Alexander in 1821 when she was 17 years old. The next thing I saw revealed to me how God had impressed on Lewellyn the truth that the only valuable use of life is to prepare for Eternity. Sadly, Evelina died one year after their marriage. *In this world, ye will have tribulation.* The message on Lewellyn's tombstone indicates that he was a highly intelligent, well-educated, deeply spiritual man. If you ever get the chance, read the writings of people who lived in centuries past (even their penmanship was impeccable; just look at our Declaration of Independence) and then look at the way people write (and talk) today. Look at the way people reverenced God in the past and then look at the way people curse and mock Him today. When you do, it will become quite evident: Man isn't coming up from the apes; no siree, man is going down from Adam – *and fast!*

Now, let's fast forward to today. Don't *you* wait until your tombstone is the only way you have to get "God's Message" out to this world. *No,* you and Jesus go tell them *NOW* – while you're still alive and able. *"Only*

one life, 'twill soon be past, only what's done for Christ will last!" (C. T. Studd). Once this day is gone, you will never be able to get it back and live it differently. Once **your life** on Earth is over, you will never be able to get *it* back and live *it* over again either. So, purpose in your heart to live the life you have *now* for **Jesus**. Don't just "spend" your life (time, *same thing*) ... *invest it* ... in **Jesus!** *And* **Eternity!** Allow your Lord to use **you** to get His Message out to the world the same way Lewellyn allowed God to use *him*. Let Jesus live out *His Life* and *His Purposes* "in you" and "through you" – **NOW**. You will be *Eternally* glad you did. *"Time's awastin', Charlie Brown!!"*

"THE ONLY VALUABLE USE OF LIFE IS
TO PREPARE FOR ETERNITY!"
(Lewellyn Hudson, 1836).

I doubt that very many people will ever read Lewellyn's message that he left behind on his tombstone. I'm glad that I took the time (my time is Jesus' time) and wrote it down. Maybe this is the Lord's way of getting Lewellyn's message out to the world after all. When I see Lewellyn in Heaven, he will probably say, *"Thank you for helping Jesus get my message out ... even though it took Him almost two hundred years!"* And I will say, *"Thank **Jesus!** He is Sovereign over all, and He knew just the right time. It was a great honor to serve at the pleasure of my King ... like you did, Lewellyn."*

Young folks (and even many ole folks) are always asking that age-old question, *"Why am I here?"* "Jesus in you" can tell them: *"You will never know 'why' ... until ... you first know 'Who.'"* You can introduce them to the **Sovereign Lord** Who created them and redeemed them with His own Blood on the Cross; *then* they will know that they are here to *receive* His forgiveness, *love* Him with all their heart and *glorify* the **Living Christ** by fellowshipping with Him and faithfully doing *His Will*. Only the Lord Jesus, our **Sovereign King**, can give them a reason to live – *The Reason – **Him!** "People don't know who they are because they don't know why they're here"* (Tony Evans).

I consider this chapter to be one of the most powerful in my book because I consider my discovery of Lewellyn's tombstone to be one

of the most profound moments of my life. I "sensed" that something *Supernatural* was going on. I still do … even as I write about it. And yet, look at how it happened. The Lord had called Charlie Home to Heaven, and I was left alone on this Earth. For quite some time, I had been aimlessly traveling here and there – wandering and wondering what my future might hold. At least Moses knew he was headed for the Promised Land. And so was I … I just didn't know it. Then came "that day" when I was just lazily killing time *("As if you could kill time without injuring Eternity" {Henry David Thoreau})*, fellowshipping with Jesus and totally unaware that He was about to part the sea of darkness with that bright Georgia sun and show me what **The Son** had been leading me to all along. My Lord Jesus is the *Producer, Director and Script Writer* of "The Life of Molly McCoy," and **He** was in every *seemingly* random event which eventually led me to Lewellyn Hudson's tombstone. *"Your life is good because God is good. And, guess what, God is in your story, and He is always at work!"* (Katherine Wolf).

Our God Reigns from His Eternal Realm where time is meaningless. Jehovah Jesus tells us that one thousand years are as a day to Him, and one day is as a thousand years. We hear those words and tend to concentrate on the "thousand years" part. So, we pray, *"**Lord!** Why is it taking You **so long** to do what I have asked You to do? Is it such a big thing, (for pity's sake)?!"* Our Lord is never caught off-guard, so He replies, *"My Little Lamb, why do you concentrate so hard on **that one thing** you want Me to do for you? Take the blinders off and look around at **all I AM doing right now**, for **Heaven's** sake!"* Once again, Jesus has to remind His Little Lamb that even when He's not doing something … *He's doing something!* So just hang on; Jehovah Jesus is well able to compress a thousand years into one day. Ever had one of those days? Maybe *this* is one of those days. If so, make sure you're filling it with "Greater Works" that will *last* for a thousand years (should our Lord tarry) and then on into **Eternity!**

A husband told his wife, *"Honey, when I die, I want you to bury me at the Mall. If you bury me in a cemetery, you'll never come to see me. But if you bury me at the Mall, you'll come to see me all the time!"* Well, I doubt that *you* are going to be buried at the Mall. So don't you see; even better than a message engraved on your tombstone is your "Personal Evangelism Ministry" – **NOW!** The people you share

the Gospel with *before* you die will impact future generations for years, even centuries, to come. You may not have a whole lot in this world, my Christian Friend, but you have **Jesus.** And He is giving you "today." Let *Him* live "through you" *today* to the Glory of our Heavenly Father. Ask Him to give you the wisdom to know how He wants to use **you** to *"impact* **Eternity.***"* Go through *every* door He opens for you and use *every* opportunity He gives you to tell others about your Saviour. As a Born-Again Christian, you can most likely trace your Spiritual Heritage all the way back to the Apostle Paul! However, there were lots of links in the chain along the way. How would *you* like to be a "link" in the chain for someone else? *What a Divine Honor!* **"But as we were allowed of God to be put in trust with the Gospel, even so we speak" Signed: Every Born-Again Christian (I Thessalonians 2:4).**

We Born-Again Christians need to be like Pheidippides *(Who?).* He was the guy who ran the first Marathon Race to Athens, Greece in 490 BC to report a great military victory. When he arrived, his last words were **"Rejoice! We Are Victorious!"** And then … he fell dead (I can't say that I blame him). My Christian Friend, let's run "The Race" that is set before us with great determination and great *Joy* (like Pheidippides)! Then, *we* can depart this world one day as *Victors in Jesus!* Daily labor for "The Lord you love" while it is yet day, for the night cometh (your death) when no man can work. Make sure you are lying in *your* coffin thinking, *"Ah, I can finally rest … because when I was walking around on Planet Earth, I gave Jesus my all. I gave everything I had in me for my Precious Lord!"* (OK, just kidding. Trust me, you will *never* make it into a coffin. Absent from your body … present with your Lord! It will be the fastest trip you ever took – and *the best one!* "Verily I say unto thee, Today shalt thou be with Me in Paradise!" Signed: Jesus.)

Maybe you're an older person getting ready to retire from your 8-5 job, and you're looking forward to having the opportunity to finally do those things you always wanted to do but never had the time. Well, let me "be Jesus" to you for a minute and broaden your horizon. Think for a moment of all those people you've known over the years who are already dead. So, why aren't *you?* One reason: **God.** The Lord is the One Who gives you every breath you take and every beat of your heart – and He does it because He has a reason for you to be here – *His Reason.* Now, I know what you're thinking, *"Wait a minute! I know what you're about*

270

*to say. You're going to tell me to spend whatever days I have left telling people about **Jesus** instead of doing all those fun things I've always wanted to do. That's not fair!! I worked hard all my life, and now I should be able to do what I want to do, for pity's sake!"* My, my, you are *still* a very sharp cookie, because you've got a pretty good grip on what I'm thinking. But calm down ... because you aren't entirely right.

Many of the folks I witness to are clerks in stores. Some of them will say that they are already a Christian and refuse my tract. When they do, I tell them to take it anyway and give it to someone who *does* need Jesus. They usually say, *"Oh no, I can't do that. My company doesn't allow me to witness on the job."* My reply is always the same, *"Well, you don't live here, (for pity's sake). Keep it, and when you leave here, you're just as free as I am to give it to whomever you wish."* What they are really saying is, *"I don't want to witness for Jesus – **ever!"*** They remind me of a couple guys I hired to do some rather difficult rehab work on my ole house a while back. After two days of very hard work, I noticed they were a little later than usual showing up. When they *did* arrive, one was wearing a tee-shirt that said: "I'm not late. I didn't want to come!" We had a good laugh over it, but I'm pretty sure that guy meant every word. Many a Christian should be wearing a tee-shirt that says: "I'm not witnessing for Jesus. I don't want to." *"A little girl was asked to describe the difference between the clergy and the laity. 'Well,' she replied, 'the clergy are paid to be good ... the laity are good for nothing'"* (Adrian Rogers).

When someone asked Harry Bollback (in his 90's) if he was retired, he replied, *"I retire every night so I can get up the next morning and find out what God wants me to do."* If you are retired, you can witness for your Lord Jesus *all you want to – even* while you're doing all those fun things you've always wanted to do. *Yes!!* The only problem is: How much do you *want* to witness for Jesus? *"If you don't want what God wants, then you won't do what God commands"* (Tony Evans). Adrian Rogers says, *"You need to get your "wanter" fixed."* And I know just **The One** Who can fix it for you. Your Lord Jesus will open your eyes to a new possibility: Now that you are no longer under the iron-rule of your boss, you can let **Jesus** be your Boss for a change. You will soon be so *in love* with your New Boss that you will be witnessing for Him all you want to ... and even when you don't want to. Don't you dare say you're too old. If God could use ole Abraham and Sarah to be instrumental in

the birthing of His Son Jesus, He can surely use *you*. Just look at Moses. Look at Corrie Ten Boon. Now go look in the mirror. You're looking at someone about to begin the *best years* of their life – **with Jesus!** *"Get out of your lazy-boy and get busy. God still has a plan for your life!"* (Greg Laurie).

One morning, the wife of a retired fellow asked him, *"So, what are you going to do today?'"* He replied, *"Nothing."* She said, *"But you did that yesterday."* He yawned and said, *"I know, but I'm not finished yet."* I know what *you* need to do today, my Friend: *Wake up* and be finished and done with doing *nothing*. Take the loooong look into **Eternity** and make sure that *something* from your life here on Planet Earth is waiting for you there. Number your days and use the ones you have left to bring *someone* to the foot of Jesus' Cross so that He can *Save them* the same way He *Saved you*. Make up your *Mind of Christ* that when *you* check out of Motel Earth, people will be remembering how much you gave (not how much you had) and how much you sacrificed for your Lord and His Kingdom (not how much you squirreled-away for yourself). Let Jesus live "His Life" through *you*, and your life will leave behind the fragrance of **Jesus**. Then, when you punch Earth's Time-Clock for the last time, you will discover that **God's** "Retirement Plan" is a Universe better than any Company on Planet Earth! *"Grow old along with Me, the best is yet to be!" Signed: Jesus, Lord of all the years you have left.*

I was on my way home from town with some grub the other day when I noticed a large marquee sign in front of a store with this message on it: **THE BOSS SAID PUT SOMETHING ON THE SIGN.** That guy reminded me of all the *less-than-fired-up* Christians who feel like they've just *got to* say *something* to someone about "Jesus." **You** be the *fired-up-for-Jesus* Christian who's **got something to say** to *everyone* about your *"Lord and Saviour Jesus Christ!!"* And Jesus will confess you before His Father Who is in Heaven!!

The Apostle Peter calls us Christians "lively stones." I like that. How lively is *your* witness for your Lord Jesus these days? Instead of being a "rolling stone," be a "living stone" in your Lord's Church and He will use you to do a lot more *Eternal Good* for His Kingdom than all the tombstones in the world! Give the winds a Mighty Voice – *your voice* – **Jesus Voice!** You just never know what your Lord might do with the God-Anointed Words you speak to that *one lost person*. Remember:

Destiny's door turns on very small hinges; so even if you only get to say a few words to a person about your Lord Jesus as you hand them a Gospel tract, little is *much* when **God** is in it. Your friends and family may tell you to give it up, you're just wasting your time, **but God** never wastes *anything* in His Eternal Kingdom … and He's not going to start now. So, put away your chisel and loosen up your God-Anointed tongue. Let **Jesus** speak through you, and He will make your life **Heaven Every Day**. Then, on that glorious day when your Lord calls you Home to Glory, you can join ole D. L. Moody in saying:

"Is this dying? Why, this is bliss. There is no valley.
I have been within the Gates.
Earth is receding. I see Heaven opening! God is calling!
I must go!!"

"WELCOME TO MY WORLD!"

FAMOUS LAST WORDS

"I come to Thee, Holy Father, keep through Thine own Name those whom Thou hast given Me" Signed: Jesus, God the Son (John 17:11).

As we come to the close of this part of my Legacy, I have bittersweet feelings. I am sad because I feel that through this Journey you and I have shared together, we have become Fast Friends ... and I hate to see you go. But go, you must. God has places for you to go, things for you to do and people for you to see. You have miles to go before you sleep – you and your Lord Jesus (your *Forever Friend*).

I hereby entrust you to Jesus' tender care; His *Great Love* for you will see you through your darkest day and your deepest valley. Give Jesus your heart, your attention, your time, your devotion, *your very life* – and Jesus will give *you* "A Wonderful Life" taking His Glorious Gospel to a world full of needy souls. So, go – and I will see you again – in Heaven. There, we will share stories, glories and Jesus' Love. For now though, I want to thank you for investing your life (time, *same thing*) in reading my book. I trust you met Jesus along the way and He blessed you in a very special way ... as only He can do. *"Unto you it is given to know the mysteries of the Kingdom of God."*

I know that I have been a bit hard on you in urging you to become a *Mighty Witnessing Warrior* in God's Eternal Kingdom, but I only did it at my Lord's request. So, if you look closely at those "hard sayings of Jesus" through your "Jesus Glasses" and "Spiritual Inspector," you will see the evidence of *Divine Fingerprints* all over them. However, if you're still not convinced, let me make amends by making you a deal. If you should choose to accept your Lord's Invitation to become a completely sold-out,

radically committed Member of "The Fellowship of The Unashamed," and upon arriving in Heaven, you're sorry you did ... look me up (Jesus will help you), and I will give you some of *my* Heavenly Reward. Our Lord tells us that one of our Heavenly Rewards is *"Joy!"* So, I will have plenty of *Joy* to share with you. And when I do ... *Ta Da* ... you'll be *GLAD* you did! *Yea!!*

Doesn't everything work out beautifully in *Jesus' World!!*

"WELCOME TO MY WORLD!"

"And that's all she wrote."
(for now)

ABOUT THE AUTHOR

Molly McCoy is a lil ole widow lady spending her last days telling as many folks as possible about Jesus and His So Great Salvation. She dwells among untrodden paths, living in obscurity as a nobody who can tell everybody about Somebody Who can "Save" anybody! And now, she's telling *you* ... so that you can take the Baton of the Gospel of Jesus Christ and spend *your* days doing the very same thing.